Presented to

_____

From

_____

Date

_____

In Touch
WITH GOD

CHRISTIAN ART
PUBLISHERS

Published by Christian Art Publishers
PO Box 1599, Vereeniging, 1930, RSA

© 2008

First edition 2020

Devotions written by Nina Smit

Cover designed by Christian Art Gifts

Images used under license from Shutterstock.com

Scripture quotations are taken from the *Holy Bible*, New International Version®
NIV®. Copyright © 1973, 1978, 1984 by International Bible Society.
Used by permission of Zondervan Publishing House.
All rights reserved.

Scripture quotations marked NLT are taken from the *Holy Bible*,
New Living Translation®, copyright © 1996. Used by permission of
Tyndale House Publishers, Carol Stream, Illinois 60188.
All rights reserved.

Scripture quotations are taken from THE MESSAGE. Copyright ©
by Eugene H. Peterson, 1993, 1994, 1995, 1996, 2000, 2001, 2002.
Used by permission of NavPress Publishing Group.

Set in 11 on 14 pt Palatino LT Std
by Christian Art Publishers

Printed in China

ISBN 978-1-64272-675-6

20 21 22 23 24 25 26 27 28 29 – 10 9 8 7 6 5 4 3 2 1

As for me, it is good

to be near **God**.

I have made the

Sovereign LORD

my refuge; I will

tell of all Your deeds.

Psalm 73:28

Contents

January

Living Close to God

The secret to success and happiness is to live close to God. As you learn to know Him better each day you will love Him more day by day. You need to diligently seek the presence of God in your life. The following prayer by St. Patrick reveals a desire for God's nearness and presence:

I arise today
through God's strength to pilot me,
God's might to uphold me,
God's eye to look before me,
God's ear to hear me,
God's word to speak for me,
God's hand to guard me,
God's way to lie before me,
God's shield to protect me,
God's host to secure me,
from everyone who desires me ill,
Christ with me, Christ before me, Christ behind me,
Christ in me, Christ beneath me, Christ above me,
Christ on my right, Christ on my left,
Christ where I lie down, Christ where I sit, Christ where I arise,
Christ in the heart of every man who thinks of me,
Christ in the mouth of every man who speaks of me,
Christ in every eye that sees me,
Christ in every ear that hears me.

First Seek the Lord's Advice

Jehoshaphat also said to the king of Israel, "First seek the counsel of the LORD*" (1 Kings 22:5).*

When the King of Israel asked King Jehoshaphat of Judah to go to war with him against Aram, he was immediately willing to do so, but he had one condition: that the Lord be consulted first before they do anything.

If you follow this advice in the new year things will fall into place for you. This year, before you follow your own lead, bring your plans to God first. The path to follow in the new year is crystal clear to Him. He already knows exactly what is in store for you: whether it will be a brilliant year full of surprises and expectations or whether it will be a year of crises and heartache.

When you regularly seek the Lord's advice and surrender your year and your life into His hands, you can be certain that even if trials and tribulations lie ahead of you, the wisdom of God will be available to you each and every day – that He will carry you even when things are extremely tough. Even then will He be with you to help and support you.

The very best New Year's resolution is to set aside more time for God this year and to work on your relationship with Him. This year, live close to God, listen for His voice and be ready to obey Him. Talk to Him and study His Word. Then you will experience the blessedness of His presence in your life every day.

Heavenly Father, I commit to seeking Your advice every day of the year that lies ahead rather than following my own bent. Please lead me daily and show me Your will for my life. Amen.

God Is with You

"So do not fear, for I am with you; do not be dismayed, for I am your God. I will strengthen you and help you; I will uphold you with My righteous right hand" (Isaiah 41:10).

God did not promise us a life of eternal happiness on earth or a problem-free existence, but He did promise that in the stillness and in the darkness He will be with us, beside us, in us and He will help us to exist. This is what Philip Yancey claims in his book *Reaching for the Invisible God.*

The people of God were often confronted with big problems in biblical times, but He was always there to help and protect them and to show them His strength. For that reason they were almost always able to get the better of their enemies.

It is highly unlikely that you will have a problem-free year this year; in fact, you can probably count on the fact that problems and crises will cross your path, but in the midst of those crises you need never be afraid or worried. After all, you have the promise that God will never let you down, that He will be with you every day of the new year to lead you and help you, that He Himself will strengthen you whenever you need extra strength, that He will hold you tight with His own hand and will help and protect you.

This is why you can enter the unknown year that lies ahead with great faith. If God is with you, then nothing will be against you.

Heavenly Father, it is wonderful that You have promised to be with me, to strengthen me and to help me, to hold me tight and to save me. I come now to lay claim to that promise! Amen.

Are You Close to the Lord?

"Is the LORD among us or not?" (Exodus 17:7).

In this passage, Israel asks a rather strange question: they want Moses to tell them if the Lord is still with them. If, after all the miracles that God worked for them during the exodus and the journey through the wilderness, they still doubted whether the presence of God was with them, they must really have been very short-sighted. They began to question God every time things went slightly wrong for them. Before we get too critical of the Israelites, we should first acknowledge that we very often do exactly the same thing!

There is a story of a group of Christians during the American Civil War who went to visit President Abraham Lincoln. "We hope that God is with us, President Lincoln," they said to him. "I reckon that's not the most important thing," Lincoln answered. The visitors stared at him in shock, until he added, "I am more concerned about whether we are with the Lord."

Perhaps this is the question that you should answer for yourself today, right at the beginning of the new year. Are you still absolutely certain of the fact that you are with the Lord? That the Lord is with you is a promise that is emphasized in various places in the Bible. But what about you? Are you with the Lord? What do unbelievers see when they look at you and what do people hear when they listen to you? Do your actions, attitudes and words all bear witness to the fact that you love God and are truly with Him?

Heavenly Father, I praise You for the promise that You will never leave me. You are with me each day of the new year. Please forgive me for the times when I act like I am not with You. Amen.

A New Future

"For I know the plans I have for you," declares the Lord*, "plans to prosper you and not to harm you, plans to give you hope and a future. Then you will call upon Me and come and pray to Me, and I will listen to you" (Jeremiah 29:11-12).*

The advice that Jeremiah gave to the Israelites in exile was that they should continue with their lives in the foreign land and should not still long for the past. God promised that He would one day return them to their own land. He planned to prosper them and had a future for them. He guaranteed them something to look forward to if they were prepared to call to Him and seek His will.

Usually at the beginning of a new year, people have all kinds of expectations about what the year ahead will hold for them. And this is not wrong. God wants His children to have positive expectations. It is His will that we should leave the disappointments of the past behind us, and that we should reach forward to a new future with Him. With the help of God you too can manage to make your dreams come true this year, to embrace a new and brighter future.

There is, however, one condition that you must not lose sight of: If you want to be able to take God's promises as your own, you must be prepared to call on Him, to seek His will and obey Him. Only then will the Lord undertake to answer you and to fulfill your expectations for the new year.

Heavenly Father, thank You so much for the promise that You have planned to prosper me in the year that lies ahead, that You want to give me a future and a hope. I want to call upon You now and I want to obey Your will. Amen.

A Vision for the New Year

"I am the LORD*, and there is no other; apart from Me there is no God. I will strengthen you, though you have not acknowledged Me"* (Isaiah 45:5).

God gives each of His children a special vision – a task He gives specifically to them. Katie Brazelton in *Pathway to Purpose* says that to have a vision is to know how God wants to use you in a powerful way to accomplish His will. It is to sense your God-given destiny and to see what remarkable, humanly impossible task God has in mind for you. It is to receive a taste of His multi-dimensional strategy for you – to be aware of the kind of person that He would like you to become and the work that He would like you to do for Him.

This year, try to find out what the personal task or vision is that God has planned for you. Pray that He will reveal it to you and that He will Himself equip you to bring it to pass. Be mindful of the fact that this vision could require a lot from you, but know too that you will be able to accomplish it because the God who gives you the vision, will also give you the strength to do it well.

If the Lord gives you a vision, He also promises to be with you and to help you fulfill it. All that He asks of you is your willingness. The only way you will be truly happy this year is if you discover your vision and, with the strength of God, bring it to pass.

Heavenly Father, please show me what task and what special vision You have set aside for me this year. Equip me to be able to do it to the best of my ability for Your glory. Amen.

The Only Important Time

Whatever your hand finds to do, do it with all your might (Ecclesiastes 9:10).

There is a time for everything, and a season for every activity under heaven, says the writer of Ecclesiastes. There is a time to be born and a time to die, a time to plant, a time to uproot, a time to break down and a time to build. God made everything to fit into a determined time (see Eccles. 3). And it is God's will that you use the time that He has entrusted to you with caution, so that you will make the most of your time and use the days of this new year in such a way that at the end of the year you will be a wiser and more mature person.

Therefore, do not waste your time in the year that lies ahead. Do everything that comes your way with enthusiasm and diligence. There is just one moment that is really important, and that is right now. "Make the most of every opportunity," Paul advised the community in Ephesus (Eph. 5:15). You cannot change anything that has happened in the past and neither can you predict the future. You do not even know what awaits you tomorrow. That is why you need to make the best use of today.

Philip Yancey, in *Reaching for the Invisible God*, rightly says that today is the only time over which we have any power. Therefore, remember, there is only one time that is really important – now! Use today as if there will be no other time.

Heavenly Father, will You please help me to use my time in the year that lies ahead with insight. To do everything I do in the very best way possible and with absolute commitment. Amen.

There Is Always Hope

We have this hope as an anchor for the soul, firm and secure. It enters the inner sanctuary behind the curtain (Hebrews 6:19).

In his autobiography, *A Long Walk to Freedom*, Nelson Mandela talks about how he was imprisoned on Robben Island for fourteen years before he was permitted to see his daughter. It was a magnificent experience for him to hold her close again after such a long time. He had last seen her when she was a young child, and now she was a woman with a baby in her arms.

She placed Mandela's first grandchild in his arms. He said that to hold a newborn baby, so vulnerable and soft in his rough hands, hands that for so long had worked with nothing but picks and shovels, was a great joy. He could not believe that any man could ever have been happier than he was that day.

According to the tradition of Mandela's tribal culture, the grandfather can choose the name of a new baby, and Mandela decided to call him Zaziwe, which means hope. He truly hoped that this baby would belong to a new generation of South Africans for whom apartheid would be nothing more than a distant memory.

The children of God also have a hope to which they can hold fast: the hope of heaven that waits for us. You can enter the new year with hope, no matter what your circumstances, because even if your hope is not fulfilled in this lifetime, you can still hold on to God's promise that heaven awaits you in the future.

Heavenly Father, thank You so much that I can put my hope in heaven. This hope is a secure anchor in my life because I know that this hope will come to pass. Amen.

Do Your Work for God

Serve wholeheartedly, as if you were serving the Lord, not men (Ephesians 6:7).

Philip Yancey tells how he visited Calcutta where the nuns who had been trained by Mother Teresa serve the poorest and most wretched people on the planet with great love. No one can understand the commitment of these sisters. They get up at four in the morning, and sing and pray together before they begin with their daily work. The calmness of these women's spirits astounded Yancey.

Mother Teresa instituted a rule that her nuns should set aside Thursdays for prayer and rest. "The work will always be here, but if we do not rest and pray, we will not have the strength to do our work," she told them. Yancey reports that these sisters work with a wonderful calmness. They do not work to complete a specific workload for a specified charitable organization. They work for God. They begin their day with Him, they bring their day to a close with Him – and everything in between is an offering to God. Only God determines their worth and measures their success.

This year you can try to follow the example of these nuns of Calcutta. Let this be your motto for the new year – to do your work for God. Look to God for guidance, because He is the only one who can determine your worth and measure your success. Make sure to set aside specific and sufficient time to be alone with Him and that you get sufficient rest. If you're willing to do this, you will be able to bring about miracles this year.

Heavenly Father, please help me this year to do everything I do for You, and to look only to You when I want to achieve success. Amen.

January 9

Carried by God

"You whom I have upheld since you were conceived, and have carried since your birth. Even to your old age and gray hairs I am He, I am He who will sustain you. I have made you and I will carry you" (Isaiah 46:3-4).

There is a beautiful contrast presented to us in Isaiah 46:1-4: While His covenanted people forsook Him and carried worthless idols in their hands, God did not stop carrying them. There are various promises in the Bible that God will carry His children – that He will care for them from their birth through to their old age, that even through times of difficulty He will carry them when their strength is weak.

Perhaps it would be good, at the beginning of the new year, to take a personal inventory: Are you still burdening yourself, like the Israelites of old, with worthless idols that are weighing you down because you refuse to let them go, or are you allowing God to carry you? Someone who is being carried has to make no effort of his or her own – he simply has to be still and allow the other person to carry the load.

For people who are willing to become still and allow God to carry them, the beautiful promise found in Isaiah is still valid today: The God who created you has undertaken to carry you every day of this new year, to save you and to hold you close, and to give you sufficient strength for each day right through to your old age.

Heavenly Father, forgive me for sometimes being weary because I carry so many unnecessary burdens with me. Lord, today I want to allow You to pick me up and carry me. Please hold me tight and save me from all danger. Amen.

With Jesus in Your Boat

Jesus got up and rebuked the wind and the raging waters; the storm subsided, and all was calm. "Where is your faith?" He asked His disciples (Luke 8:24-25).

In May 2005 I had a moving experience. The Bizweni congregation invited me to spend a morning with a class of severely disabled children.

There were five teachers who cared for about sixteen children. Each teacher was given the chance to tell the same Bible story in his own words and show the pictures in a children's Bible to his little group of children. The story was the one where Jesus was awoken by His disciples when a storm broke out on the sea. I listened in awe to the group of five teachers who repeated the same story five times and wondered how much the children, whose ages ranged from four years to twelve years, had actually understood of it. Not one of them was in a position to be able to communicate verbally in any way. When it was the turn of a young black teacher to show his group the pictures, he ended his story with words that I will never forget, "If you have Jesus in your boat with you, you can laugh in the storm."

Make sure that Jesus is in your boat of life this year. Then the storms of life can come against you but you will not need to fear. Not only can He calm any storm, but He also keeps you safe, even after you die.

Lord Jesus, thank You for the privilege of being able to laugh in the storm because You are in my boat of life and I can be certain that with You by my side I am completely safe at all times. Amen.

Live as God Asks You To

He has showed you, O man, what is good. And what does the LORD require of you? To act justly and to love mercy and to walk humbly with your God (Micah 6:8).

Some psychologists suggest a treatment in which patients should act as if a certain situation is true, even though the circumstances might reflect the complete opposite. If you are unhappy in your marriage you need to treat your husband like you did when you were first married; if you are struggling to forgive someone, act as if you have already done so; and if you do not like someone, behave as if that person is your best friend. Such a lifestyle ensures that these positive actions can influence your whole life positively.

Through the mouth of the prophet Micah, God showed His people how He wanted them to live. He expected more than sacrifices from them. Their relationship with Him needed to be right and their love for Him should be reflected in the way they live: they should do what is right, be faithful to Him, love Him and live humbly.

Try to apply God's command to the prophet Micah in your own life. This year, behave in the way that the Lord asks you to, do the things that are good and right in His eyes. If you ask Him, God will make it possible for you to treat all people with fairness and righteousness, and to let your love and faithfulness for Him and others be evident in the way that you live before your God.

Heavenly Father, this year I truly desire to live as You long for me to do. It is my prayer that You will teach me to do what is right, to approach You as well as all other people with love, faithfulness and humility. Amen.

Be Holy

To be made new in the attitude of your minds; and to put on the new self, created to be like God in true righteousness and holiness (Ephesians 4:23-24).

If you want to be like Jesus, it is necessary for you to start living a holy life, just as He is holy, to begin thinking in a new way and to fulfill God's will.

In *Reaching for the Invisible God*, Philip Yancey refers to Thomas Merton's reflection and meditation in which he ponders how we can even begin to know God if we do not at least begin to be somewhat like He is. We do not see and then act, but act and then begin to see.

An active relationship with God is only possible if you make up your mind to obey His commands, to set aside sufficient time to spend with God, if you get to know Him better through studying His Word and doing His will.

We can begin to understand God's holiness if we try to behave as Jesus did. John writes, "Whoever claims to live in Him must walk as Jesus did" (1 John 2:6). If you do not really understand what this means, then go and read the four Gospels through from beginning to end so that you can see how Jesus lived and behaved. And then, as Jesus recommended to His disciples after He had told them the parable of the Good Samaritan, "Go, then, and do exactly the same!" Because it is only when you focus your whole life on acting just as Jesus did that you will be able to begin living a holy life.

Lord Jesus, it is my deepest desire to become more like You each day. Renew my thoughts and my soul, help me to live a holy life and to obey Your will in all things. Amen.

First Do and Then You Will See

Then Jesus told him, "Because you have seen Me, you have believed; blessed are those who have not seen and yet have believed" (John 20:29).

Thomas refused to believe that Jesus had really risen from the dead; he insisted that he could not believe unless he saw Him with his own eyes. Then Jesus appeared to Thomas and invited him to look at His nail-pierced hands and to put his hand into the wound in Jesus' side. Thomas was awestruck. All that he could manage to utter was, "My Lord and my God!"

If you truly want to become like Jesus, it is necessary to start behaving as if you believe it and then you will see how the things that you believe will become true, as we read yesterday.

Thomas Merton goes on to say that the person who first wants to see clearly before he believes never actually sets out on the journey. The writer of Hebrews is very clear on this matter. He writes, "Now faith is being sure of what we hope for and certain of what we do not see" (see Heb. 11:1). If you still insist on visual evidence before you are prepared to believe in God, you will not get very far. Trust God even if you cannot see what lies ahead in the future. Trust Him to help you in all your undertakings that lie ahead of you in this new year. If you take Him at His Word – even though His promises have not yet come true for you – you will reap the fruit of your faith.

Lord Jesus, sometimes I really struggle to believe when I don't see. Please forgive me, and make it possible for me to take You at Your Word this year. Amen.

Faith Is a Choice

"'If you can'?" said Jesus. "Everything is possible for him who believes" (Mark 9:23).

The children of God need to commit themselves to attempting to act like Jesus; to believe in Him without insisting that what they believe in must be made visible. And yet it is not that easy to keep on believing when the promises of God just do not seem to come to pass in your own life. There is then only one thing left for you: *choose to believe in God.* Sheldon Vanauken declares that to choose is to believe. All that we can do is to choose. It is not that we do not ever doubt, but we do ask for help to overcome our doubt after we have made the decision. We are, in effect, saying, "Lord I believe; help my unbelief."

This year you can choose to believe in God once again. Perhaps there will be days when you may still doubt. On those days simply hold fast to the promises of God that He has mapped out for you in His Word and be obedient to the things that He highlights for you in His Word.

There are many things that we will never be able to understand with our human minds and yet every Christian can choose day by day to trust God. The prophet Isaiah reminds us that He is the one you can trust every day of your life (see Isa. 33:6), and of all the people who have trusted in God through the ages, not one has been disappointed.

Lord Jesus, I want to put my trust in You today and choose to continually believe in You in spite of my negative circumstances. Please help me in the areas where I still doubt. Amen.

Two Extremes

What is man that You are mindful of him, the son of man that You care for him? You made him a little lower than the heavenly beings and crowned him with glory and honor (Psalm 8:4-5).

The Bible is full of paradoxes: the last shall be first; a person needs to lose his life in order to gain it; children are the most important people in the kingdom of God; if you truly want to be great, you need to be prepared to serve others; we are sinners from the moment of our birth and we are made in the image of God.

An old Jewish rabbi once remarked that every person should carry two stones in his pocket. One on which should be written: *I am but dust and ashes*; while the message written on the other should be: *The world was created for my benefit*. The rabbi went on to explain that we should use each stone as needed.

What a valuable lesson for the new year that lies ahead: be aware of how worthless and incomplete you are every day, but know also that God has placed you on this earth as His image-bearer and that He sacrificed His Son so that the price of your sins could be covered.

You must never become big-headed about your achievements, but you need also never succumb to feelings of inferiority. On the days that you feel really good about yourself, remind yourself that you are made of dust, but when you sit on the ash heap with Job, think about the fact that you are the crown of God's Creation, His image-bearer. Between these two extremes you should manage to live a balanced life this year.

Heavenly Father, help me never to become proud and arrogant but always to remember my shortcomings. Yet I worship You because You have made me so wonderful that I can be Your image-bearer. Amen.

Life Is Difficult

"I have told you these things, so that in Me you may have peace. In this world you will have trouble. But take heart! I have overcome the world" (John 16:33).

It is interesting to note that the book that has spent the longest time at the top of the *New York Times* Best-Sellers List is *The Road Less Traveled* by M. Scott Peck – a book that begins with the words: Life is difficult.

Job says that man is born to trouble (Job 5:7). Before Jesus was crucified He also warned His disciples that life is hard. That is why you can reasonably expect your share of difficulties this year. Because we are people who live on a planet that is interspersed with sin, it is inevitable that hardship will at some or other time come your way. It might be that your new year will include a sickbed; perhaps you will be disappointed because your dreams will not be realized; you might experience financial setbacks. But in the midst of all these difficulties you can depend on the fact that Jesus has already overcome the world and that He is on your side.

On top of this, hardships always have a positive side as well – it is in fact your hardships that cause you to draw more closely to God, that help to reveal your own inabilities. Fortunately, the children of God know that He is with us when we go through hard times. Trials are good because they nurture perseverance, so writes Paul to the church in Rome; and in its turn, perseverance develops sincerity of faith, and sincerity of faith develops hope (see Rom. 5:5). This year, use your allotment of hardship to help you to grow in faith.

Lord Jesus, over and over again I have found that life is difficult. Thank You that hardship can be an advantage because it keeps me very close to You, and because it develops perseverance and sincerity and faith. Amen.

Hold Fast to Your Faith!

Let us throw off everything that hinders and the sin that so easily entangles, and let us run with perseverance the race marked out for us. Let us fix our eyes on Jesus, the author and perfecter of our faith. Consider Him ... so that you will not grow weary and lose heart (Hebrews 12:1-3).

Philip Yancey says that faith will always mean that you believe something that cannot be proved, and that because of it you commit yourself to something of which you can never be absolutely sure. Someone who lives by faith is compelled to proceed on incomplete evidence and to believe in something up front that will only make sense in retrospect.

It is rather difficult to keep believing when there are few visible signs around you to which you can attach your faith. Perhaps it would be good if every Christian were to realize that it is not all that easy to believe. And that it is impossible to believe from our own self if God does not put faith into our lives. God makes it possible for you to believe. The fact that you believe in Him is not the result of your own cleverness, but is pure grace.

The road of your earthly journey will at the very best of times be full of potholes and it is doubtful if you will succeed on your own in living the way God expects you to. Yet you can be sure that if you persevere, if you hold fast to your faith and keep your eyes focused on Jesus the Author and Perfecter of your faith, you will not become spiritually weary, but will eventually one day arrive at your heavenly destination.

Lord Jesus, I praise You that You have made it possible for me to hold fast to my faith, to keep my eyes focused on You so that I will one day arrive at the right destination. Amen.

Unfulfilled Expectations

Hope deferred makes the heart sick, but a longing fulfilled is a tree of life (Proverbs 13:12).

Perhaps you should, at the beginning of a new year, make peace with the fact that not everything you are hoping for this year will happen. The reason that we sometimes become disillusioned and disheartened is simply because we want things to be different from what they actually are.

If you apply for a job and are reasonably certain that you will get it, you are floored if your application fails; if you have planned a trip overseas in great detail and your plane is three hours late, you will be upset about the time that has been wasted. It is also understandable if you are disappointed because your child has not done as well in his course at university as you expected him to.

There is, however, a way in which you can limit disappointments in the year that lies ahead. Learn not to nurture so many expectations that will probably not work out, and trust God with your dreams. Focus on Him, be prepared to exchange your will for His and ask Him to intervene on your behalf in the new year; that He will give you the strength to handle your crises in the right way.

Do not see yourself as the victim of every disaster, but learn from it. And hold fast to the promise in Romans 8:28, that ultimately the Lord will cause all things – even the disasters – to work out for your good if you love Him.

Heavenly Father, please help me this year to handle my expectations that do not work out in the right way. Thank You for Your assurance that ultimately You will work all things out for my good. Amen.

When You Need Help

Lord, there is no one like You to help the powerless against the mighty.
Help us, O Lord our God, for we rely on You, and in Your name we
have come against this vast army. O Lord, You are our God; do not
let man prevail against You (2 Chronicles 14:11).

Take some time to read through the exciting story of war in 2
Chronicles 14. King Asa of Judah was confronted by a huge army.
It seemed like the only outcome of the battle against the Cushites
would be total annihilation. Asa had 500,000 soldiers who were
armed only with shields, spears, bows and arrows while the Cushite
Zerah's army consisted of a million men and 300 chariots. It was
crystal clear to King Asa that only God could help them now, and
he prayed that things would work out as they had so many times
before in the history of Israel.

As always, God listens when His children come to Him asking
for help. He answered King Asa's prayer for help and in verse 12 we
read that the Lord caused the Cushites to be defeated by Judah. So
many Cushites were slaughtered that King Zerah was never able to
restore his army.

The Lord is fighting on your side this year. When you have to face
moments of crisis that you are not able to deal with on your own,
you can confidently seek His help. He can still help the weak against
an army. With Him on your side you can be sure that you will be on
the winning side every day of the new year.

Heavenly Father, it is wonderful to know that I can simply come and
ask for Your help this year when crises unravel in my life, I know that
I am always a winner because You are on my side. Amen.

Seek the Lord Purposefully

The LORD is near to all who call on Him, to all who call on Him in truth (Psalm 145:18).

Walter Ciszek wrote a remarkable book called *He Leadeth Me*. All through his life, Ciszek struggled to reconcile the negative situations he faced every day while he was in a labor camp in Siberia with God's will. His hard life taught him bit by bit to trust in God with a childlike faith, but he continued to seek a clearer experience of the presence of God in his life. Eventually he found it in a somewhat unlikely place: in the camp where he was being held a prisoner.

In *Reaching for the Invisible God*, Philip Yancey writes about how Ciszek came to the realization that through faith we can know that God is present everywhere and is always there if we simply turn to Him. It is therefore us who need to place ourselves in the presence of God; we who need to turn to Him in faith. We need to look beyond the image to the faith – in fact the realization – that we are in the presence of the loving Father who is always ready to listen to our childish stories and respond to our childlike faith. Ciszek had to learn that life is really not fair and that God does not simply smooth the road for us with a wave of a magic wand.

Even though all things will not fall in exactly the right places for you this year, you can know that you will find God if you seek Him, that He is close to all those who call on Him in righteousness, that He will lead you if you ask Him to do so.

Heavenly Father, thank You very much for the assurance that You are always there when I call on You in righteousness – even in those times when things go wrong for me – in the year that lies ahead. Amen.

January 21

Dependence on God

Now listen, you who say, "Today or tomorrow we will go to this or that city, spend a year there, carry on business and make money." Why, you do not even know what will happen tomorrow. Instead, you ought to say, "If it is the Lord's will, we will live and do this or that" (James 4:13-15).

Sometimes we wrongly imagine that we are in control of ourselves, our time and our future. People who think this are mistaken. Not one of us knows what will happen tomorrow. At the beginning of a new year you do not know if by the end of the year your whole life will have turned upside down.

The future remains a closed book to people. And yet the children of God can dream dreams and make plans for the future – just as long as they realize that their plans must fit in with God's plans for His kingdom, and as long as they are willing to submit their plans to the will of God. Ultimately He is the only One who holds the future in His hands. And because you know for certain that He loves you, you also know that nothing happens by chance in the life of a Christian. God already knows what He has planned for you in the new year.

Acknowledge your absolute dependence on God right now. In the Sermon on the Mount, Jesus told the people that those who know that they are dependent on God will receive the kingdom of God (see Matt. 5:3). To live within the will of God and to be completely dependent on Him is the only guarantee that you will be successful and happy in the year that lies ahead.

Heavenly Father, forgive me for so reluctantly surrendering control of my life to You. This year I want to live within Your will, in complete dependence on You. Please help me to do so. Amen.

Leave the Baggage of the Past!

One thing I do: Forgetting what is behind and straining toward what is ahead, I press on toward the goal to win the prize for which God has called me heavenward in Christ Jesus (Philippians 3:13-14).

Paul tackled the challenges that lay ahead of him with the right attitude. He was not concerned with the things that had gone wrong in the past, but reached forward to the new things that lay ahead of him. He made every effort to be the first to cross the finishing line so that the heavenly prize to which God had called him, could be his.

Many people start the new year while they are still staggering under the heavy baggage of the year that has past. And it is so unnecessary. Harvey Cushing says that even the strongest man will give way when the burden of yesterday is carried together with that of tomorrow.

Perhaps you too have mistakes and faults that you have made in the year that has past. Begin this year without the burden of the things that are behind you and gird yourself up to reach the finishing line. Usually there is only one winner, but the children of God can all be winners. There is a heavenly prize that waits for each one of us.

Right now stop stressing about all the things that went wrong in the year that has past. Forget about your mistakes. Or better yet, learn from them and do not make the same mistakes again.

Heavenly Father, help me to leave the unnecessary baggage of the past behind me, to live this year with commitment and enthusiasm and to exert myself so that Your heavenly prize will be mine. Amen.

Hold Fast to God's Promises

Being fully persuaded that God had power to do what He had promised (Romans 4:21).

Abraham succeeded in continuing to hope in God and to believe in His promises long after it seemed completely impossible for the promises to ever come true. And God rewarded Abraham's persistent faith. Even though he and his wife were much too old to be able to have children, God fulfilled the promise that He would give them a son. Isaac was born because Abraham held fast to the promises of God, because he was one hundred percent convinced that God's power was sufficient to do what He had promised.

When someone ends up in the depths of despair, it is good to be reminded of the promises of God. The Bible even tells us that we should remind God of His promises (see Isa. 62:6).

Every promise of God is built on four pillars, so writes L. B. Cowman in her well-known devotional *Streams in the Desert.* The first two are the righteousness and holiness that will never allow God to deceive us, the third is His mercy that will not allow Him to forget. The fourth is His truth that will ensure that He will not change, but guarantees that He will carry out all that He has promised. You can count on this in the year that lies ahead!

Heavenly Father, just like Abraham, I hope in You and believe that You have the power to do what You have promised. Thank You that I can hold fast to Your promises in the year that lies ahead. Amen.

Your Time Is Precious!

> *Do this, understanding the present time. The hour has come for you to wake up from your slumber, because our salvation is nearer now than when we first believed. The night is nearly over; the day is almost here (Romans 13:11-12).*

Paul delivered this sermon almost 2,000 years ago – in this letter he wanted to teach the Christians in Rome that time is precious; that the return of Jesus is imminent. There is no better time to reflect on this Scripture verse than at the beginning of a new year. Not one of us knows how much more time we have to live. We simply do not have the time to live a life that is not established according to God's expectations.

There is a story about the renowned evangelist Dwight L. Moody who, one night, addressed a large crowd about sin and the judgment of God. He then invited everyone to return the next evening so that he could talk to them about the mercy of God and His salvation. That night the hall in which the meeting had been held burnt down and Moody never again had the chance to speak to that specific group of people. He reproached himself his whole life because he had not used the time he had to present the salvation message.

This year, use every opportunity that comes your way; live as God asks you to do, so that you will not later regret making better use of your time. Time that is wasted can never be reclaimed.

Lord Jesus, I realize that the time of Your return comes closer day by day. Teach me to use my time properly and to live as You ask me to. Amen.

Quiet Time

"Let My teaching fall like rain and My words descend like dew, like showers on new grass, like abundant rain on tender plants" (Deuteronomy 32:2).

How I get up in the morning determines my whole day. If I jump out of bed in a hurry in the mornings and have only five minutes to read my Bible and pray, my whole day goes wrong from the beginning. Everything I plan seems to fail, I run on a short fuse and am rushed; nothing seems to work out well.

But if I wake up early enough so that I can spend an hour alone with God and His Word and can discuss my day with Him, everything runs smoothly. I am relaxed and can solve every problem that arises with God's wisdom and His strength. As the day proceeds I am more and more aware of the presence of God in and around me.

You too can enter each day of the new year with self-confidence and confidence in God with the certain assurance that this day will be a day of victory for you because you have God with you. But you need to make time for God's instructions – you need to let His words refresh you every morning like dew.

If you neglect your quiet time, you will suffer much harm for the rest of your day. Always remember: the busier your day will be, the more you have need of your quiet time with God. The most foolish thing you can do is to neglect your quiet time because you have too many other things that demand your time.

Heavenly Father, I praise You for the privilege of being able to spend times of refreshing and restoration with You. Thank You that the words of Your Word can refresh me like morning dew. Amen.

Continue to Wait on the Lord

On one occasion, while He was eating with them, He gave them this command: "Do not leave Jerusalem, but wait for the gift My Father promised, which you have heard Me speak about" (Acts 1:4).

Jesus asked His disciples to remain in Jerusalem and to wait for the gift that His Father had promised them. If they had not listened to Him they would not have been there when the Holy Spirit was poured out.

When someone once had the opportunity to ask Abba Anthony, one of the desert fathers what a person should do to bring pleasure to God, he was immediately ready with his answer. There are three things, he said, that bring God pleasure. The first two are obvious: that we should always be aware of the presence of God and that we should obey His Word. The last one is, however, somewhat surprising: that we should not be too hasty to leave the place where we find ourselves at present.

Perhaps you are trapped in a town, job or marriage at the moment that does not seem to work out for you. Perhaps, here at the beginning of a new year you have the desire to pack up your tent and move somewhere far away. Rather diligently take heed of Abba Anthony's advice: stay where you are. This is the place where the Lord wants to use you this year, even though you are not quite happy there at the moment.

Stop being dissatisfied with your present circumstances. Rather make peace with your situation and ask God to use you in a special way this year right where you are.

Lord, I am sorry that I am so dissatisfied with my surroundings and situation. Make me willing to be used by You right here where I am. Amen.

Principles for a Better Life

I saw that wisdom is better than folly, just as light is better than darkness (Ecclesiastes 2:13).

During a series of interviews with juvenile prisoners, the writer Katie Brazelton asked each one of them what three things they would do should they be released that day. She then summarized the answers of the prisoners into six principles for a better life:

1. Live one day at a time. Do not run ahead of yourself. If you realize you are beginning to go off track, immediately make a plan to get back on.
2. Think positively. Avoid negative people and influences. Better yet, find role models and mentors who will help you when things start to become difficult.
3. Relax. Live light. Do not take yourself so seriously. Laugh more readily at yourself and with others. Enjoy good, innocent fun.
4. Give to others much, much more than you expect from them.
5. Talk to God about every decision so that you can learn to focus on the bigger picture concerning your purpose in life, and do not focus on your own desires all the time.
6. When you discover that certain something that inspires you, respond to it immediately. It will help you to stay out of trouble.

When I read these principles I realized that they are the perfect New Year's resolutions for each one of us. If you could manage to keep these six principles this year, you will also find that it is much easier to stay out of trouble!

Heavenly Father, will You please help me to follow these principles for a better life so that this year will be a good year for me. Amen.

Do Not Be Afraid!

There is no fear in love. But perfect love drives out fear, because fear has to do with punishment. The one who fears is not made perfect in love (1 John 4:18).

The command to not be afraid appears 365 times in the Bible, more than any other command, precisely because each day we encounter things that can make us afraid. And most people tend to begin the new year with a little quiver of fear in their inner being. It is hard not to be afraid of the unknown. We don't know all that lies ahead for us this year. We are afraid that we might not get through the year.

The good news is that you do not need to be afraid if you love God. God's love for you should be able to drive every fear from your life. In *Reaching for the Invisible God* Philip Yancey writes that the antidote to fear is not a change in your circumstances but a deep understanding of the love of God. This year, when you want to give in to fear, think of God's immeasurable, incomprehensible love for you. If you grasp the extent of that love your fear will simply dissolve of its own accord.

John describes this love for us in 1 John 4: 19, "We love God because He first loved us." God loved you long before the world existed declares the Bible. Right back before time began, He had already chosen you to be His. This year you can with absolute confidence take all your fears and worries to Him – He wants to give you His peace in exchange for them.

Lord Jesus, thank You that Your love will cause every fear in my life to dissolve. I praise You that I can enter the year that lies ahead under the banner of that love. Amen.

Beware of Sin

If I had cherished sin in my heart, the Lord would not have listened (Psalm 66:18).

One of the things that disturbs our relationship with God the most is sin. Unconfessed or deliberate sin has a way of building a wall between God and us so that He no longer hears our prayers.

Unfortunately we live in a society where sin has become cheap. Nothing is actually seen as wrong anymore in the eyes of the world. Living together, adulteress relationships, swearing, using drugs, watching explicit movies, lying and cheating have all become such a part of everyday life that even Christians have become used to them. But God's rule against sin remains the same – the Bible's understanding of sin has never changed.

If the wrong things around you cause you to live the wrong way, it is time that you see the red danger light flickering ahead. What you do still matters to God. He still asks you to obey His Word and His commands if you want to live close to Him. He sees sin in such a serious light that He let His Son die so that you can be forgiven for the wrong things you do.

This year, therefore, make an effort to study the Bible again so that you will know how God wants you to live. Only then will He listen to your prayers and will you live close to Him every day.

Father, please forgive me for becoming so accustomed to sin that it no longer disturbs me. Show me once again through Your Word and Your Spirit what Your will for my life is. Amen.

Live Close to God

This is what the LORD Almighty says: "In those days ten men from all languages and nations will take firm hold of one Jew by the hem of his robe and say, 'Let us go with you, because we have heard that God is with you'" (Zechariah 8:23).

The prophet Zechariah prophesied that a great number of people would go to Jerusalem to seek the will of God and to ask His advice. These people would say to the Israelites that they wanted to go with them because they could see that God was with them.

If you live close to God you have the assurance that God will also be close to you and that He will even change the way in which you think and live so that day by day you will become more like Jesus. "Come near to God and He will come near to you," writes James. He also goes on to tell us how to do it: "Wash your hands, you sinners and purify your hearts you double-minded" (James 4:8). If you are serious about drawing closer to God, you will need to be prepared to bid your sins farewell because sin will always bring about distance between you and God. If you want to live close to God, your life should demonstrate this closeness. Christianity is not a fact that you can hide away. Other people "read" your life, and that is why you ought to live in such a way that they will become jealous and will want to follow your God because they too long for the joy and peace that they see radiating from your life.

May it be true for you this year that people who look at you will want to go with you because they can see that God is with you.

Heavenly Father, I want to live in such a way that all who look at me will be able to see that You are with me. Please help me to inspire other people to also learn to know You. Amen.

Desire God

As the deer pants for streams of water, so my soul pants for You, O God. My soul thirsts for God, for the living God. When can I go and meet with God? (Psalm 42:1-2).

A person can only survive for three days without water, although he can go for forty days without food. It is therefore much more serious to be without water than it is to be without food.

The psalmist compares his longing for God in a time of hardship with the physical thirst of a deer. It is God Himself who places this desire to want to live closer to Him in our hearts and lives. The church father St. Augustine once wrote, "I invite You into my soul which has been prepared to receive You through the desire which You have placed in it."

When you truly live close to God, you cannot get by without Him and you constantly long for His presence in your life. Then you find it a joy to study the Bible, to think about God, to talk to Him and to testify about Him. Then you will be like Peter and John who, in spite of the fact that the Jewish Council forbade them to speak about Jesus, answered that they would rather obey God than people (Acts 4:19).

When you find yourself in a crisis situation you want God to be with you. You walk around all day with a longing to live even closer to Him, to have an even more intimate relationship with Him. This year satisfy your spiritual longings for God through living close to Him every day and making His Word part of your life.

Heavenly Father, I long for Your presence in my life as a deer thirsts for water. Thank You that I can experience Your closeness every day and that my relationship with You can grow stronger. Amen.

rayer

Heavenly Father,
This year I truly want to draw closer to You every day –
I want to set aside more time to spend with You,
and seek Your advice before I do anything.
Thank You for the assurance that You will be with me
every day of the new year.
I praise You because You have planned
a prosperous future for me
and You have a special vision for my life.
Teach me to understand how important today is.
Help me to use the time given to me to the best of my ability
and to take hold of every opportunity that comes my way.
I want to anchor my hope in You and work only for You –
I choose now to have faith in You.
How good You are to promise to carry me day by day!
Make it possible for me to live as You ask me to,
to be holy, to be ready to continue believing,
even when there is no visible evidence for my faith.
I want to hold fast to this faith
and run the race of faith in such a way
that I will one day win the heavenly prize.
Even if my expectations are not fulfilled
I know for certain that You will help me when I need You.
I confess my absolute dependence on You, Lord,
which is why I want to wait on You, avoid sin
and unburden all my fears on You.
My heart longs for You.

Amen.

February

Knowing the Word of God

Your Bible is extremely precious and indispensable if you really desire your relationship with God to grow and increase in depth and intimacy.

Pam Farrel, in her book *Woman of Influence*, declares that, "Each woman can build her relationship with God by hearing, reading, studying, memorizing and obeying God's Word. Within its pages you will find everything you need for a life of hope and meaning."

Every child of God has a desperate need for a personal and intimate knowledge of His pure Word. Kay Arthur says that God gives us a lifetime, which is how long it will take, to mine the treasures of His Word.

How precious is your Bible to you? It is my prayer that by the end of this month you will not only have a better understanding of your Bible, but will have experienced a more intimate relationship with God.

Find Your Joy in the Word!

Blessed is the man who does not walk in the counsel of the wicked. But his delight is in the law of the LORD. He is like a tree planted by streams of water, which yields its fruit in season and whose leaf does not wither. Whatever he does prospers (Psalm 1:1-3).

In Psalm 1 we are given a beautiful description of what a person looks like when God's Word is a joy and delight to him; the kind of person who spends time in the Word. Such a person is like a tree that grows beside streams of water. Because his roots are always receiving water, his leaves remain green and he bears fruit in season.

Things always go well for such a person and the Word of God and his relationship with God are a constant source of joy to him. On the other hand, people who live far from God, are like chaff that is blown away by the wind and their road through life leads to a dead end.

If you set aside time to study God's Word then you will be like the psalmist's tree that is planted near streams of water and you will be a source of strength for others and you will bear spiritual fruit for God. God also undertakes to make you prosperous because He will bless you in all that you do.

The choice is ultimately yours. You alone can choose if you want to be like a tree planted beside streams of water, taking pleasure in God's Word and finding your joy in it ... or like chaff that is blown away by the wind because you do not know the Word of God. Choose today what you want to be.

Heavenly Father, I choose now to find my joy in Your Word, to bear fruit for You and to be a source of strength. Please prosper me and bless me in all that I do. Amen.

Your Bible Is Amazing

You will do well to pay attention to it, as to a light shining in a dark place, until the day dawns and the morning star rises in your hearts (2 Peter 1:19).

Most of us take our Bibles for granted, we see it as a well-known and well-loved book that sits on our bedside tables. We do not fully realize what a remarkable book the Bible really is. Through the centuries, the Word of God has often been questioned, yet scientific research has proven the declarations in it to be true time and time again. It has been compiled from sixty-six separate books that were written by more than forty writers in three languages over a time period of more than three thousand years. And yet it has a common thread and a central message that runs through it and everything in the Bible makes perfect sense!

In the Old Testament we find the history of the people of God and the promise of the coming Messiah. The New Testament deals with the birth, life, death and resurrection of Jesus and the spreading of His joyous message over the whole of the then known world.

To fully understand the Bible, you need the input of the Holy Spirit. Only He can clarify the Word for you. The message of the Word should also not be kept to yourself – you should not only be staying in its light, but you should carry the light of the Word to all people you meet, so that they too can experience the wonder of the Word for themselves.

Heavenly Father, I praise You for the wonder of Your Word. Send Your Holy Spirit to explain it to me, so that I can live in the light of Your Word and convey its message to everyone I know. Amen.

Road Map for Life

The unfolding of Your words gives light. Direct my footsteps according to Your word (Psalm 119:130, 133).

When sinful people read the words of a holy God, a miracle happens: the Word opens up for us, gives us wisdom and insight and at the same time keeps us on the path which God Himself has outlined for us.

It is almost impossible to try and find your way in a strange city if you do not have a map to show you the right road you need to take to get to your destination. You will be so lost that it will take you hours to find the right address.

Your Bible is like a road map that God has given to you so that you can know exactly how He wants you to live. With the help of this Road Map you will not get lost on all kinds of detours and diversions, but you will eventually arrive at your destination.

It is necessary to consult your Road Map every day. Ask the Holy Spirit to reveal God's Word to you each time you open the Bible. Ask Him to explain it to you so that it will give you insight on how to carry out the instructions in the Word. If you set aside sufficient time each day for Bible study, you will definitely stay on the right road.

Heavenly Father, thank You so much for the Bible, the Road Map that comes directly from You, and that gives me light on my path through life and insight into Your will. I pray that Your Word will always keep me on the right road. Amen.

Walk According to the Word

Blessed are they whose ways are blameless, who walk according to the law of the LORD. Blessed are they who keep His statutes and seek Him with all their heart (Psalm 119:1-2).

The commandments of God are set out in detail in His Word for you so that you can learn exactly what His will for your life is. The better you know the Bible, the better you will know what God desires of you. The psalmist says that those people who organize their whole lives according to God's Word and obey His will with their whole heart have the promise that it will go well with them.

God wants His children to walk according to His Word, that they will do exactly what His Word asks of them. The reason that His commands are so clearly presented in the Bible is so that we can carry them out completely and exactly.

To walk in obedience to God involves a slow, but steady progression in His Word. If you are serious about staying involved with the Word of God, wanting to learn to know it intimately, and to live according to it, you can be assured that you will make progress and move ahead in your spiritual life.

You will change for the better day by day so that as the years go by you will become more and more like Jesus.

Lord, teach me to carry out the commandments found in Your Word. Provide me with the right insight so that I can obey Your law and make it possible for me to live irreproachably and to walk according to Your Word. Amen.

February 5

Read John 17:13-23

The Word of God Is the Truth

"Sanctify them by the truth; Your word is truth. My prayer is not for them alone. I pray also for those who will believe in Me through their message" (John 17:17, 20).

In the High Priestly prayer, Jesus prayed for His followers who were to remain behind in the world. He sent them into the world to continue with His work and to make disciples. Just like Jesus when He was on earth and revealed the Father to them, they were now to carry His gospel message to others and be completely yielded to Him through the Truth.

The Bible puts an extremely high premium on the Truth. The Truth encompasses all that is good and right. The Word of God is the Truth. This Word keeps God's children on the right track so that in word and deed, heart and mind they will live more and more in line with the law of God. Through their actions, the Word of God will be made known throughout the whole world and His power will be clearly seen. Jesus also prayed for those people who would come to believe in Him through the testimony of His disciples.

In order for Jesus' mission to the world to be successful, it is imperative that the content of His Word should be made known to all people so that they will come to believe in Him. Jesus expects you to make the Truth of His Word known on the earth so that those people who hear it will come to know Him and love Him.

Lord Jesus, thank You for Your Word that is the Truth. I want to live in such a way that I will be completely surrendered to You in truth and spread Your Word so that all those who hear will come to believe in You. Please make this possible for me. Amen.

The Word Is Close to You

"The word is near you; it is in your mouth and in your heart," that is, the word of faith we are proclaiming: That if you confess with your mouth, "Jesus is Lord," and believe in your heart that God raised Him from the dead, you will be saved (Romans 10:8-9).

In Deuteronomy 30 Moses speaks to the Israelites about what is written in the law of God. In Deuteronomy 30:10, he promised them, "The LORD will again delight in you and make you prosperous, just as He delighted in your fathers, if you obey the LORD your God and keep His commands and decrees that are written in this Book of the Law and turned to the LORD your God with all your heart and with all your soul" (Deut. 30:9-10). The blessing of God and His care for His people is seen here to have a condition: The people must undertake to obey the laws and commands that have been recorded in the Book of the Law.

In Romans 10 Paul gives the church in Rome a practical explanation of how to become a Christian. The redemption of God is as close to you as His Word. If you study your Bible you will know exactly what to do to come to faith. And faith is still the only requirement for your salvation.

The Word of God should be in your heart and in your mouth. With your mouth you confess that Jesus is Lord and with your heart you believe that He died for your sins and that He rose from the dead. This is *all* that you need to be saved.

Lord Jesus, Your Word is near to me, in my mouth and in my heart. Give me the boldness to confess my faith and to share it with others so that they too can believe in You. Amen.

A Living Word

The word of God is living and active. Sharper than any double-edged sword, it penetrates even to dividing soul and spirit, joints and marrow; it judges the thoughts and attitudes of the heart (Hebrews 4:12).

God means what He says. What He says goes. His powerful Word is as sharp as a surgeon's scalpel, cutting through everything, whether doubt or defense, laying us open to listen and obey. Nothing and no-one is impervious to God's Word. We can't get away from it – no matter what" says Hebrews 4:12 (*The Message*). The Word of God is alive. Martin Luther said that the Bible is alive and that it spoke to him in every life circumstance. It had feet and ran behind him, it overtook him when he tried to get away from what said; it had hands and it seized him.

When you become involved in the Word, you cannot stay the same. The Bible points out your sins to you, it penetrates your innermost being. It changes you and evaluates the things that you say and think. Even your hidden thoughts and intentions are brought to light. By the time you have finished with the Word your whole life will lie open before God, and you will realize exactly how big a sinner you are.

Therefore, listen to what the Word has to say to you and be prepared to be thoroughly changed through the Word.

Lord Jesus, thank You for Your powerful Word that penetrates deep into my innermost being and exposes my deepest feelings. I want to become what Your Word asks of me, Lord. Help me to be obedient to You. Amen.

February 8

Be Taught by the Word

He chose to give us birth through the word of truth, that we might be a kind of firstfruits of all He created. My dear brothers, take note of this: Everyone should be quick to listen, slow to speak and slow to become angry (James 1:18-19).

The children of God need to read the Word of God with meekness and humility. We ought to pay careful attention to what the Word of God has to say to us. We also need to be willing to allow the Word of God to teach us.

How do you respond to the Word of God? James warned us not to get upset if we do not agree with what the Word has to say. You are not free to impose your own interpretation on it or only read specific things in the Bible that correspond with your own opinions. You must be willing to open your heart to what the Lord wants to say to you.

If you do this, you will not only be able to serve the Lord better, but you will also discover that as you begin to obey the Word your life will take on new meaning and direction.

A life that is disconnected from the Word can never really be happy because the Word saves you from inner brokenness and prevents you from making mistakes. Therefore, be open to receive the Word of God so that you can be open to the things that God wants to share with you.

Lord, it seems impossible to think that You personally speak to me each time I open Your Word. Help me to be prepared to live my life according to the guidelines of Your Word and to be obedient to it. Amen.

A Doer of the Word

Do not merely listen to the word, and so deceive yourselves. Do what it says. Anyone who listens to the word but does not do what it says is like a man who looks at his face in a mirror and, after looking at himself, goes away and immediately forgets what he looks like (James 1:22-24).

The Bible hits the center of the bull's eye regarding the affairs of people. The Bible clearly stipulates what is required of you in order to live a meaningful life. If you stray from this law your whole life will fall apart, but if you obey it your life gains new meaning and significance.

The moment you begin to follow and obey the Word of God you will be happy. The Greek word that is translated with "do" in this Scripture verse means that you will "look deeply into" something with intense interest. The same word is used when the disciples came to the tomb of Jesus and looked into the empty grave. This is the kind of attitude that you require in your time spent with the Bible.

Many people read their Bibles but what they read goes in one ear and out the other. If you are in the habit of reading your Bible absent-mindedly and immediately forget what you have read, you will miss an awful lot. Decide right now what you will do with the message of the Bible that is directed at you. Are you prepared to study it intensely and obey it?

Heavenly Father, You know that I love Your Word. Teach me to read my Bible with careful attention and make me willing to obey to the letter Your commands that are written in the Bible. Amen.

The Secret to a Happy Life

The man who looks intently into the perfect law that gives freedom, and continues to do this, not forgetting what he has heard, but doing it – he will be blessed in what he does (James 1:25).

God speaks out in His Word. James writes that someone who takes the trouble to learn all about the Word of God and is prepared to listen to the will of God will be set free from all the wrong things that can turn a person's life upside-down. Someone who has such an interest in the will of God and does those things that he hears in the Word is the one who is truly happy and has discovered the real meaning of life.

James uses four verbs to emphasize this focus on the Word: you need to *look* intently into the Word, *continue* in it, not *forgetting* what you have heard but *doing* it, then you will be blessed (see James 1:25).

In the mirror of God's Word you can see yourself for who you really are. If you are willing to take the Word of God seriously and to obey the things that have been recorded in it and remember them, God guarantees that you will have a blessed life.

Ronald Reagan said that within the pages of the Bible are the answers to all the problems that people have ever experienced. The Bible is able to touch hearts, put minds in order and refresh souls.

No wonder the Bible can make us happy!

Heavenly Father, thank You that You talk to me every time I open the Bible and that I can find solutions for all my questions and problems in it. I want to look more deeply into Your Word, persevere in it, remember what I have heard, and do it. Please help me to do this. Amen.

A Light for Your Path

Your word is a lamp to my feet and a light for my path (Psalm 119:105).

During the electricity power cuts we experienced in 2006, in the Western Cape, many people were left in pitch darkness on some winter mornings. It was rather traumatic to have to light candles, like in the old days, in order to see. And to have to do without morning coffee if you did not have a generator or gas stove; not to speak of the chaos on the roads in the busy early morning traffic without any working traffic lights.

Unexpected, sudden darkness has a way of disorientating people – even in familiar surroundings. While these power cuts continued, I counted my blessings more than ever that we no longer live in the Middle Ages, and that I am not blind.

Every person goes through dark times in his or her life. And in those times it is only the Bible that can serve as a light and the promises of God that can brighten your day.

In the dark world in which we live, the Bible is the lamp that shows us the way. It shows us where and when to walk, it makes us aware of dangers and makes it possible to see. With the Word of the Lord as a light, we can, in the darkest times of life, travel with joy.

Heavenly Father, I praise You for the light of Your Word that shows the right path for me every day, that points out dangers to me and that makes it possible for me to pursue my life's journey joyfully and safely. Amen.

Meditate on the Word

Do not let this Book of the Law depart from your mouth; meditate on it day and night, so that you may be careful to do everything written in it. Then you will be prosperous and successful (Joshua 1:8).

When Joshua took over from Moses as the leader of the Israelites, God told Joshua that the Book of the Law should direct his words; he should meditate on it and carry out all that is written in it.

To really understand the Bible it is necessary to meditate on it day and night and make the truths that are found in it your own. You can, therefore, not just quickly scan through it like with a storybook, but you should really take to heart what is written in it and think it over.

Martin Luther often said that people should have a thought from the Holy Scriptures in their minds when they go to bed at night and then fall asleep meditating on this thought. So that when they wake up the next morning this thought will come back to them and bear fruit.

When you have made a specific part in the Bible your own, God asks you to do all that is written in it. If you are willing to do this He guarantees you success – then He will make sure that you will succeed in all you do.

Heavenly Father, I pray that You will help me to make Your Word my own by helping me to meditate on it and to be obedient. Thank You for the promise that You will make me prosper in all that I do for Your glory. Amen.

God's Word Touches Your Life

If anyone considers himself religious and yet does not keep a tight rein on his tongue, he deceives himself and his religion is worthless (James 1:26).

When you come to know the depths of God's Word and are prepared to obey it you will be blessed, as we read yesterday. But the Word of God does not only make you happy, it touches your whole life. With the Word of God as your guideline even your own words will be affected and changed.

You will no longer use the name of God in vain. Instead, you will find that you are able to hold your tongue; to speak words of truth and encouragement to other people.

The Word of God affects your *ears* because you can hear the cries of help from orphans and widows. The Word of God affects your *hands* to be able to do things for those who are helpless. The Word of God touches your *heart* to keep you pure from the sinfulness of the world, from all the things that defile people on the inside.

In short, the Word of God completely changes your way of life. You no longer live far away from God, but His words are in your heart and they guide your life. Your faith is no longer meaningless, but it becomes the most important thing in your life. Do not put off exposing yourself to the Word of God in this way.

Heavenly Father, I praise You for Your Word that touches my tongue, hands and heart and inspires me to obey You and to follow You with my whole life. From now on I want to live with Your Word as my only guide. Amen.

Learn the Word

Jesus replied, "You are in error because you do not know the Scriptures or the power of God" (Matthew 22:29).

The Pharisees and scribes tried to trap Jesus time and again through their questions, but they did not succeed because He knew the Scriptures too well. When He was tempted by the Devil in the wilderness, He was able to trump the Devil three times with answers from the Scriptures.

In today's Scripture passage it was the Sadducees who did not believe in the resurrection and tried to catch Jesus out with their question. If a woman was married to each of seven brothers, whose wife would she be when the resurrection takes place, they wanted to know from Him. Jesus made short shrift with them. His answer was focused on two aspects: the correct knowledge of Scripture and the power of God. They wandered from the truth because they did not know the power of the Scriptures or of God, Jesus said.

If you are willing to take your study of the Bible seriously, you, like Jesus, will know how to answer people who try to ask you trick questions. It is good to read books that explain things in the Bible such as concordances and commentaries, as well using various Bible translations. In this way, each time you study the Bible, a verse or passage will be seen from a different angle and your knowledge of the Bible will increase.

The more confident you become with the Word of God, the more wisdom and insight you will receive.

Heavenly Father, there is so much insight and wisdom locked up in Your Word. Help me to study it and to consult other books that can explain Your Word to me so that I can truly know my Bible and use it to answer people's trick questions. Amen.

The Bible Comes from God

All Scripture is God-breathed and is useful for teaching, rebuking, correcting and training in righteousness (2 Timothy 3:16).

We clearly understand that the Bible is not just a book that came into existence through the effort and knowledge of people when we read the history of how the Bible was written. The Bible itself is very clear about the fact that it was inspired by God and that the preaching of the Word also takes place through the working of the Holy Spirit.

Peter writes, "For prophecy never had its origin in the will of man, but men spoke from God as they were carried along by the Holy Spirit (2 Pet. 1:21). "Every part of Scripture is God-breathed and useful one way or another," states 2 Timothy 3:16 in *The Message*.

The more you read your Bible, the more time you give to studying it, the better you will understand God's message to you. Even though dedicated, sustained Bible study will demand much discipline from you, it is always worth the effort because the words in your Bible are not human words but a love letter from God Himself.

For that reason you must not just read your Bible, but become actively involved in it: pray before you begin to read the Bible and ask God to open His Word to you. Pray again when you have finished reading and answer God on His Word. By reading your Bible you will receive a personal message directly from God every day. Make sure that you do not only discover the message but also live it out every day.

Heavenly Father, my Bible is very precious to me. I know that the content of my Bible comes directly from You. It is very exciting to hear You speak to me each day when I read my Bible. Please help me to be obedient to the commands in Your Word. Amen.

What the Bible Does

As for you, continue in what you have learned and have become convinced of ... and how from infancy you have known the holy Scriptures, which are able to make you wise for salvation through faith in Christ Jesus. All Scripture is God-breathed and is useful for teaching, rebuking, correcting and training in righteousness (2 Timothy 3:14-16).

Even though Timothy's father was a Greek, he knew the Scriptures from a young age because his mother and grandmother were God-fearing women. In this letter, Paul asks Timothy to steadfastly hold on to the things that he had learned when he was young and in which he believed. He also tells him what the Scripture can do: through reading it you find out how to be saved; it helps you to know when you deviate from the right path; it also makes it possible for you to help other people find the right way when they are on the wrong path. The better Timothy knew the Scriptures, the better he would be able to tell other people how God wants them to live.

Your Bible still does the same today: people who know their Bibles are equipped to work for God because they know what God expects of them. They can help other people to find the right way and set misconceptions right by helping them to nurture the right way of living.

The studying and lifestyle of people who enter into the service of God should be determined by the Bible. Try to learn and to live out the things that you read in your Bible.

Heavenly Father, thank You that I have been able to know and read Your Bible. It helps me to believe in You and to help other people to find the right way when they are on the wrong path. Amen.

When the Word Opens Up ...

The unfolding of Your words gives light; it gives understanding to the simple. Direct my footsteps according to Your word (Psalm 119:130, 133).

Through the centuries, thousands of preachers have received new insight and enlightenment from their Bibles every Sunday when they preach to their congregations. The more sermons I listen to, the more I marvel at the wonderful inspiration that people gather from their Bibles. I am amazed, too, when I am busy with my own Bible study to find that things that were at first unclear suddenly become clear as I read a specific part of Scripture.

When the Word of God suddenly opens up for people, it really does bring light and gives insight to people who are inexperienced. It fills ordinary people with wisdom. If you do not know right from wrong, you simply have to turn to the Bible. Also when you most need to hear the voice of God, in times of hardship or crises, the right advice can be found in your Bible. You will also find that time after time well-known, trusted Scripture verses suddenly have a fresh new meaning for you. You hear the voice of God so clearly that it seems almost unbelievable.

But it is only the Holy Spirit that can reveal the Word of God to people. That is why you should never read your Bible haphazardly or open it randomly. Read your Bible prayerfully in such a way as not to take the Scripture verses out of context.

Spirit of God, I pray that You will open the Word to me so that it can fill me with wisdom and can inspire me. May Your Word always keep me on the right path. Amen.

The Bible Keeps You from Sin

I have hidden Your word in my heart that I might not sin against You (Psalm 119:11).

In the Scripture verse for today the psalmist writes that he has hidden the Word of God in his heart so that he will not sin against God. Sins are specified in the Word of God. If you read your Bible carefully you will know exactly what things God forbids His children to do.

The Bible is a mirror in which God shows us our sins. The commandments of God are crystal clear throughout the Bible. In the Old Testament He gave His people the Ten Commandments as well as dozens of other laws to teach them what things are right and what things are wrong. Although the ceremonial laws are no longer necessary in the New Testament environment, the things that God will never accept are clearly set out in the New Testament. Paul writes to the church in Galatia, "The acts of the sinful nature are obvious: sexual immorality, impurity and debauchery; idolatry and witchcraft; hatred, discord, jealousy, fits of rage, selfish ambition, dissensions, factions and envy" (Gal 5:19-20).

The better you know the Bible the better you will know what wrong things in your life you need to change so that the Spirit will direct your behavior in future.

Holy Spirit, I pray that You will clearly show me in the Word what things are right for me and those things that are wrong. Please make it possible for me to renounce the sins in my life and to live only for You from now on. Amen.

Before You Go to Sleep

In your anger do not sin; when you are on your beds, search your hearts and be silent. I will lie down and sleep in peace, for You alone, O LORD, make me dwell in safety (Psalm 4:4, 8).

Many of us read our Bibles before we go to sleep at night. And the Word of God always has a calming effect on His children. You must, however, guard against going to bed so late that you are too tired and sleepy to make time for God. There are also many people who lie awake at night because they are fearful and restless.

This is unnecessary if you are a Christian. When you, before you go to sleep, think about the Bible passage that you have just read, it is much easier for you to fall asleep peacefully – you know without a doubt that the Lord will protect you through the night and will care for you.

"My Son, keep your father's commands," urges the writer of Proverbs. "When you walk, they will guide you; when you sleep, they will watch you; when you awake, they will speak to you" (Prov. 6:22). If you should find yourself lying awake, talk to God rather than counting sheep. Use the time that you are lying awake to pray for people whom you do not usually find time to pray for during the course of every day: your childhood friends, missionary workers or someone whom you've read about in the newspaper. Time that is spent with God is never wasted.

Heavenly Father, it is wonderful to read Your Word every evening before I go to sleep and to talk to You as well. Help me to fall asleep peacefully at night and protect me while I sleep. Amen.

And When You Wake

The arrogant cannot stand in Your presence; You hate all who do wrong. For surely, O LORD, You bless the righteous; You surround them with Your favor as with a shield (Psalm 5:4, 9).

A wonderful thing happens when you fall asleep at night while thinking about the Bible passage that you have read: you wake up in the morning with that Scripture still in your thoughts and with a special awareness of the presence of God. There is no better way to start the day than with God. Yesterday's Scripture verse from Proverbs 6 ends like this, "When you awake, they will speak to you" (v. 22).

David made it a habit to begin his day with God. "I will sing of Your strength, in the morning I will sing of Your love" (Ps. 59:17). If you make time every morning to lay all the day's responsibilities before God, to ask His blessing on them and allow Him to guide you, you will find that your day will run smoothly right from the start.

All through the day you will be aware that the Lord is with you, ready to help you, and you will find that His power is available to you. My husband often says that a day that begins with a song of praise will inevitably be a day of victory.

Heavenly Father, it is a joy for me to be able to start my day with You and to have a song of praise in my heart. Thank You for the assurance that You will be with me every day and will act on my behalf. Amen.

Let the Word Live in You

Let the word of Christ dwell in you richly (Colossians 3:16).

When an overweight person joins a gym and starts to follow a healthy diet, the positive results will quickly become visible. In the same way, other people should be able to see by the way you live that the Word dwells in you. In *The Message* this Scripture verse reads as follows, "Let the Word of Christ – the Message – have the run of the house".

If you really want to live close to God you should remain involved with the Word of God, continuously meditate on it and make the guidelines that are found in it a part of your life. "To live effectively, we must saturate our thoughts in the Word of our God. When we meditate on the Scriptures, we experience a heightening of all the powers of the personality, enabling us to gain a degree and quality of life that is divine. Let this fact be burned into our minds – meditation is the combination which gives us access to God's locked treasures of life and power," writes Selwyn Hughes.

Rick Warren says that it is not enough simply to believe in the Bible; your mind needs to be full of it so that the Holy Spirit can transform you with its truth. Read your Bible in such a way that you will carry the content of it with you and the treasures of God will be available to you. Allow the message of the Word to refresh you every day, to lead and guide you, to comfort and to encourage you.

Heavenly Father, help me to live in such a way that the message of Your Word in all its fullness will remain in me so that all those who look at me will see that my whole way of living has been influenced by Your Word. Amen.

Eat the Word!

He said to me, "Take it and eat it. It will turn your stomach sour, but in your mouth it will be as sweet as honey." I took the little scroll from the angel's hand and ate it. (Revelation 10:9-10).

My husband received a copy of one of Eugene Peterson's books as a gift at the Denver Book Festival in July 2006. The title of the book interested me: *Eat This Book*. Peterson took the name from Revelation 10:9 where the angel told John to eat the book that he had given him. After John had eaten the book he received the command from God to proclaim His message, "You must prophesy again about many peoples, nations, languages and kings" (Rev. 10:11).

In his book, Peterson encourages Christians to "eat" the Word of God through studying it until they know it so well, it has become a part of them, until it flows in their blood vessels and they "digest" it like the food that they eat.

If you really want to know which of the things that are proclaimed by the world these days are right or wrong you can do so through "eating" your Bible – by going back to the Bible and testing the way of life today against it. When people order their lives according to biblical measures and obey God's guidelines rather than those of the world, they will find it is still possible to be whole and healthy in the midst of corruption and immorality.

Heavenly Father, please make it possible for me to eat Your Word so that it will become an integral part of my life and that I will be able to measure all things according to it. Amen.

Your Bible Is a Weapon

Then the men of Israel retreated, but he [Eleazar] stood his ground and struck down the Philistines till his hand grew tired and froze to the sword. The LORD brought about a great victory that day (2 Samuel 23:9-10).

Our Scripture reading for today tells the beautiful story of the brave Eleazar, one of David's "three heroes". Because the might of the Philistines was so great against them, the army saw no reason to carry on fighting – instead they turned around and ran away. Everybody except for Eleazar – he remained standing and confronted the Philistines. He clung so tightly to his sword that later on he could not open his hand to let go of the sword. Because Eleazar trusted in God, God "brought about a great victory."

Sometimes it feels as if we too are fighting against an army that is too powerful for us. Disappointments, responsibilities and disasters rain down on us like an enemy army until we want to admit defeat and flee like the Israelites. Fortunately, you too have a sword that you can use. When Paul describes the armor of God with which believers can defeat the Devil, he writes, "Take the sword of the Spirit, which is the word of God" (Eph. 6:17).

You can also use the sword of God's Word until your hand grips it so tightly that after a while you are unable to loosen your hand from the grip. With that sword you will be able to withstand all the attacks of the Evil One, and God will bring about a great victory for you too.

Heavenly Father, I praise You for the sword of the Spirit, my Bible, with which I can resist all the attacks of the Evil One. Thank You that You bring about victory for all those who use Your sword as a weapon. Amen.

The Word Is a Treasure

I rejoice in Your promise like one who finds great spoil (Psalm 119:162).

When the well-known blind singer and writer Jennifer Rothschild was asked during a television interview what she would choose to see if she were given the chance to see just one thing for one moment, she answered that it was like potato chips for her – you can never have only one! She then went on to explain why she gave this answer – she was scared that she might make the wrong choice and that she would regret it for the rest of her life. When she returned home, the question haunted her. What would she choose: the faces of her parents that she had last seen when she was fifteen years old, the faces of her husband and two sons that she had never seen, a sunset or a flower? Eventually she came to a decision about the choice she would make if this were to be given her: she would choose to be able to read Psalm 36:10 in her own Bible, because all things change and the Word is the one thing that remains the same: "With You is the fountain of life; in Your light we see light."

This story helped me realize anew how precious our Bibles are and how privileged we are to be able to open them at any moment during the day or night and read from them. Do not allow this great privilege – to be able to read your Bible for yourself – to ever pass you by. Use it!

Heavenly Father, how good You are to me that I am able to read the truths in Your Word and make them my own. Thank You too that You are the source of my life and that I can live in the light of Your Word. Amen.

The Word Builds You Up

Now I commit you to God and to the word of His grace, which can build you up and give you an inheritance among all those who are sanctified (Acts 20:32).

In this passage Paul is speaking to the elders in Ephesus. He tells them that the Holy Spirit sent him to Jerusalem and that he did not know what would happen to him there but that he was expecting imprisonment and persecution (see v. 23). Yet he counted his life as unimportant – all that he wanted to do was to complete his life's work – to bring the gospel to the heathen nations. He entrusted the elders to God and to the word of His grace. He told them that the word is powerful to build them up and to bring them to a place where they could share in God's inheritance.

The work of God cannot be accomplished without the Word of God. Not only spiritual leaders, but every Christian needs to be equipped by the Word of God and allow it to build them up if they want to grow spiritually.

In Deuteronomy 6:7 the people of God are commanded to live according to the commands and instructions of God and to teach them to their children, "Impress them on your children. Talk about them when you sit at home and when you walk along the road, when you lie down and when you get up."

You need your Bible to build you up spiritually if you want to become a stronger and more mature Christian and it is your responsibility to share the truths of the Word with your children.

Lord, teach me how to use my Bible correctly so that I can be built up spiritually and can share in the blessings that You have promised as an inheritance to Your children. Amen.

Make the Word a Part of You

"If you remain in Me and My words remain in you, ask whatever you wish, and it will be given you" (John 15:7).

In this well-known parable of Jesus – that He is the true vine and His Father is the gardener and His children are the branches – He says that we need to remain in Him as the branch remains on the vine if we want to bear fruit for Him. Without being connected to the vine, a branch of a vine is worth nothing – it cannot grow and neither can it bear fruit. But if we remain in Him we have the assurance that we will bear much fruit.

There is another promise: if we remain in Jesus and His words remain in us we will be able to ask Him for anything and we will receive it.

When someone has an intimate relationship with Jesus and makes the Word of God a part of his or her life and way of thinking, such a person will not ask something that will conflict with the will of God.

You can make the words of Jesus a part of your life if you make the words of His Word your own. Memorize Scripture verses from your Bible so that the Word will constantly be at your fingertips – even if you do not have a copy of the Bible with you.

Obey the Word and study it so that it will become part of you. Only then will you be able to claim this promise as your own; then you will live so close to Jesus that His will becomes your will, and then He will give you all that you ask of Him.

Lord Jesus, it is my heart's desire to remain in You so that Your words will remain in me and Your will becomes mine. Thank You for the promise that You will then give me all the things that I ask. Amen.

The Hammer of the Word

"Is not My word like fire," declares the LORD, *"and like a hammer that breaks a rock in pieces?" (Jeremiah 23:29).*

In this passage God reproved the prophets who presented their false dreams as His Word to Israel. Through the mouth of the prophet Jeremiah He tells them that they should keep their dreams to themselves, and that they should never offer up their own visions as His word.

The Word of God, said Jeremiah to them, is like nutritious wheat and not like the worthless straw of the words of the false prophets. The Word of God also does not just flow through a person without affecting that person – it always has a powerful effect on your life. It is like a fire or like a hammer with which stones can be crushed. These false prophets were not doing the people any favors by working carelessly with the Word of God. Instead, they were simply confusing them.

When you become occupied by your Bible it should always have a powerful effect on your life. Make sure that you do not read things into the Bible or offer up your own views and interpretations as Bible truths. You must never, like the prophets in Jeremiah's day, distort the message that is contained in your Bible to support your own opinions.

Ask the Holy Spirit to make it possible for you to be able to make a fine distinction between what is really written in the Word of God and your own interpretation. Do not offer straw to other people and proclaim that it is wheat!

Holy Spirit, will You please clarify the Bible to me so that I can clearly distinguish between the commands of God and my own interpretation. Help me to carry out the message of Your Word with great responsibility. Amen.

Comfort from the Word

*Remember Your word to Your servant, for You have given me hope.
My comfort in my suffering is this: Your promise preserves my life
(Psalm 119:49-50).*

In times of tribulation the psalmists always gave themselves over to
the promises of God. Each one of these promises is recorded in the
Bible for us and they still comfort us in difficult situations. Immanuel
Kant testified that one single line of the Bible was able to comfort
him more than all the other books that he had ever read.

Christians need never find themselves without comfort because
we always have God with us. He knows about all the things that
make life difficult for us. And the comfort that we can receive from
Him is able to equip us so that we can bring the same comfort to other
people who are going through hard times. In your own difficulties
and times of heartache you receive the very best comfort from the
Word of God. For example, when you are afraid, you can turn to
Psalm 23:4, "Even though I walk through the valley of the shadow
of death, I will fear no evil, for You are with me; Your rod and Your
staff, they comfort me."

From now on, underline and mark your favorite comforting
Scripture verses; better yet, make sure that you know them off by
heart so that they will be at hand when you need them. Then you
will be able to testify together with the psalmist, "When I said, 'My
foot is slipping,' Your love, O LORD supported me. When anxiety
was great within me, Your consolation brought joy to my soul" (Ps.
94:18-19).

*Heavenly Father, I want to thank You for all the times in the past
when I was comforted by Your Word. Help me to pass this comfort on
to other people who are going through hard times. Amen.*

The Word Remains Forever

Your word, O LORD, is eternal; it stands firm in the heavens. Your faithfulness continues through all generations; You established the earth, and it endures (Psalm 119:89-90).

In the world in which we live there are very few things that are permanent. Everything is constantly changing. Fortunately, the Word of God will never change. Every word that is written in it still stands firm today. Peter testifies, "The word of the Lord stands forever" (1 Pet. 1:25).

Many people these days try to water down the Word of God by insisting that the commands that are in it do not apply to us today. They try to make it more people-friendly and try to adapt it to our modern way of thinking and living. But the Bible warns that the words of God will never pass away. "Heaven and earth will pass away but My words will never pass away," says Jesus in Luke 21:23. The Bible is just as relevant today as it was thousands of years ago. The commandments in it are still valid for the children of God. It remains fresh and new because it is the Word of God and we cannot change it to suit ourselves.

There is a warning regarding this in the very last book of the Bible, "If anyone takes words away from this book of prophecy, God will take away from him his share in the tree of life and in the holy city, which are described in this book" (Rev. 22:19).

Heavenly Father, please forgive me for sometimes wondering if Your Word is still relevant today. I now know that Your Word remains steadfast eternally in the heavens and that I may not change anything in it. Amen.

rayer

Heavenly Father,
I praise You for the miracle of Your Word
which I have available every day
so that I can read, study, memorize and obey it.
Thank You for the joy that Your Word brings to me, for the wisdom and
insight that it gives me. From now on I want to walk according to Your
Word and order my whole life according to it.
Your Word is the Truth, Lord. It is a living Word that has the power
to change me and to judge everything that I think and do.
I want to be taught by Your Word and obey it
so that I can be truly happy and blessed by it.
Your Word is a light on my path through life, it shows me the right way.
I want to meditate on Your Word
so that it can change my whole life for the better.
I want to spend time in Your Word and
learn to know it better each day so that it can equip me to work for You.
When Your Word opens up to me it brings light,
it gives me insight even though I am still inexperienced.
Please reveal Your Word to me each time I read it
and show me which sins in my life I need to repent of.
Help me to live in such a way that the message of Your Word will remain
in me so that people who look at me will be touched by my life.
I want to eat Your Word so that it will become a part of me
and so that I can test all things against it. I want to use it as a weapon
to resist the attacks of the Devil.
Teach me each day how valuable Your Word is.
Thank You that it comforts me in times of hardship
and that it remains steadfast forever.

Amen.

March

Generosity and Gratitude

March is the month of Lent. At this time Christians remember the crucifixion of Jesus. Lent makes us once again thankful for the incomprehensible generosity of God who sacrificed His only Son, so that we, if we believe in Him, will one day live forever.

Generosity is always interwoven with gratitude – we are more ready to give to others because we are grateful for what God has given us.

This month we will spend some time considering what we can learn through the generosity of God – and once again look at the quality of our own gratitude. Hopefully by the end of the month we can know exactly what the generosity of God encompasses and also be prepared to be generous toward others in the future. Discover how to show your thankfulness in every aspect of your life.

How Much Do You Give?

Remember this: Whoever sows sparingly will also reap sparingly, and whoever sows generously will also reap generously. Now he who supplies seed to the sower and bread for food will also supply and increase your store of seed and will enlarge the harvest of your righteousness (2 Corinthians 9:6, 10).

In this passage Paul uses the image of a farmer who is sowing his seed so that he will be able to harvest it later. It goes without saying that the farmer who only sows a few seeds will only have a few plants to harvest, but the farmer who sows abundantly will more than likely also have an abundant crop to harvest.

It is the same in the kingdom of God. People who are stingy with their money and possessions will one day bring in a scant harvest for the Kingdom simply because they have little that can grow. The size of your spiritual harvest is also always linked directly to the amount of seed that you have sown. In the same measure that you have given, you will receive. Give more and you will receive more.

A friend of mine often says that you can measure some people's faith by the amounts that they give. How does your life look? Are you already giving of your money in such a way that you will one day have an abundant harvest for God, or are you still sowing so grudgingly that there is scarcely any harvest to talk of in your life?

Heavenly Father, please forgive me for sowing so grudgingly that my spiritual and material harvest will be meager. Help me from now on to be more generous so that my life will yield a rich harvest for You. Amen.

The Fruit of Generosity

Out of the most severe trial, their overflowing joy and their extreme poverty welled up in rich generosity (2 Corinthians 8:2).

In this Scripture passage Paul asks the church in Corinth to finalize their collection for the poor Christians in Judea and Jerusalem. He encourages them to be generous. As an example for the Corinthians of what Christian generosity should look like, Paul refers to the residents of Macedonia. Even though things were not particularly easy for these Macedonians, they were rich in their abundant generosity. They too were going through hard times and were very poor and yet they insisted on giving Paul a monetary offering. And this offering, as Paul writes in 2 Corinthians 8:3 was more than what they actually had to give. It is this kind of abundant generosity that is the key to joy in a person's life.

The Macedonians in Paul's day are still an example to us of how we ought to give. They did not wait until they had enough for themselves, they did not give out of their excess as we usually do. (It is after all so much easier to give those things that we do not actually need.)

Rather, they gave where it hurt, above their capacity. Only when you are willing to distance yourself from the things that you really need, only when you give more than what you can afford, only then will you taste the true joy of generosity like the Macedonians experienced.

Lord, please forgive me for my inherent selfishness and help me to be excessive in my generosity so that I will be prepared to sacrifice more than what I can afford for Your sake. Amen.

The Generosity That God Requires

They did not do as we expected, but they gave themselves first to the Lord and then to us in keeping with God's will (2 Corinthians 8:5).

The Macedonians surprised Paul with their overwhelming generosity, but their generosity did of course grow out of the fact that they were Christians. God does not want your money and things if your heart does not belong to Him. He does not need your possessions in order to build His kingdom because all the riches of the world already belong to Him. His will is that you firstly offer your life to Him and then as a matter of course make your money and goods available to Him.

Therefore, first work on your relationship with God and ask Him to make you more generous. Because it is only when your heart is set right that you, like the Macedonians, will insist on helping other Christians financially and will be aware of the people who really need your help.

You should attempt to focus on being truly generous, to really care for other people and always be willing to put your hand deeply into your pocket so that your generous lifestyle will reflect your faith.

C. S. Lewis says that all people believe that generosity is a wonderful Christian value until they have to give away something specific. Make sure that this will never be true of you!

Heavenly Father, I want to give myself to You right now. Take my life, Lord, and make me willing to give my money and my possessions to You as evidence of my salvation. Open my eyes to people in need. Amen.

The Extravagant Generosity of God

Thanks be to God for His indescribable gift! (2 Corinthians 9:15).

God was prepared to give us an "indescribable gift", His only Son, so that we could be saved. Jesus Himself was prepared to put His life on the line, to die on the cross to make our salvation possible.

I am usually quite prepared to put my hand into my own pocket so that other people can be helped and so that God's kingdom can be extended, but I would not even begin to consider putting the lives of my children or grandchildren on the line to show my generosity. This is not negotiable. Neither do I think that I could sacrifice my life to save someone I do not even know. And yet this is exactly what God has done. He gave His Son.

God is so magnanimous toward us simply because He loves us so much. Because He loves *you* so much. "God so loved the world that He gave His one and only Son, that whoever believes in Him shall not perish but have eternal life," (John 3:16). Paul writes to the church in Rome and tells them that, "God demonstrates His own love for us in this: While we were still sinners, Christ died for us" (Rom. 5:8).

Consider whether God's extravagant generosity finds an echo of generosity in your own life.

Heavenly Father, thank You for Your inexpressible gift, for letting Your Son die so that I can live. Lord Jesus, thank You that You were willing to die for me while I was still a sinner. I praise You for Your generosity. Amen.

The Selfless Generosity of Jesus

Your attitude should be the same as that of Christ Jesus: Who, being in very nature God, did not consider equality with God something to be grasped (Philippians 2:5-6).

Generosity always assumes that we will be prepared to sacrifice certain things for the sake of others. People find it easy to give away things that they know they will never use again, but when there is a possibility that they might need it in future, their own little bit of generosity gets a little bogged down.

Most of us look for excuses for why we cannot be more generous. Jesus became poor for us so that we could be rich, wrote Paul to the church in Corinth, "You know the grace of our Lord Jesus Christ, that though He was rich, yet for your sake He became poor, so that you through His poverty might become rich" (2 Cor. 8:9). We tend to easily forget that Jesus is Himself God and that He was prepared to sacrifice His position as King of heaven to come to a sinful world that not only misunderstood Him, but also did not accept the sacrifice of love that cost Him His life. Jesus gave His life so that His people could come to God; but what did they do – they let Him die the most cruel death.

Jesus' sacrifice is still applicable today. He died so that you can live. He sacrificed His heavenly glory so that one day it could be yours. What have you done with this generous gift?

Lord Jesus, I praise You for Your unbelievable generosity that caused You to sacrifice heaven to come to earth as a person so that heaven could be mine. Amen.

Give with Gladness

Each man should give what he has decided in his heart to give, not reluctantly or under compulsion, for God loves a cheerful giver (2 Corinthians 9:7).

The person who gives with gladness will quickly find that his reward is happiness. The congregation in Macedonia offered their contributions to God with gladness. They even insisted on giving a contribution to the Christians in Judea even though Paul did not expect it from them because things were not particularly easy for them either. The rich inhabitants of Corinth on the other hand had to be nagged before they were prepared to put their hands into their pockets.

Each time I stood with a collection tin on the street in the past, I could not help but notice how many smart and respectable-looking people looked the other way, while people who seemed quite poor came to throw a few cents into my tin, with a smile.

God looks more at the attitude with which you give than at the amount that you give. After all, He does not actually need your contribution. That is why you should always give cheerfully – not out of compulsion or to feel good or because you secretly believe that God ought to bless you if you give generously.

Try to give especially to those who deserve it least. The grace of God is like water – it always flows downward. Make sure that your generosity flows in the direction of people who do not deserve it at all.

Heavenly Father, please forgive me that my own generosity is put to shame over and over again by people who have so much less than I have. Make me prepared to give with gladness, especially to those who do not deserve it. Amen.

Decide for Yourself How Much

Each man should give what he has decided in his heart to give, not reluctantly or under compulsion, for God loves a cheerful giver. Now He who supplies seed to the sower and bread for food will also supply and increase your store of seed and will enlarge the harvest of your righteousness (2 Corinthians 9:7, 10).

It does not help to be generous with a negative attitude. God loves people who are prepared to give to Him with joy, writes Paul to the church in Corinth. And He Himself will make sure that your generosity will reap a rich harvest. But the amount that you give depends entirely on you – you need to decide for yourself how much you are prepared to give.

There is, however, an indication of how much we should give – the Bible indicates that we should give a tithe of our income. A little while ago I listened to a conversation where everyone vehemently declared that no one these days can afford to give their tithe. But is this really true? Have you ever tested God in this matter? God is absolutely faithful; He provides abundantly for the needs of the people who put Him first, "'Bring the whole tithe into the storehouse ... Test Me in this', says the LORD Almighty, 'and see if I will not throw open the floodgates of heaven and pour out so much blessing that you will not have room enough for it'" (Mal. 3:10).

I have personally witnessed how faithful God is to this promise. Perhaps the time has come for you to test God in this matter.

Lord, I am somewhat fearful to give a full tithe of my income to You. But I really do want to test You in this – and I trust You to open the windows of heaven for me. Amen.

God Gives More than Enough

God is able to make all grace abound to you, so that in all things at all times, having all that you need, you will abound in every good work (2 Corinthians 9:8).

During the last eighteen years of my husband's ministry we lived in an area of South Africa where there are a lot of very wealthy people. Many times I was amazed at the luxury cars and lavish houses of some people, and I often listened as the women told of their overseas holidays and the clothes and shoes that they bought from designer stores.

Sometimes I secretly wished that we could have that much money! But the children of God need never long for earthly riches. Your heavenly Father is the richest person ever. All things belong to Him. And He is more than able to let you share in His abundance.

"Every good and perfect gift is from above, coming down from the Father of the heavenly lights, who does not change like shifting shadows" (James 1:17). You have most likely already discovered that God knows exactly what you need – even before you ask Him. God will give all these things to you in abundance. "God can pour on the blessings in astonishing ways so that you're ready for anything and everything, more than just ready to do what needs to be done" promises *The Message*.

Heavenly Father, how good You are to me! I praise You for giving me all things in abundance every day so that I will always have more than enough of everything. Thank You so much for that! Amen.

God Gives So That You Can Give

Now He who supplies seed to the sower and bread for food will also supply and increase your store of seed and will enlarge the harvest of your righteousness. You will be made rich in every way so that you can be generous on every occasion, and through us your generosity will result in thanksgiving to God (2 Corinthians 9:10-11).

God gives to us to make us givers. And He will reward our generosity in His own time by making sure that one day we will reap a rich harvest.

When the psalmist described the righteous person, one of the most important qualities that he emphasized is the willingness to "scatter abroad his gifts to the poor" (see Ps. 112:9). God blesses the people who are willing to be generous toward others. He gives more than enough to us so that we in turn can share with those people who have less than we do.

Giving to the poor means responding to the love of God in your life by showing love for others. In this way other people will see that the seed which God has planted in you is bearing fruit for Him. The seed, the power to grow and the harvest belong to God; all that you need to do is to be willing to take something of what God has given you and to share it so that you will bring in a rich harvest for Him. And this generosity, as Paul writes in verse 11, results in God being thanked.

Heavenly Father, thank You so much for all the things that You have given to me, even though I do not deserve them. Help me to be willing to give to those who have less than I do so that people who see my generosity will thank You. Amen.

Give without Ulterior Motives

"Everything they do is done for men to see. They love the place of honor at banquets and the most important seats in the synagogues" (Matthew 23:5-6).

Most people are prepared to give, but their reasons for giving differ very widely. Many people give because they want to score bonus points with God. Others are generous because it makes them feel good. Yet others give to be seen by other people. "Be careful not to do your 'acts of righteousness' before men, to be seen by them. If you do, you will have no reward from your Father in heaven" warns Jesus in the Sermon on the Mount (Matt. 6:1).

The Pharisees in Jesus' day also gave huge amounts, but they did so to gain honor and esteem for themselves. This kind of generosity does not earn anyone any points. Jesus often reprimanded the people for their double standards and insincerity. In Matthew 23:11 He warns that the one who is greatest among them serves others.

Sometimes people suppose that God will notice their excessive generosity and that He will reward them for it. Unfortunately it does not work like that. When you make your contributions do so without any ulterior motives as Paul did, "We are not trying to please men but God, who tests our hearts" (1 Thess. 2:4).

Heavenly Father, I am sorry that I am often generous, but with the wrong motives. Help me to give all my offerings to Your kingdom without ulterior motives and with joy. Amen.

Don't Give to Be Seen ...

"So when you give to the needy, do not announce it with trumpets, as the hypocrites do in the synagogues and on the streets, to be honored by men. But when you give to the needy, do not let your left hand know what your right hand is doing" (Matthew 6:2-3).

We conducted a most delightful experiment in our church a few years ago. We assigned a "secret friend" to each member of the ladies' group. Each woman was then expected to plan surprises for her secret friend, like an anonymous birthday present and all sorts of other wonderful surprises. I received a beautiful bouquet of flowers from my secret friend, and she also asked someone to deliver a wonderful warm loaf of freshly baked bread to my door. At the end of the year the names of the secret friends were revealed. You could discover whether you were now a new friend richer or if after all it was one of your close friends who had spoilt you so wonderfully through the year.

Everybody loves surprises. When you help poor people you should do it in such a way that no one knows about it – just like the secret friends in our congregation had to go about their giving.

Christian love and generosity should be done in such a way that no one apart from yourself and the person who is on the receiving end will know about it. Only then will God reward you for your service to your neighbor.

Lord, I am sorry that sometimes I do things for other people to be noticed so that I can be honored for it. Help me from now on to go about things in such a way that my left hand will not know what my right hand is doing. Amen.

Give Now

"Do not withhold good from those who deserve it, when it is in your power to act. Do not say to your neighbor, 'Come back later; I'll give it tomorrow' – when you now have it with you" (Proverbs 3:27-28).

The saying rightly goes that we should make hay while the sun shines. When a person makes up his mind to do something for someone else, it so often happens that the good deed is continuously put off and delayed – until to their despair they find that it is too late to do anything. This happened to me when I kept putting off going to visit a sick elderly woman in one of our previous churches, and I regretted it for months after because she suddenly died before I got around to my planned visit.

Now is the time to care for people who have less than you do; now is the time to give things that are obvious to you but that other people so desperately need. First begin with the people you know who are nearby: find out if there is a family in need in your church. When you have finished helping the people around you, you can enlist with a soup kitchen in your community or go and help by pouring tea at your local hospital.

"If anyone has material possessions and sees his brother in need but has no pity on him, how can the love of God be in him?" (1 John 3:17). Therefore, make it your priority to get involved right now.

Heavenly Father, please forgive me for putting off doing good things for others and show me where You want me to be more generous. Amen.

March 13

Thankfulness Expressed in Deeds

Is not this the kind of fasting I have chosen. Is it not to share your food with the hungry and to provide the poor wanderer with shelter – when you see the naked, to clothe him, and not to turn away from your own flesh and blood?" (Isaiah 58:6, 8).

Suze Orman says that giving is an action that needs to come from deep within us, it must spring from a desire to express thanks for what we receive. If what she says is true every Christian woman ought to be a giving person, someone who will convert her thankfulness into deeds because we receive so much from God every day that we cannot help but share our abundance with other people.

Unfortunately thankfulness can be somewhat selfish; when people only say thank You to God for all that He has given them but conveniently forget to reach out to other people. Just like a person's love, one's thankfulness should not simply be words and lip service but it must be seen in your actions.

What God longs for from you is that you will give food to those people who are hungry, that you will give clothes to those people who have nothing to wear, and help those people who need you.

If you are willing to obey this command you can take the beautiful promise in Isaiah 58:10 and 11 for yourself.

Heavenly Father make me so grateful for all that I receive from You that my thankfulness will be expressed in my deeds by helping those people who have less than I do. Amen.

You Have More than Enough!

Better what the eye sees than the roving of the appetite. This too is meaningless, a chasing after the wind (Ecclesiastes 6:9).

If you are reading this devotional it is probably a given that you have a house, a car, enough food and enough clothes to dress coolly when it is hot and to be warm when it is cold. It is quite possible that you also have money in your wallet, money in the bank and that you are a member of a medical aid fund.

If this is true of you, you have more material possessions than 99% of the world's population. You are rich, extremely rich, and it is about time that you stop yearning for the unnecessary things that you want like that new car, those designer clothes and a house by the sea. You should also teach your children to see how blessed you are as a family, how God has actually given you an advantage because there are millions of people who do not have a roof over their heads and who go to sleep hungry.

Thankful people should guard against always wanting more. "Whoever loves money never has money enough; whoever loves wealth is never satisfied with his income" (Eccles. 5:9). Be careful you do not become one of those people who are never satisfied with what they have.

Heavenly Father, please forgive my ingratitude and my unquenchable yearning for bigger and better. Make me satisfied with what I have received from Your hand and teach me again that what I have is so much better than the things that I long for. Amen.

God Is Satisfied

Now finish the work, so that your eager willingness to do it may be matched by your completion of it, according to your means. For if the willingness is there, the gift is acceptable according to what one has, not according to what he does not have (2 Corinthians 8:11-12).

Paul tells the church in Corinth that their eagerness to collect money for the kingdom of God should not wane. Their enthusiasm to finish the collection should be just as great as their willingness in the beginning.

Unfortunately, sometimes we begin putting aside money for a good cause with great enthusiasm but then our eagerness begins to wane if the work becomes too much or if it requires too much of our time and money. At other times again, we are exceptionally generous but this willingness to give also declines after a while. Make sure that you remain enthusiastic in collecting offerings and in giving to the kingdom of God.

It is of utmost importance to God that your offerings to Him are both collected and given out with the right attitude. He will never ask for more than what you have to give. Paul asks the church in Corinth to make the contributions from their available resources. Therefore, you never have to put yourself in debt in order to be generous. If someone is willing to make what he has available to God, God is satisfied.

Heavenly Father, please help me to be enthusiastic in putting aside money for Your kingdom. Help me to be willing to put that which I have at Your disposal. Amen.

A Nation United in Giving

The people rejoiced at the willing response of their leaders, for they had given freely and wholeheartedly to the LORD. David the king also rejoiced greatly (1 Chronicles 29:9).

It was the life-long dream of King David to build a temple for God. But God did not fulfill David's dream. Through the prophet Nathan, God let David know that he would not be the one to build His House. David's son, who would be king after him, would have this privilege (see 1 Chron. 17:4, 11-12).

Rather than being disappointed about this, David accepted God's decision. He placed his dream on the shoulders of his son, Solomon, and in a selfless gesture he gathered all the materials that would be needed for the building of the temple. He donated large amounts of gold and silver and requested all the people to open their hands and bring a gift to the Lord. When the people willingly committed themselves to doing this, a whole nation was united in their willingness to give.

Many Christians are very reluctant to give of their money and possessions to their church so that the work of God can be carried out on earth. Ask God to make you more generous so that you will gladly contribute to the extension of His kingdom, and follow the example of David by encouraging your Christian friends to do the same thing!

Heavenly Father, forgive me for being so reluctant to commit my money and things to You. Make me as generous as Israel of old, willing to give so that Your work can be done on earth. Amen.

Everything Belongs to God

Yours, O LORD, is the greatness and the power and the glory and the majesty and the splendor, for everything in heaven and earth is Yours. Everything comes from You, and we have given You only what comes from Your hand (1 Chronicles 29:11, 14).

The whole nation of Israel was willing to dig deep into their pockets, together with their king, for the house of God to be built. After collecting gold, silver, bronze and copper, David prayed the beautiful prayer of thanksgiving that is found in 1 Chronicles 29:10-19 where he acknowledged that all the gifts that they brought together actually belonged to God anyway because everything they had, they had received from Him (1 Chron. 29:14).

Before deciding what or how much you are going to give to God's kingdom there is one fact that you need to take note of: All your possessions come from God. None of the things that you regard as your own property, therefore, actually belong to you. All that you can do is to give the things back to God that you have already received from Him.

As soon as you realize this it becomes easier to give your tithe. You no longer ask how much of your money and possessions you will set aside for God, but rather how much of the things that belong to God you are willing to give back to Him. Always give willingly and cheerfully as Israel did.

Heavenly Father, I now realize for the first time that everything that I have comes from You and that I can only give back to You the things that belong to You. Thank You very much for Your generosity toward me – make me generous toward others. Amen.

Generosity and Gratitude

You will be made rich in every way so that you can be generous on every occasion, and through us your generosity will result in thanksgiving to God. This service that you perform is not only supplying the needs of God's people but is also overflowing in many expressions of thanks to God (2 Corinthians 9:11-12).

People who have been on the receiving end of generosity once, never forget it. In fact, these people are usually also grateful people. Paul encouraged the church in Corinth to be generous by telling them that their generosity will have two positive results: the needs of the believers in Judea would be provided for and God would receive thanks and honor from them.

The believers in Judea would praise God for the obedience of the Corinthians to God and also for their generosity toward them. There was also a third benefit: the Christians in Judea would intercede with God for the Corinthians and thank Him for His grace toward them.

When you show generosity toward other people, a little seed of thankfulness always sprouts in their lives. They are thankful to God because their needs have been provided for and they bring honor to God. Through your generosity you can ensure not only that the needs of other Christians are met, but also that God will be glorified. Above all you can know for sure that the people who have been on the receiving end of your generosity will pray to God for you.

Lord Jesus, make me so generous toward other Christians that they will be grateful to You and honor You because they can see how great Your mercy is in my life. Amen.

Grateful for Salvation

Giving thanks to the Father, who has qualified you to share in the inheritance of the saints in the kingdom of light. For He has rescued us from the dominion of darkness and brought us into the kingdom of the Son He loves, in whom we have redemption, the forgiveness of sins (Colossians 1:12-14).

Paul tells the church in Colosse that they are saved because they believe in Jesus. It is their faith in Jesus that gives them the right to become children of God and one day they will be able to take possession of their heavenly inheritance.

Because Jesus paid the ransom for their sins on the cross, their sins no longer have any power over them. All the people who had been caught in the power of darkness have been set free from their sins once and for all through the work of Jesus. For this salvation they ought to be thankful to God.

There are millions of people in the world who will never have the privilege of hearing the gospel message, while it is more than likely that you grew up hearing it. You must never lose sight of the great privilege you have had in hearing the gospel and that you were able to make a decision for God. If you are not sure of your salvation do not wait any longer – ask God to make you His child now. There is no prayer that He would want to answer more.

Lord Jesus, I praise You for the privilege I have of knowing You and of being able to make a decision to follow You. Thank You so much that You made it possible for me to be set free from my sins forever. Amen.

Thankful in All Things

Speak to one another with psalms, hymns and spiritual songs. Sing and make music in your heart to the Lord, always giving thanks to God the Father for everything, in the name of our Lord Jesus Christ (Ephesians 5:19-20).

There is one characteristic that every Christian ought to have: to be thankful in all situations and in doing so succeed in thanking God for everything.

It is not particularly hard to be thankful when things are going well, but when they take a turn for the worst it is much more difficult. Yet, God asks you to be thankful in *all* things. The longer you live, the more reasons you will have for being thankful. Yet, it is only when your thankfulness is directed at God and not your circumstances that you will be truly thankful – even for the things that you wish were different.

On top of that your thankfulness should not be kept to yourself. Paul urges the church in Ephesus to sing of their thankfulness – so often we forget to sing a song of thanks when we pray, simply because there are so many requests that we want to bring to God.

God wants your thankfulness, it makes His heart glad when His children are thankful. And if you succeed in being thankful in *all* things He cannot help but bless you.

Heavenly Father, I pray that You will make it possible for me to be thankful in all things. I know that I will only be able to do this if my gratitude is anchored in You. Amen.

Be Thankful for Your Daily Bread

When you have eaten and are satisfied, praise the LORD your God for the good land He has given you (Deuteronomy 8:10).

Moses promised the Israelites that God would give them a land with, "Streams and pools of water, with springs flowing in the valleys and hills; a land with wheat and barley, vines and fig trees, pomegranates, olive oil and honey, a land where bread will not be scarce and you will lack nothing" (Deut. 8:7-9). He also reminded them that when they had enough to eat they ought to thank God for the good land and for the food that He has given them.

My husband and I both love eating! We are so used to having enough (or too much!) food that I must shamefully confess that I am sometimes so wrapped up in my thoughts when we sit down to eat that I often can't remember if my husband has said grace or not.

You should never take the food in your house for granted, but consciously thank God each time you eat. There are thousands of people around the world who do not have enough food to eat. When Jesus taught us to pray for our daily bread it literally means that we must also provide for others around us.

Therefore, reach out to people who are hungry and don't ever forget to thank God for your food.

Lord, I want to come to You and thank You for the abundance in our house. Thank You for the food that we have received from Your hand. Help me to be truly thankful for it and make me willing to share my abundance with others. Amen.

Express Your Thankfulness

Nor should there be obscenity, foolish talk or coarse joking, which are out of place, but rather thanksgiving (Ephesians 5:4).

It seems as if the members of the church in Ephesus were more interested in talking about worldly things than being thankful to God. Gratitude isn't a topic on which we spend much time. And yet thankfulness is a characteristic that should be evident in all God's children.

"We so easily forget to be grateful for the little things that we receive from the hand of God. But how can God entrust great things to those who do not receive the little ones with thankfulness from His hand," writes Dietrich Bonhoeffer.

How often do you tell other people about your thankfulness to God for the grace that He has given to you so undeservedly? Most likely you do not talk about crude or frivolous topics, but it is likely that you do complain – like most people do – about the prevailing crime, violence and corruption you see around you.

Do remember, however, that thankfulness to God is appropriate. You should develop the habit of saying thank you to people for what they do for you and for the things that you receive from them. Why not decide right now to change your focus and speak less about all the things that annoy you and more about the things for which you are grateful? Learn to express your thankfulness to God and other people every day.

Heavenly Father, please forgive me for complaining so much about the things that irritate me because in the process I completely forget to be grateful to You. Help me to be a more grateful person from now on. Amen.

Speak of Your Thankfulness

I will give You thanks in the great assembly; among throngs of people I will praise You. My tongue will speak of Your righteousness and of Your praises all day long (Psalm 35:18, 28).

In Psalm 35 the psalmist begs God to save him from his enemies who laugh at his troubles and threaten his life even though he has done only good toward them. When God answered his prayer and punished the people who sought his life, the psalmist promised to testify before the whole congregation of his thankfulness to praise God each and every day for His faithfulness.

It is unfortunately true that many people are quick to hold prayer meetings for rain or for peace, but if God answers these prayers we completely forget to thank Him.

We should all make more time to testify to other people about all the things we are grateful for and tell them of God's faithfulness towards us. Perhaps you could begin to keep a journal about all the things you are thankful for – through the day write down the reasons you have for being thankful and each evening thank God for them.

Get your whole family involved in saying thanks. You could even make a game of it by thinking of new things to say thank you for and then try to tell God how grateful you are for at least one thing each day.

Lord, I am sorry that I seldom testify to others of my gratitude to You. Help me to be like the psalmist so that I will be able to speak in front of my church and that each day I will praise You for the things that I am grateful for. Amen.

Peace and Thankfulness

Let the peace of Christ rule in your hearts, since as members of one body you were called to peace. And be thankful (Colossians 3:15).

When a person breaks free from his sinful lifestyle he becomes a new person who should begin to live like a different person, and become more and more like Jesus. From verse 12 onwards Paul tells the church in Colosse exactly how this person's life in Christ should look.

Christians ought to be compassionate, kind, humble, gentle and tolerant toward one another. They should be patient and forgive one another just as God has forgiven their sins. Above all, they ought to love one another because love is the bond that binds them together in perfect unity. Only then will the peace that Christ gives come to full expression in their lives.

It is important for Christians to try to guard this peace at all costs; to look for a peaceful solution in every situation. We should also try our best to nurture a lifestyle of gratitude and learn to take nothing for granted, but to be grateful for every little thing that comes our way.

Grateful people are people who live with peace in their hearts, whose lives are so full of joy that they cannot help but share their joy with others.

Heavenly Father, thank You that I can break free from my old, sinful lifestyle and that I can be a new person; a person who experiences Your peace in my life each day. Help me to be thankful in all things. Amen.

March 25

Prayer and Thanksgiving

Do not be anxious about anything, but in everything, by prayer and petition, with thanksgiving, present your requests to God. And the peace of God, which transcends all understanding, will guard your hearts and your minds in Christ Jesus (Philippians 4:6-7).

The Scripture verse for today is amongst my favorites in the Bible. It clearly spells out that we do not have to worry about anything; all that we need to do is to ask God for what we truly want while we thank Him for hearing and answering our prayers! If we can get this right God will give us His peace, which is beyond all understanding.

While Paul is delivering this impressive message, he is not relaxing on holiday. He is sitting in jail – not exactly a place swarming with grateful people! And yet he manages not only to succeed in being thankful in spite of his dreadful circumstances, but the whole letter that he writes to the church in Philippi is so full of joy that it is often referred to as the joyful epistle.

If you find yourself stressed and worried at the moment, listen to Paul's good advice: Go and speak to God about your problems and at the same time thank Him because you know that He will present a solution for each one. Trust God to give you His peace to stand guard over your heart and mind.

Heavenly Father, You already know about the things that concern and depress me. I bring them to You certain in the knowledge that You will bring about solutions for me. Thank You so much for that! Amen.

Remember to Thank God

Thanks be to God, who always leads us in triumphal procession in Christ and through us spreads everywhere the fragrance of the knowledge of Him (2 Corinthians 2:14).

Here Paul uses the image of a king who has emerged as a victor in a battle and now leads a triumphal procession with great festivity to celebrate his victory.

Christ is the one who has triumphed over all the evil and wicked forces in the world – He conquered Satan when He hung on the cross – although the final victory over the forces of darkness will only happen when He returns. As His children, we are victors with Him and we too are able to resist the Devil in His strength. Thank Jesus for giving us the ability to defeat Satan.

You are victorious too through the strength that God gives. He has chosen you to spread the knowledge of Christ in the world. Together with Paul you should thank God for the triumphal procession of the gospel. Not many of us remember to be thankful to God for this. We ask God for things and when He responds to our prayer requests we are like the ten lepers whom Jesus healed. We completely forget to go back to Him to thank Him (see Luke 17:12-19).

Do not forget any longer to be thankful. Thank God for every blessing that you receive from His hand. Thank Him for the privilege you have of being more than a conqueror through Him and that He has chosen you to spread the knowledge of Jesus like a beautiful fragrance.

Lord, please forgive me for my inherent ingratitude and help me from now on to remember to thank You for every blessing that I so undeservedly receive from Your hand. Amen.

Grateful Service

Therefore, since we are receiving a kingdom that cannot be shaken, let us be thankful, and so worship God acceptably with reverence and awe (Hebrews 12:28).

One of the greatest reasons why Christians should be thankful is the fact that God makes us part of His eternal kingdom when we believe in His Son, Jesus. Sinful people can never deserve this heavenly inheritance, but we can show our thankfulness for this by serving God with respect and awe, and by committing our lives to His kingdom.

When you are extremely thankful towards someone you really want to show your gratitude by giving that person something or serving him in some way that will show how grateful you are.

You owe God your eternal gratitude – He was willing to sacrifice His Son so that you could one day be in heaven. You should also be grateful to Jesus. He was prepared to give His life so that your debt of sin could be paid. You should thank Him by offering your service to Him. "Whoever serves Me must follow Me; and where I am My servant also will be" (John 12:26). "The fear of the LORD is a fountain of life" (see Prov. 114:27).

Show your thankfulness by reporting for service in the kingdom of God and be prepared to serve Him and obey Him for the rest of your life.

Lord Jesus, I will never be able to show my gratitude to You sufficiently. I want to report for duty to serve in Your kingdom – I am prepared to serve You for the rest of my life and to obey You always. Amen.

The Giver of All Gifts

Who makes you different from anyone else? What do you have that you did not receive? And if you did receive it, why do you boast as though you did not? (1 Corinthians 4:7).

In this passage Paul is talking to the Christians in Corinth about their relationship with the apostles. Apostles are simply servants of Christ who, in His absence, have been put in charge of congregations. Their task is to teach the congregation more about God. Some of the members of the congregation in Corinth considered themselves to be better than the rest because of certain gifts they had. Paul tells them very clearly that they have nothing to boast about because everything that they have comes from God. They should rather remain within the limits that God has set for them and do the work that He has asked them to do.

If you have more talents than your friends you need to tread lightly so that you do not fall into the same trap as the Christians in Corinth. You have nothing to boast about, "No one may boast before Him. Let him who boasts boast in the Lord" (1 Cor. 1:29, 31).

God is the one who gives you all gifts and talents and He is also the one who blesses you so that things go well with you and gives you success in your endeavors.

Heavenly Father, I am sorry for sometimes acting rather arrogantly. Humble me and help me to always realize that You are the Giver of all gifts and that all that I have comes from You. Amen.

A Gift of Grace

For it is by grace you have been saved, through faith – and this not from yourselves, it is the gift of God (Ephesians 2:8).

Some people are natural givers. They are always busy sharing things. I have a friend who has this characteristic and it bewilders me. If I admire something that she has she insists on giving it to me, and I have to struggle long and hard to persuade her against the idea!

Dirkie Smit, in a South African newspaper column, writes that generosity means being compelled by the knowledge that we live by grace and so are obliged to show mercy to others. We must remember that we have nothing that we did not first receive, that nothing really belongs to us and that what we have has not been given to us just for our own satisfaction. We owe it to one another to use our gifts and opportunities with the heartfelt desire to serve those who have less than we do. This is the core of the Christian life.

Only when you realize that everything you have comes from God, will you discover the secret of true generosity. You no longer have to be stingy about your possessions, because they do not really belong to you anyway. You can freely be as generous towards others as God is to you.

All that you are is pure grace. And because God is so merciful to you, you are compelled by His love to be merciful to others.

Heavenly Father, thank You for the gift of Your grace that compels me to offer my mercy and generosity to other people. Make me generous in every respect because You are so generous towards me. Amen.

Use Your Gifts to Serve

Each one should use whatever gift he has received to serve others, faithfully administering God's grace in its various forms. So that in all things God may be praised through Jesus Christ. To Him be the glory and the power for ever and ever (1 Peter 4:10-11).

Most people say that you are generous when you are willing to share your possessions with other people. But true generosity embraces far more than just the giving of your belongings. "What we are is God's gift to us. What we become is our gift to God," says Eleanor Powell.

God has given you special gifts with which you can serve Him and your fellow Christians. Who and what you are is expressed in these gifts that God has given you. In her book *Walking on Water* Madeleine L'Engle writes, "The important thing is to recognize that your gift, no matter what size, is indeed something given to you by God. You can take no credit for it, but you can humbly serve, and in serving, experience wholeness and refreshment."

Abundance does not relate only to money, but more specifically to your gifts. Are you prepared to demonstrate your generosity through your willingness to employ the gifts that you have received from God and to serve your fellow believers?

Heavenly Father, forgive me for being generous with my money but stingy with my gifts. I praise You for the gifts that I have undeservedly received from You. Make me willing to use these gifts to serve You and other people. Amen.

Communion – Feast of Generosity

The Lord Jesus, on the night He was betrayed, took bread, and when He had given thanks, He broke it and said, "This is My body, which is for you; do this in remembrance of Me." In the same way, after supper He took the cup, saying "This cup is the new covenant in My blood; do this, whenever you drink it, in remembrance of Me" (1 Corinthians 11:23-25).

Jesus offered His body and His blood on the cross so that you could come to God, so that your sins could be forgiven on the grounds of His work of reconciliation. The celebration of Communion is therefore a feast of generosity. Jesus sacrificed His life so that we could live forever.

When partaking in Communion, you must never forget that it must be in remembrance of Jesus. When you eat the bread, you are reminded of the body of Jesus that He gave for you; and when you drink the wine, you are reminded of the blood of Jesus that flowed for you on the cross.

Communion is also your guarantee that Jesus bore the punishment for your sins on the cross and it helps you to look forward to the day when Jesus will return and will receive you to Himself for ever.

You must never become accustomed to this generosity of Jesus, but with each Communion you should praise and thank Him for it. If it were not for His generosity you would never have had the privilege of becoming a child of God.

Lord Jesus, I praise You for Your generosity that made You go to the cross where Your body was broken and Your blood flowed so that my sins could be forgiven. Thank You for redeeming me. Amen.

Prayer

Lord Jesus,
During this month I want to stand quietly at the Cross and think
especially of the extent of Your generosity towards me –
thank You that You were prepared to sacrifice Your life for me.
By remembering Your suffering, I also want to
examine my generosity toward others.
I am sorry for being so stingy in my life
and investing so little in Your kingdom.
Help me to be like the Macedonians –
prepared to be excessive in giving.
But before I give my money, I first want to give my life to You –
thank You for the promise that You will always care for me abundantly.
I realize that I have nothing that I have not received from You
and that You always give to me in abundance so that
in turn I can give to others who have less than what I do.
Help me to always give with the right motives
and not just to be seen by others.
Today I want to offer my help; I want to help
people who need me and turn my gratitude into deeds.
Make me grateful in all things and give me the right words
so that I can express this thankfulness to You
and testify in front of other people.
Lord, every day I want to clearly declare the reasons for
my thankfulness to You, and serve and obey You for the rest of my life.
I want to offer my talents to Your service because this is also
a gift of grace from Your hand.
Thank You that every time I take communion
I am reminded of Your generosity.

Amen.

April

Blessing from Pain

Time and again I have found that the things that bring the most pain are in fact the ones that bring the greatest blessings. During the course of his or her life, each person encounters hurt, pain and loss. This month we are going to focus on the suffering that Jesus went through on the cross, and the great blessing of salvation that it means to us. We will learn through Scripture passages on adversities what great blessings so often lie hidden in difficulties. You can apply these lessons of pain in your own life so that you will eventually realize that every bit of pain that God allows into your life will ultimately be the cause of great blessings for you.

April 1

When God Leaves You ...

When envoys were sent by the rulers of Babylon to ask him about the miraculous sign that had occurred in the land, God left him to test him and to know everything that was in his heart (2 Chronicles 32:31).

When King Hezekiah fell seriously ill, the Lord had mercy on him and healed him. After this things went very well for Hezekiah and he was prosperous in all that he did. And then follows the rather odd statement that God left Hezekiah, apparently without reason. Hezekiah was after all one of the strong kings of Israel. He trusted in God, cleansed the temple and caused it to be used once again as a place of worship. God blessed him and while he was king things went well for the nation.

And then, all of a sudden, God left Hezekiah. The reason for this was that He wanted to "test him and to know everything that was in his heart," claims our core text. His sickness and the time when the Lord left him was a difficult period in Hezekiah's life – but when he looked back on it he could testify that it had actually been for his own good, "Surely it was for my benefit that I suffered such anguish. In Your love You kept me from the pit of destruction," he testified in Isaiah 38:17.

Adversity sometimes leaves you feeling as if the Lord has abandoned you, when actually it works the other way around: Hardship causes you to flee to the Lord, because you realize that you have now reached a point where only He can help you. For this reason adversity is in fact beneficial. Not only for Hezekiah but also for you and for me.

Lord, I realize now that You sometimes leave me so that I can know my own heart. Thank You for the difficulties that cause me to draw nearer to You. Amen.

Is Adversity the Will of God?

It was the LORD's will to crush Him and cause Him to suffer. After the suffering of His soul, He will see the light of life and be satisfied; by His knowledge My righteous servant will justify many, and He will bear their iniquities. For He bore the sin of many, and made intercession for the transgressors (Isaiah 53:10-12).

The Lord's Servant of whom Isaiah is talking here would have to go through many difficulties and, furthermore, this hardship was the will of God. He was despised and rejected by people, a Man who would know suffering and pain – yet He took the suffering of people upon Himself and carried their sicknesses. His suffering was, therefore, to their advantage. After He had endured this suffering, He would once again see the light and know the Lord, writes Isaiah.

Adversity is not usually the will of God. It was, however, the will of God that Jesus should suffer. He had to die on the cross so that the debt for our sins could be paid in order for us to become children of God and to know Him. This portion from Isaiah was also applied by Jesus to Himself in Luke 22:37 when He said to His disciples, "It is written: 'And He was numbered with the transgressors'; and I tell you that this must be fulfilled in Me. Yes, what is written about Me is reaching its fulfillment." On the cross Jesus took your sins upon Himself. His suffering is advantageous to you because through it He completely settled the cost of your sins.

Lord Jesus, I praise You because Your suffering was for my benefit. Through it You paid the price of my sins once and for all so that God is now willing to forgive me. Amen.

April 3

God's Exchange

To proclaim the year of the LORD's favor, to comfort all who mourn, and provide for those who grieve in Zion (Isaiah 61:2-3).

Here the prophet Isaiah brings a bit of good news to the discouraged people of God who were in great difficulty at the time because they had been taken away into exile: God Himself promised that He would show them great mercy, He would punish their enemies and comfort those who mourned, prophesied Isaiah. God also undertook to enter into a wonderful exchange transaction with them: He would give the nation honor instead of punishment, joy in the place of sorrow and gladness rather than heartache.

People are mostly the main reason for our heartache. They disappoint us or persecute us. We are also heartbroken when we lose people whom we love. Whatever the source of your heartache, God really wants to enter an exchange transaction with you just as He did with His people in the time of Isaiah. He undertakes to exchange your funeral clothes for party clothes, to give you honor instead of pain, joy in the place of sorrow and gladness in the place of heartache. He wants to make a covenant with you as He did with Israel of old. If you are willing to do this, you will be able to rejoice in your God and be able to sing a song of praise to His glory!

Lord, Your exchange transaction sounds to me like the best news ever! I really want to come and exchange my heartache for Your joy so that for the rest of my life I can be Your covenant child and can also rejoice in You and be glad. Amen.

Fear Is Unnecessary

The LORD is my light and my salvation – whom shall I fear? The LORD is the stronghold of my life – of whom shall I be afraid? Wait for the LORD; be strong and take heart and wait for the LORD (Psalm 27:1, 14).

The psalmist begins this psalm by expressing his faith and trust in God. Because God is his light and salvation, he does not have to be afraid of anyone or anything. In verse fourteen he reveals the secret of how he has managed to get rid of the fears in his life: he trusts in the Lord to help him.

If you belong to God, you also do not need to be afraid. God undertakes to rescue you. That is why your fear is not actually necessary, although it is human nature to be scared. In some dangerous situations fear is in fact unavoidable. What is important is how you choose to respond to your fear. There is an anonymous quotation that says, "Fear came knocking at the door; faith went to answer – and there was no one there." The answer to the things about which you are afraid is to exchange your fears with faith.

Trust in the Lord as the psalmist did. Take each one of your fears to God and tell Him about it. If you trust in Him you will discover each time that your fear will disappear like mist before the sun. Because it is a given that most things which we fear will not even happen to us.

Lord, I am sorry that there are still so many things that frighten me and make me anxious. I now want to bring my fears to You, and replace each one with faith and trust fully that You will help me. Thank You that no one who has trusted in You has ever been disappointed. Amen.

In the Depths of Despair

"I will refresh the weary and satisfy the faint" (Jeremiah 31:25).

People in the Bible often realized that problems brought them nearer to God. Through the mouth of the prophet Isaiah God also undertakes to give new strength to His people who have been taken away into exile, and to exchange their despair for courage. If problems in your own life are filling you with despair, you can be certain that these emotions do not come from God. It is never God's will for His children to be in despair.

In his book *If You Want to Walk on Water You've Got to Get Out of the Boat*, John Ortberg tells about a time when he asked one of his spiritual mentors how one can measure one's spiritual condition. This friend gave him a very interesting answer. The first thing he needed to do was ask himself if he had been more discouraged in the last while. "Because," he said to Ortberg, "if I'm walking closely with God, if I have the sense of God being with me, I find that problems lose their ability to damage my spirit."

Do not allow despair to get the upper hand over your thoughts. If you feel as though you would like to join Job on his ash heap, go and talk to God about the things that are discouraging you, and ask Him to give you new courage. He is the God who gives strength to people who have no more strength – He will pick you up out of the pit of despair and once again set your feet firmly on the rock!

Lord, forgive me for letting myself be so easily overcome by feelings of despair. Please give me Your strength so that I will once again be full of courage. Amen.

Suffering Leads to Perfection

In bringing many sons to glory, it was fitting that God, for whom and through whom everything exists, should make the author of their salvation perfect through suffering (Hebrews 2:10).

Jesus came to the earth to pay the price for our sins. He did this by dying on the cross because in the eyes of God sin always deserves the death penalty. The result of the death and resurrection of Jesus is that the lives of the people who believe in Him are completely changed. His suffering resulted in the fact that we can now become perfect, that we can be led into glory. But for this to be possible, He first had to suffer for our sake. He achieved perfection through this suffering and made it possible for us to be made perfect and acceptable to God.

God brought His Son to perfection through suffering. And He does the same with His children. Our earthly suffering very often results in our being led to glory, because it makes holier people of us. Therefore, as a result of our suffering we live that much closer to God, we realize our dependence on Him and it is easier for us to obey His commands. The next time you go through difficulties, recognize that your portion of personal suffering is God's way of leading you to glory, and stop complaining about your suffering.

Lord Jesus, I praise You because You saw Your way clear to suffering on the cross in my place so that God can now forgive my sins based on Your merit. Lead me through my own suffering to perfection and help me from now on to see suffering as part of Your endeavor with me. Amen.

Spread the Fragrance of Christ

Thanks be to God, who always leads us in triumphal procession in Christ and through us spreads everywhere the fragrance of the knowledge of Him. For we are to God the aroma of Christ among those who are being saved and those who are perishing (2 Corinthians 2:14-15).

One of my friends who had cancer tells of how someone came to visit her when she was at her worst and brought a bag full of leaves. She wondered if these leaves had some kind of healing properties and if she should place them on the parts of her body where there was the most pain, but the person asked her to take the leaves in her hand and to crush them. When she did so, the special fragrance of the leaves filled the room. "Sometimes the Lord needs to crush us so that our true fragrance comes out," the person said to her.

My friend immediately knew that that was what the Lord was busy doing with her. He had taken her, allowed her body to become sick and touched her spirit so that she – broken and sore – would ask Him what He wanted to say to her through this illness. This wonderful understanding came together with the brokenness and the pain: God wanted the fragrance of His love to be spread wherever she went. This portion of pain was not to remain in her, but she needed to work through it so she could spread the beautiful fragrance of God everywhere, in all things, forever.

Think about this when you are once again broken by life. Perhaps this is God's way of setting the fragrance of Christ free in your life.

Lord, I really want to spread Your life-giving aroma through my difficulties to every person I come into contact with. Please make this possible for me. Amen.

God Gives Joy and Heartache

LORD, You have assigned me my portion and my cup; You have made my lot secure. The boundary lines have fallen for me in pleasant places; surely I have a delightful inheritance (Psalm 16:5-6).

In this psalm David testifies that everything he has received comes from God. At that moment he was experiencing only good things from the hand of God. Unfortunately this is not always the case. Sometimes God also sends His children less wonderful times. When the life of Job was turned upside down when God allowed adversity to be brought into his life, it looked as if Job was content in his difficulties, "Shall we accept good from God, and not trouble?" he asked his wife (Job 2:10). And yet the suffering of Job later became too much for him and he longed to get answers from God about why things were going so badly for him.

In difficult times we are often at first more acutely aware of our dependence on God, we receive a greater awareness of God's love, mercy and nearness. But the longer these hardships continue, the more difficult it becomes to accept the fact that God gives us both joy and heartache. In times when your own difficulties get too much for you, you can know that God walks with you on your road of suffering. He undertakes to be with you in the dark times. Even in the valley of the shadow of death you can hold onto Him and depend on Him because even there you will be completely safe in His hand.

Lord, it is difficult for me to accept that You allow the difficult times into my life. Thank You that I can trust You to never forsake me because I know You will always protect me – even in times of danger. Amen.

God Speaks through Your Sickness

God does speak – now one way, now another – though man may not perceive it. Or a man may be chastened on a bed of pain with constant distress in his bones (Job 33:14, 19).

The three friends of Job did their best to encourage him with their words but they did not really succeed! Then Elihu joined the conversation. He told Job that God speaks to people in various ways – and one of these ways is through serious illnesses.

It is completely possible that God purifies people through pain and suffering so that they will live closer to Him, but Job was already a God-fearing man who lived close to God. So the advice of Elihu really did not apply to him. People simply do not always have ready answers about sickness, as Elihu had. Yet you can, when you are sick and discouraged, listen carefully to hear if God has a specific message for you through your illness.

When one of my friends contracted Parkinson's disease and I went to visit her, she said something that I will never forget, "Today I asked the Lord to teach me to listen carefully so that I will know exactly what He wants to say to me through this illness," she testified to me. The next time you are ill you too can decide to hear the voice of God speaking to you in your illness.

Lord, I know that You speak to Your children in various ways. At the moment I do not really understand what You are wanting to say to me through my illness. Help me to listen carefully so that I will be able to hear Your message to me very clearly. Amen.

Your Redeemer Lives!

I know that my Redeemer lives, and that in the end He will stand upon the earth. And after my skin has been destroyed, yet in my flesh I will see God; I myself will see Him with my own eyes – I, and not another. How my heart yearns within me! (Job 19:25-27).

Things were really going badly for poor Job – yet there was one fact that broke through the darkness like a ray of light: he never doubted his faith, but he continued to believe that his Redeemer lived and that he would see Him face-to-face one day.

If things are really going badly for you physically, may you, like Job, hold fast to the promise: Jesus lives – He is already in heaven where He is busy preparing a place for you. One day after you die you will see Him face-to-face. Then there will be no more hardship. Negative things like sickness, death and suffering will then belong to the past forever. All that will remain will be the faith, hope and love of which Paul writes in 1 Corinthians 13.

In heaven, which is waiting for you, you will be able to enjoy the presence of Jesus for all eternity. You will be able to enjoy the light and warmth of the Son of righteousness for ever. You will be able to see God face-to-face and you will eventually become the person God has always wanted you to be.

Lord Jesus, thank You that I can already long for heaven. It is wonderful that in the midst of my difficult times I can hold on to the promise that You live, that You are preparing a place for me in heaven where there will be an end to all hardship and where I will be able to see You with my own eyes! Amen.

April 11

The Best Way to Witness

We who are alive are always being given over to death for Jesus' sake, so that His life may be revealed in our mortal body (2 Corinthians 4:11).

While Christians are on earth they will always be exposed to tribulations. Just as Jesus suffered, so too do His children suffer. Yet the strength of Jesus is always available to us, and through our suffering God gives us opportunities to witness.

While you are suffering you get an opportunity to testify about your faith and this witness carries far more weight than when things are going well for you. Tribulation has a way of making Jesus visible to others in your life. It is the way that you behave during your suffering that shows other people that you have a secret source of strength available to you; an inner joy that does not depend on your physical circumstances; a peace that can only come from God; a hope that is renewed day by day by God. The children of God are indeed given over to suffering and death in the world so that the life of Jesus will be visible to others through their mortal lives.

Ask God to make it possible for you to live in such a way that in the midst of your hardship, people will be aware of Jesus in your life and give God the honor for it. Then your prayers of thanksgiving will at the same time increase and God will receive the glory, as Paul says in 2 Corinthians 11:15.

Lord Jesus, thank You for the new bit of insight that it is in fact my trials that make it possible for me to be a powerful witness for You. Help me to show others through my positive response in my trials that I love You. Amen.

In the Fire of Tribulation

"When you pass through the waters, I will be with you; and when you pass through the rivers, they will not sweep over you. When you walk through the fire, you will not be burned; the flames will not set you ablaze. For I am the LORD" (Isaiah 43:2-3).

Each one of us gets our turn to end up in the fire of testing. God does not safeguard His children from hard times but He never leaves them alone in the fire. When Daniel's three friends were thrown into the furnace because of their faith, the people could see four figures walking around in the fire. An angel of God was waiting for them in the fire, and the fire did not even scorch them. The people who had thrown them into the fire were burnt to death, but Daniel's friends were unscathed.

God sometimes uses fires of oppression to purify His children, just as fire is physically applied to extract pure silver from silver ore. Trials strengthen your faith and build your character. Through trials you also develop a hopeful anticipation that God will give you all those things that He has promised you in His Word (see Rom. 5:3-4).

When you are purified through the fires of tribulation, you can be sure of one thing – you are not alone. God is with you in the middle of that fire. When your problems increase it becomes more difficult to focus on God. But God promises that if you are willing to trust Him in the midst of your trails, He will rescue you from them.

Heavenly Father, I praise You for the assurance that You will never leave me alone while I am being purified in the fires of tribulation but that You will wait for me in the fire and will rescue me out of it once again. Amen.

God Cannot Disappoint You

Not only so, but we also rejoice in our sufferings, because we know that suffering produces perseverance; perseverance, character; and character, hope. And hope does not disappoint us, because God has poured out His love into our hearts by the Holy Spirit, whom He has given us (Romans 5:3-5).

Tribulation always bring about positive transformation in your life: It forms and shapes you so that you are able to trust God even more firmly than before. This trust then helps you to develop a Christian character and it causes you to fix your hope on heaven that awaits you. Furthermore, people who put their hope in God will never be disappointed because He fills our lives each day with His love through the indwelling Holy Spirit.

No one who has trusted in God has ever been disappointed, the Bible teaches us, "He will be the sure foundation for your times," writes the prophet Isaiah (Isa. 33:6). There is a level of trust in God that you can only reach when you realize that He is all that you have. "When God is all that you have, you discover that He is all that you need," is a well-known saying. Your earthly suffering thus strengthens your faith and trust in God because it allows you to discover that you can find the strength in Him to persevere through your suffering time after time. Faith often prepares the way for God to take control of your life and also for Him to take your problems to His own account.

Heavenly Father, thank You very much for the assurance that I can hold fast to You with great trust and can hope in You because I know that You will never disappoint me. Amen.

Sometimes God Makes You Wait ...

I have stilled and quieted my soul; like a weaned child with its mother, like a weaned child is my soul within me. O Israel, put your hope in the LORD both now and forevermore (Psalm 131:2-3).

In times of difficulty God sometimes does not immediately answer the requests of His children for Him to help them. Sometimes He leaves us to wait for His answers. In Psalm 131 David declares that he is prepared to wait on God. He would no longer tire himself out over things which he could not do anything about, but would be satisfied to be with God and wait on Him calmly and peacefully until God, in His perfect time, would bring the solution.

When things once again become tough for you and God delays in giving you help, you can take a page out of David's book. Go ahead and ask God for the things you need; pray for strength to persevere in your crisis situations and become still in His presence. Be prepared to wait on Him – to wait until the promises in His Word become true for you.

This waiting on God is a special kind of waiting. It asks for you to be prepared to become quiet before God and trust in Him completely; with just the same kind of surrender as a baby who is soothed in his mother's arms. There in the arms of God, no one and nothing can do you any harm and there you find the assurance that God will once again in the future bring about a resolution for you.

Heavenly Father, I am sorry that it is so hard for me to wait on You. Make me calm and peaceful in Your presence, like a baby in his mother's arms, with the certain knowledge that You will resolve the issues for me. Amen.

A Reason for Joy

Consider it pure joy, my brothers, whenever you face trials of many kinds, because you know that the testing of your faith develops perseverance (James 1:2-3).

Trials are a reason to rejoice, states James. We will experience nothing of this rejoicing while we are in the process of suffering – then we are more likely to be struggling just to keep our heads above water each day so that we do not drown in our own negative circumstances. But just as God is with us in the fire of tribulation, He is also there when we have to go through deep waters as a result of our circumstances. We do not rejoice because of the pain, but we can manage to be glad in the midst of our difficult circumstances because it is in our pain that we experience the mercy of God. Perseverance follows when our faith has stood the test.

Although things might be difficult for you at the moment, you can still know for certain that heaven awaits you at the end of your suffering. For this reason you can be glad about your earthly trials – because God promises that the heavenly joy will be your portion in the hereafter. You also have the promise of God that your trials on earth are really negligible and that they will soon pass and will eventually result in an "eternal glory that far outweighs them all" (see 2 Cor. 4:17).

Heavenly Father, please make it possible for me to still be glad in the midst of trials and tribulations, because I know that if my faith withstands the test it will place me in a position where I am able to persevere. Thank You for the eternal glory that You promise. Amen.

Courage in Suffering

The God of all grace, who called you to His eternal glory in Christ, after you have suffered a little while, will Himself restore you and make you strong, firm and steadfast. To Him be the power for ever and ever. Amen (1 Peter 5:10-11).

Jesus was willing to endure great suffering on the cross because He loved us so much. When Isaiah wrote about the Servant of the Lord, he said that He would be pierced for our transgressions and bruised for our iniquities, that the punishment that would bring us peace would be on Him and that through His wounds we would be healed (see Isa. 53:5).

Sometimes difficult situations in your life threaten to drag you under but God is always stronger than your suffering; He will support you. He knows the depths of your suffering because He Himself endured far greater suffering. Run to God in adversity because that is the very best place for you. The only place where you will find real healing for your wounds is with Him. And because in your own times of hardship you share in His suffering, you become more like Him and will also one day share in His glory. He promises to build you up again once you have suffered for a short while and to make you strong and courageous and able to stand. Trust Him for this!

Lord Jesus, I praise You because You were willing to endure inhuman suffering on the cross so that I could be saved. Make me strong and courageous and able to stand firm so that I will one day be able to share in Your glory. Amen.

Hardship As a Disciplinary Measure

"I know your deeds, that you are neither cold nor hot. I wish you were either one or the other! So, because you are lukewarm – neither hot nor cold – I am about to spit you out of My mouth" (Revelation 3:15-16).

When I was little, people still believed in corporal punishment. And – perhaps because I was somewhat difficult – I was often acquainted with the wooden spoon when I did not want to listen to my parents. When my mother opened the kitchen drawer I knew exactly what she was saying to me! Discipline is one of the ways in which God speaks to you. He punishes and disciplines each one whom He loves because He does not want any of us to be lost. Hardships, as God's disciplinary measure, should therefore result in you hearing the voice of God clearly speaking to you, and you turning away from your wrong lifestyle in repentance.

If you are driven closer to God through your suffering, He promises to come into your life – He has been knocking for a long time and waiting for you to invite Him into your life. But He will never force you to give the control of your life to Him – the decision always rests with you. You will have to open the door to your life for Him yourself. And usually it is your adversities that cause you to hear that knocking and to open the door of your life to God.

Lord, thank You that the hard times that I experience cause me to hear Your voice. I now want to open the door of my life to You and turn to You so that You will be with me for the rest of my life. Amen.

Shelter from the Storm

My soul clings to You; Your right hand upholds me. They who seek my life will be destroyed; they will go down to the depths of the earth (Psalm 63:8-9).

God's children have the assurance that they are always safe with Him, that they can confidently seek shelter under the shadow of His wings in dangerous situations and that they can stay close to Him with the certainty that His hand will support and protect them.

Hannah Whitall Smith wrote a book with the title *Safe within Your Love*. In it she used a beautiful image to explain the safe hiding place for Christians under the wings of God: She writes, "I feel just like a little chick who has run out of a storm and under his mother's wings and is safe there. I hear the raging of the storm and I am utterly unable to comprehend it or measure the damage it is doing, but I am safe under His wings. He can manage the dark storm, but I cannot. Why then should I worry or feel anxious? When I feel hopeless or fear, I know I need to get back under His wings."

The next time a storm erupts in your life, you can readily go and find shelter with God and ask Him to protect you. There is always protection to be found for you under His wings. He is still able to calm every storm in your life and to keep you safe in dangerous situations.

Heavenly Father, I praise You for always offering me a safe haven when storms break out in my life. I know that there under Your wings I will be completely safe for now and for always. Amen.

A Fire That Purifies

See, I have refined you, though not as silver; I have tested you in the furnace of affliction. For My own sake, for My own sake, I do this. How can I let Myself be defamed? I will not yield My glory to another (Isaiah 48:10-11).

During our visit to the East German town of Dresden we admired the beautiful porcelain items that are made there. I so wished that I could buy some and take them home with me but unfortunately the price was somewhat out of our range! A long time after that tour I read that the exceptional Dresden porcelain is so expensive because it is placed in the kiln three times instead of just once. It is in fact this repeated application of intense heat that makes the colors of Dresden porcelain so especially bright and clear and so sought after by collectors.

Through the mouth of the prophet Isaiah, God announced that He was planning to purify His people in the furnace of affliction because they would not listen to Him. After this process they would be pure and new; useful instruments that could be used by Him. This purifying process was carried out so that God would receive the glory that was due to Him.

God still purifies His children in the crucible of adversity. During this purifying process He removes all the unnecessary elements from our lives so that we can be of better use to Him. The longer you are placed in this furnace of suffering, the more brightly your colors will shine and the more committed you will be to Him.

Heavenly Father, thank You that Your purifying process in the furnace of adversity will always make a more committed Christian of me. Purify me and sanctify me so that I will be a useful instrument in Your hand. Amen.

Incense for Christ

Thanks be to God, who always leads us in triumphal procession in Christ and through us spreads everywhere the fragrance of the knowledge of Him. For we are to God the aroma of Christ among those who are being saved and those who are perishing (2 Corinthians 2:14-15).

Paul here describes the triumphal march of the gospel through the world as a festive parade that he compares with the processions that kings who have achieved great victories would hold. During these parades, incense would be burned so that the people who came to see the parade could not only see the good news, but smell it too.

In Old Testament times incense was offered to God in the temple as an offering (see Exod. 30). In Revelation 5:8 the prayers of the believers that rise up to God are compared to this incense. Before the aroma of incense can be released it first has to be set alight. Incense is therefore also seen as a symbol of the trials that are sometimes necessary to set the fragrance of Christ free in the lives of people.

Only after you have been exposed to adversity will you develop the exceptional spirituality and holiness that God expects of His children. Just as in the case of incense, the fire of adversity is needed before the fragrance of Jesus can be completely released through your life. The next time you go through difficulties and want to rebel against them, rather see them as the only way in which you can really spread the fragrance of Christ.

Heavenly Father, make my portion of adversity like an offering of incense to You so that the fragrance of Jesus can be released in my life through it. Amen.

Return to God!

When you are in distress and all these things have happened to you, then in later days you will return to the LORD your God and obey Him (Deuteronomy 4:30).

Adversity makes us experience the grace of God in a completely new way. My granny used to say that children needed a "hearing smack" on the days they were very naughty. According to her, the only thing that would help to make them obedient was a good hiding! God very often uses the same method. With the "hearing smack" of hardship in our lives He causes us to turn back to Him, "Before I was afflicted I went astray, but now I obey Your word," testifies David in Psalm 119:67.

In Deuteronomy 4:31 Moses gives Israel a beautiful promise if they return to God in their times of difficulty, "The LORD your God is a merciful God; He will not abandon or destroy you or forget the covenant with your forefathers." God was prepared to forgive His people each time they turned back to Him and confessed their sins. This promise is still valid for us. When things are hard and you find yourself in trouble, the only advice is to turn back to God and obey His Word. Then He will take compassion on you and change your circumstances so that things will once again go well for you.

Heavenly Father, thank You that You are always there for me when the pressure rises. I praise You for the grace that You always make available to me and for Your promise that You will never let me down, but will use my hard times to bring me back to You. Amen.

Suffering for the Sake of Faith

If you suffer, it should not be as a murderer or thief or any other kind of criminal, or even as a meddler. However, if you suffer as a Christian, do not be ashamed, but praise God that you bear that name (1 Peter 4:15-16).

The sort of suffering that Peter is talking about here is the suffering that you undergo because you are a Christian and do the will of God. Suffering is never pleasant for anyone, but suffering for the sake of your faith is always beneficial for you.

It is the kind of hardship that you experience when you come to repentance and then afterwards find that your previous friends no longer really want anything to do with you. You might also be discriminated against in your workplace because of your faith. When these kinds of things happen to you, you should actually be glad because they mean that you are sharing in the suffering of Jesus. And, Peter writes, when you share in the suffering of Jesus you will overflow with joy on the day on which He returns (see verse 13).

Secondly, suffering for the sake of your faith is proof that the Holy Spirit is actually present in your life. "If you are insulted because of the name of Christ, you are blessed," writes Peter. "The Spirit of glory and of God rests on you" (verse 14). If, as a result of your faith, you once again experience opposition, follow the advice of Peter in verse 19 – commit your life to God and keep on doing what is good.

Lord Jesus, make me willing to endure hardship for the sake of my faith, because I know that it is the guarantee that I will one day experience joy when You return and at the same time have the assurance that Your Spirit lives in me. Amen.

A Shepherd in Times of Despair

*The L*ORD* is my shepherd, I shall not be in want. Even though I walk through the valley of the shadow of death, I will fear no evil, for You are with me; Your rod and Your staff, they comfort me (Psalm 23:1, 4).*

In Psalm 23 the psalmist declares that there is nothing that he lacks because God is his Shepherd. Just three verses later however, he talks of dark depths which he has to go through. Yet even then he is not afraid because his Shepherd is also present in the darkness and will lead him through it. In the hands of the Shepherd he is safe forever.

If you are a Christian you too have God as your Shepherd and you can know that He will always make sure that you have everything that you need. Yet the presence of God in your life does not safeguard you from the dark depths and danger zones.

Like the psalmist, you too can tackle these dark depths with confidence because you know that God will still be with you, that He will Himself support and protect you, that He will carry you through those dark depths until you eventually, at the end of your life, arrive safely home in heaven.

This too is emphasized by the psalmist: "Surely goodness and love will follow me all the days of my life, and I will dwell in the house of the LORD forever" (Ps. 23:6).

Lord Jesus, thank You very much for the assurance that You are my Shepherd and therefore I will lack nothing. I praise You because You are always there to protect and keep me when hard times cross my path. You will carry me through them until I arrive at home with You one day. Amen.

Time to Calm Down

*Therefore we will not fear, though the earth give way and the mountains fall into the heart of the sea. The L*ORD* Almighty is with us; the God of Jacob is our fortress (Psalm 46:2, 11).*

At the moment this is still a difficult command for people to keep. We know that God is a refuge and a shelter for us, we believe that He can and will protect us and yet there are so many things that make us restless and cause us to toss and turn at night with worry.

The writer of Psalm 46 knew what it felt like to be scared and anxious and yet trusted so completely in God that his desperate physical circumstances no longer had the ability to make him anxious. In verses 2-3 he testifies, "Therefore we will not fear, though the earth give way and the mountains fall into the sea ... and the mountains quake with their surging."

Can you say with all honesty that you, in the midst of the reigning chaos and violence in our own land, can come to a place of calmness because you know that God, in spite of the catastrophes that you see happening around you and of which you read each day in the newspapers, is completely in control? And that He also has the ability to protect His children in dangerous situations? Then you can take the promise in verse 11 as your own, "The LORD Almighty is with us; the God of Jacob is our fortress."

Heavenly Father, thank You very much for the promise that You are with me, that You are a refuge and a shelter for me, a help in times of trouble. Make it possible for me to be calm in the midst of trouble and to acknowledge that You are God. Amen.

You Belong to God

"Fear not, for I have redeemed you; I have summoned you by name; you are Mine. Since you are precious and honored in My sight, and because I love you, I will give men in exchange for you, and people in exchange for your life" (Isaiah 43:1, 4).

The people of God in the time of the prophet Isaiah had many reasons to be afraid. As a result of their disobedience they were taken away into exile and their land was destroyed. Yet God still looked after them. He comforted them by promising that He would once again free them from this exile. He promised them that He knew them by name, that He loved them and that they were very precious to Him.

In today's world we have many reasons to be fearful. But you too have been called by God by name on that day when you gave your life to Him. Even though there are many millions of people in the world God knows you personally – you belong to Him. You are so precious to Him that He is prepared to give people in your place, and nations in exchange for your life. He was even prepared to let His Son die on a cross in your place so that your debt of sin could be paid. For this reason you no longer need to fear anything. After all, you belong to God – and if He has set you free there is nothing in the world that can ever separate you from His love again.

Heavenly Father, it is wonderful that I can belong to You, that You have called me by name and that I am precious to You. Thank You that You not only give nations in exchange for my life, but that You also gave the life of Your Son. Amen.

Give Your Life to the Lord

Commit your way to the LORD; trust in Him and He will do this. He will make your righteousness shine like the dawn, the justice of your cause like the noonday sun (Psalm 37:5-6).

I must admit that at the moment I worry and am upset every single morning when my husband brings me the newspaper, together with my morning coffee. On practically every page there are reports about burglaries, murders, violence and crime. And it seems as if very few of the criminals are ever apprehended. And if they are actually apprehended they are set free because there is insufficient evidence. It seems to law-abiding citizens as if the justice system is currently one hundred percent on the side of criminals! Furthermore it is becoming more and more dangerous to venture outside your own house – you are no longer safe even in the big shopping malls.

Perhaps the time has come for Christians to not get so upset about these issues and instead focus on God. Then we will once again choose to surrender our lives to Him and trust in Him steadfastly. He is after all the Almighty. He can do all things and He offers you protection. In any case, these criminals that cause so much worry will in the long run "disappear like the grass," says the Bible. Therefore, trust in God – He will care for you and is completely able to keep you safe in the midst of the reigning crime situation.

Heavenly Father, I am sorry that I worry so much about the negative things that are happening at the moment in the world. Help me to look away from the reigning crime and violence and surrender my life to You with the certain knowledge that You will care for me. Amen.

Ask God for Help

"Then I will go back to My place until they admit their guilt. And they will seek My face; in their misery they will earnestly seek Me" *(Hosea 5:15).*

When His people left Him, God pulled back from them. This caused the people to once again turn to Him. They decided that they would once again surrender themselves to Him anew. The result of this is that God refreshed them like spring rains refresh the ground (see Hosea 6:3).

There is a well known story about a little boy who went crying to his father because he could not manage to lift a very heavy rock. "Well," his father said to him, "you did not ask me to help you." He pushed his hands under those of his son and together they easily picked up the heavy rock.

There are many crises and problems that are too heavy for us to overcome on our own. Sometimes God actually allows these problems into our lives so that we can admit our own inability and turn to Him for help. It is not all that easy to admit your own inability! We all want to prove our independence. When you, in your own times of trouble go and seek God's help He is always prepared to assist you. And when God places His hands under yours there is no problem too big and no crisis too heavy that cannot be overcome with His help.

Lord God, I am sorry that it is so hard for me to admit my dependence on You. Thank You that You are always willing to help. I now, in my trouble, want to come and ask You for help and commit myself to You anew. Amen.

When God Is with You

Have I not commanded you? Be strong and courageous. Do not be terrified; do not be discouraged, for the LORD your God will be with you wherever you go" (Joshua 1:9).

Moses was a formidable leader who not only freed the people out of Egypt but also managed to lead them through the desert for forty years. But now, on the threshold of the Promised Land, Joshua had to take over the leadership from Moses. This was no easy task. But God assured Joshua that he could be strong and courageous, that he did not have to be afraid of the big responsibility that would now be laid on his shoulders because God Himself would be with him wherever he went. With God's support and strength, Joshua even succeeded in taking over the enemy cities.

God still gives His children the instruction to be strong and courageous in times of trouble, to not be afraid because He will be with us. It's possible to handle the heaviest responsibilities and to overcome the greatest difficulties if you have the assurance that God is with you to help you. And He promises you that He will be near you – for this reason you do not need to be afraid of anyone or anything. Make use of His support. After all, you know that He will be with you wherever you go.

Heavenly Father, I now take Your promise for me – thank You that I can exchange my fear for Your strength and can be courageous because You will be with me wherever I go. Amen.

God Uses Your Troubles

Consider it pure joy, my brothers, whenever you face trials of many kinds, because you know that the testing of your faith develops perseverance (James 1:2-3).

A certain John Baillie wrote a striking prayer, "Teach me, O God, so to use all the circumstances of my life today that they may bring forth in me the fruits of holiness rather than the fruits of sin."

God can use everything that happens in your life – even your difficulties – to mold you spiritually so that you will become the person that He intended you to be. James explains it like this at the beginning of his letter: we ought to be glad about our hard times because they make our faith stronger. If your faith has passed this test it puts you in the position where you can persevere, and if this perseverance continues to the end you will come out on the other side spiritually richer. There are two conditions necessary for this: You must persevere to the end and never give up your faith, and You must endure in prayer until God has given you the things that you are praying for.

In the midst of the worst suffering, you can still hold on to the fact that your life is in God's hands and that He can and will use your hardship of the moment to form you into a more mature and holier Christian.

Heavenly Father, thank You that You can use each thing in my life to mold me into a holier, more mature child of Yours. I know that You can use even this portion of suffering with which I am wrestling at the moment to bring about good in my life. Amen.

Pray in Your Trials

Is any one of you in trouble? He should pray. Is anyone happy? Let him sing songs of praise. Therefore confess your sins to each other and pray for each other so that you may be healed. The prayer of a righteous man is powerful and effective (James 5:13, 16).

The very best advice for times of trouble is to put aside more time for prayer. God knows you and your circumstances but He really wants you to communicate with Him when things are tough. And it is after all natural to pray more when things are going badly than when they are only going well for you.

For this reason tribulations are actually beneficial – your pain holds blessing for you because it keeps you on your knees and causes your relationship with God to be deepened and become more intimate. Hardship also makes you spiritually stronger – it is a support for your faith to see how God answers your prayers and brings about a solution for you. It is not coincidental that James writes that the prayer of a believer has a powerful outcome, because when His children pray, God works.

Elisabeth Kübler-Ross, the German psychologist who became well known for her work with the dying, claims, "The more wind storms you can survive, the better you can work through your hardships, and the better you know that you are never given more than you can handle. When you go through the mill, it is your own choice how you will come out on the other side: finely ground or beautifully polished." In future use your portion of suffering to make a better, more mature version of yourself.

Heavenly Father, thank You that I can talk to You and can ask for Your help in times when I am hurting. I believe that You will help me each time just as You have done in the past and that my pain of the moment will ultimately contain a great blessing for me. Amen.

rayer

Heavenly Father,
Thank You for the life lesson that it is indeed the times
of pain in my life that hold the greatest blessing for me.
I know that my many fears are really not necessary
because You will never disappoint the people who trust in You.
You use the suffering in my life for my own good
because it makes it possible for me
to spread the fragrance of Christ.
Please forgive me for so quickly letting myself be
dragged down by emotions of despair and depression – and please
exchange my heartache for a lasting joy.
Everything in my life comes from You: sorrow and joy;
You talk to me through sickness and adversity
and I can hold fast to Your promise that You will one day in heaven
put an end to sorrow forever.
Show me that it is in fact the hard times in my life
that make me a more powerful witness for You.
I praise You because You will never leave me alone.
You are with me every moment – especially in the fire of adversity.
It is wonderful that You make it possible for me to be glad when I go
through times of trouble because it teaches me to persevere
and to keep my hope in You.
Sometimes You use adversity as a disciplinary measure to
bring me close to You again – it teaches me to be dependent on You:
it compels me to return to You: to seek help from You.
I now want to surrender my whole life to You with the certain
knowledge that You care and you will ultimately
exchange every tiny piece of pain for a great blessing for me.

Amen.

May

Spreading the Good News

If you have God in your heart, you cannot help but spread the good news of Jesus.

Jesus promised His disciples that the Holy Spirit would make them witnesses so that His message could be spread in Jerusalem, Judea, Samaria and to the ends of the world.

The whole book of Acts is a testimony of what exceptional witnesses the early Christians were.

Paul writes to the church in Corinth that we can speak to others about our faith because we have the Spirit of faith to empower us (2 Cor. 4:13).

During this month we are going to focus on how to be spontaneous witnesses so that the good news of the love of God will be spread through our words and our deeds.

Help for the Task of Witnessing

The LORD said to him, "Who gave man his mouth? Who makes him deaf or mute? Who gives him sight or makes him blind? Is it not I, the LORD? Now go; I will help you speak and will teach you what to say" (Exodus 4:11-12).

In the Old Testament already we hear that God wants His children to spread His message. He tells Moses that he does not have to be afraid to testify because God, who gave people their mouths, would help him to speak and tell him exactly what to say. Moses, however, just like us, continued making one excuse after the other. In his defense, we must admit that Moses had a physical problem – he stammered!

Perhaps you too have a physical reason that makes it hard for you to witness. If so, take God's promise to Moses for yourself. He will help you to be a powerful witness. He will help you speak and teach you what to say if you are willing to be used by Him.

Like the disciples long after Moses discovered, God never gives us the task to be His witnesses without being with us. "I am with you always, to the very end of the age," Jesus promised them when He sent them out as witnesses (Matt. 28:20). You too can trust God to do that for you!

Lord Jesus, thank You for the assurance that You will teach me what to say when I speak to people about You and for the promise that You will be with me. Amen.

God's Witnesses

On the evening of that first day of the week, when the disciples were together, with the doors locked for fear of the Jews, Jesus came and stood among them and said, "Peace be with you!" Again Jesus said, "Peace be with you! As the Father has sent Me, I am sending you" (John 20:19, 21).

The first time that Jesus appeared to His disciples after His resurrection, He had a very important message for them, "As the Father has sent Me, so I am sending you." The work that Jesus came to accomplish on earth was to proclaim the message of salvation – an obligation that He carried out with great diligence up to His crucifixion and death. God Himself equipped Jesus for this task.

The time came for Jesus to return to His Father, but He left His followers behind to continue His work on earth. As Jesus was sent by God, He also sent His disciples to proclaim His joyful message further. During the three years that they had worked with Him, they were prepared by Jesus for this important work – and their time had come to tell people who did not know Him yet. Jesus breathed on them and said, "Receive the Holy Spirit" (v. 22).

If you belong to God you are automatically one of His witnesses – you actually have no choice in this matter. A disciple is at the same time also a disciple-maker, otherwise he completely misses his purpose.

Fortunately for you, you have also received the Holy Spirit to help you with this task.

Holy Spirit, I praise You because You are with me to equip me to witness for God in the world. Please help me with my work on earth. Amen.

Today Is the Day!

"In the time of My favor I heard you, and in the day of salvation I helped you." I tell you, now is the time of God's favor, now is the day of salvation (2 Corinthians 6:2).

Paul urges the church in Corinth not to receive the grace of God in vain. God answered their prayers at the right time; today is the day of their salvation. They had to treat their salvation seriously; the salvation that God brought about for them and which Paul explained to them. In verse 11 Paul writes that his heart was wide open to the people of Corinth and he asked that they would open their hearts to him.

The worst thing that any witness can do is to put off his work of witnessing. There is no better time to testify of your faith than today. You can confidently put God to the test in this matter – He wants you to be His witness today, and to tell other people of His love (even if you are shy, or young, or find it difficult to talk).

You cannot afford to remain silent – if you do so, someone might forfeit their last chance to accept God into their lives.

Heavenly Father, I am sorry that I often put off witnessing for You. Help me to realize the urgency of Your message of redemption so that I will no longer keep it to myself, but will share it with other people today. Amen.

Out of the Overflow of His Heart ...

"The good man brings good things out of the good stored up in his heart, and the evil man brings evil things out of the evil stored up in his heart. For out of the overflow of his heart his mouth speaks" (Luke 6:45).

To be a witness for Christ is a natural outcome of faith. The mouth speaks of what the heart overflows with. Jesus said this to His disciples after He told them that a tree is known by its fruit.

The truth of this saying can be seen very clearly if you listen to grannies swapping stories about their grandchildren! The things that you talk about show other people what is truly important to you. From your words people will very quickly hear that you are a Christian, just as they can see from your deeds that you belong to God.

"I believed; therefore I have spoken," Paul wrote to the church in Corinth (2 Cor. 4:13). From the day of his conversion on the road to Damascus, Paul never stopped witnessing. His whole life was dedicated to telling people why they should believe in Jesus.

If you are a Christian, other people should know about it. Are you able to speak about your faith in such a way that people can see that your heart is filled with the love of God?

Lord Jesus, my heart is indeed full of You – give me the right words to tell other people about You, so that my mouth will overflow with the things that live in my heart. Amen.

Who Will Go?

Then I heard the voice of the LORD saying, "Whom shall I send? And who will go for us?" And I said, "Here am I. Send me!" (Isaiah 6:8).

God gave the prophet Isaiah a vision of His majesty: Isaiah saw God sitting on a high throne and the train of His robe filled the temple. Surrounding Him were angels who praised Him with the words, "Holy, holy, holy is the LORD God Almighty; the whole earth is full of His glory!" (Isa. 6:3). When Isaiah saw this vision and realized how mighty and holy God is, he was immediately aware of his own sinfulness and confessed his impurity before the Lord. At this, one of the angels touched his lips and he heard that God had forgiven his sins.

Directly after this the Lord asked whom He could send as a messenger for Him, and Isaiah was ready for the challenge. "Here am I. Send me!" he answered. Unlike Moses before him and Jeremiah after him, Isaiah did not have a list of excuses for why he could not carry out God's command, but he was immediately willing to do it.

God still uses people in His service to carry His message to others. Like Isaiah, you are a sinner, but God can purify you and forgive your sins so that He can use you as His messenger. God wants to call you and send you today. Are you willing to be His messenger?

Lord God, You know me very well and You know that I am a sinner. Touch me as You did Isaiah so that my sins can be forgiven and that I will be prepared to be sent as Your messenger. Amen.

A Light for the Nations

The LORD says ... "I will also make you a light for the Gentiles, that you may bring My salvation to the ends of the earth" (Isaiah 49:6).

God had a specific task in mind for the exiles from Israel who were now returning to Jerusalem – it was His will that they would not just keep the covenant promise to themselves but that they would carry it out to the rest of the world. He had called them for this task even before they were born, wrote Isaiah, and He promised to make their mouths like sharp swords (Isa. 49:1-2). The prophet Isaiah told the people of this commission, "I am making you a light to the nations so that you will bring my salvation to the ends of the earth."

God has also called you before you were born to be His witness on the earth and to carry the message of His joyous salvation to others. He wants to make you a light for the nations so that His salvation will reach all people so that everyone will have the opportunity to believe in Jesus.

Are you prepared to do this? Then the promise in verse 5 is also for you, "I am honored in the eyes of the LORD and my God has been my strength."

Heavenly Father, it is wonderful that You have called me, as You called the Israelites of old to be a light to the nations and to spread the Good News of Your gospel so that it will reach the farthest corners of the earth. Thank You for the promise that You will give me the strength to do this. Amen.

The Testimony of a King

"He rescues and He saves; He performs signs and wonders in the heavens and on the earth. He has rescued Daniel from the power of the lions." So Daniel prospered during the reign of Darius and the reign of Cyrus the Persian (Daniel 6:27-28).

By listening to his jealous officials, King Darius issued a decree that anyone in his kingdom who, in a period of thirty days, worshiped anyone except him would be thrown into the lions' den.

When Daniel trespassed against this decree and continued to worship God, King Darius had no other choice but to throw him into the lions' den. After a sleepless night, early the next morning the king went to the lions' den to see what had happened to Daniel. When he saw him fit as a fiddle among the lions, the king knew that the God of Daniel was the only true God. He did not hesitate to issue another decree: this time the instructions read that the God of Daniel was to be honored and feared throughout his kingdom. On top of this the king gave a wonderful testimony of God, "He rescues and He saves; He performs signs and wonders in the heavens and on the earth," he said.

Daniel's unshakable faith in his God led his king to come to repentance and to also worship God. Furthermore, on the command of the king the whole country was instructed to follow his example.

Heavenly Father, I pray for a faith like that of Daniel that will encourage other people to believe in You and to testify of You. Amen.

Jesus' Command to Testify

"As you go, preach this message: 'The kingdom of heaven is near.' But when they arrest you, do not worry about what to say or how to say it. At that time you will be given what to say" (Matthew 10:7, 19).

It was of the utmost importance to Jesus that the message for which He had come to earth was spread further. He, therefore, sent His disciples to go and do this. They were to proclaim through the whole of Israel that the kingdom of God was at hand. He also warned them that this work of witnessing would not always be easy; they could expect to be persecuted.

Yet, He promised that they need not worry about what they would say because God Himself would give them the right words to speak. He also added, "For it will not be you speaking, but the Spirit of Your Father speaking through you" (Matt. 10:20).

Jesus still sends His followers into the world to carry His message that the kingdom of God is at hand. If you are willing to be one of His sent ones, you also need not worry about what you will say. Through the working of His Spirit who lives in you, God will give you the right words to say each time. But the warning of Jesus also still applies to you: to be a witness is never an easy task – you can expect opposition. Prepare yourself for this!

Lord Jesus, I am prepared to be one who proclaims the coming of Your kingdom. Thank You for Your promise that Your Spirit will give me the right words and that You Yourself will support me. Amen.

John's Life Mission

There came a man who was sent from God; his name was John. He came as a witness to testify concerning that light, so that through him all men might believe. He himself was not the light; he came only as a witness to the light (John 1:6-8).

Even before the birth of John the Baptist, his father Zechariah, prophesied that his son would one day be the predecessor of the long awaited Messiah. "You will go on before the Lord to prepare the way for Him," he prophesied in Luke 1:76-77. And John fulfilled his father's prophesy. He fulfilled his mission that he had received from God. He himself said that he came to bear witness to the light so that all those who listened to him would come to believe in Jesus. John also made it abundantly clear that he was not the light, but that he had only come to tell people of the light. "The life appeared; we have seen it and testify to it, and we proclaim to you the eternal life, which was with the Father and has appeared to us," writes the apostle John (1 John 1:2).

Through his testimony, John did his part to ensure that the light of Jesus shone brightly in the darkness, and that the darkness could not extinguish it. Every person who testifies for Jesus helps to spread His light though the world, and ensures that the reign of the Devil over the world receives a deathblow. Because no matter how cruel the world looks to us, Jesus has overcome the world.

Lord Jesus, use my testimony to enrich the knowledge other people have of You so that Your light can be spread throughout the world. Amen.

The Testimony of an Elderly Woman

There was also a prophetess, Anna, the daughter of Phanuel, of the tribe of Asher. She was very old. Coming up to them at that very moment, she gave thanks to God and spoke about the child to all who were looking forward to the redemption of Jerusalem (Luke 2:36, 38).

Anna, who spent so much time in the temple, was an example for every believing Israelite. Even though women did not play an important role in biblical times, she, in spite of her advanced age, did not stay away from the temple where she served God night and day through fasting and praying.

When she saw the Baby Jesus in Simeon's arms, she immediately believed the words of Simeon: "Sovereign Lord, as You have promised, You now dismiss Your servant in peace. For my eyes have seen Your salvation, which You have prepared in the sight of all people" (Luke 2:29-31). She did not keep the good news to herself, but began to speak to all those who had been waiting for the Messiah.

Anna is still a worthy example worthy for us to follow today. Perhaps you neglect your church attendance because you are no longer all that young, perhaps you no longer pray as much as you did before and perhaps you shy away from witnessing to others simply because you are using your age as an excuse.

There are still many people these days who have not heard the message of Jesus. If Jesus is a part of your life, it is your responsibility to speak to them about salvation.

Heavenly Father, make me a witness like Anna was, and help me not to hold back from speaking to others about my salvation. Amen.

Do Not Be Ashamed to Witness ...

So do not be ashamed to testify about our Lord, or ashamed of me His prisoner. But join with me in suffering for the gospel, by the power of God (2 Timothy 1:8).

Paul was never ashamed to speak to others about the message of Jesus, and he was also not ashamed to go through hardships for the cause of Jesus. For this reason he could speak to Timothy with authority about witnessing. Paul told Timothy he should not be embarrassed to proclaim the message of the Lord.

Some people find it much easier to witness than others do. Some of my friends can spontaneously initiate a conversation with perfect strangers and ask them about their faith. If I try to do this, I blush and every word I thought of saying flies out of my head. At least, this was until I learned the secret of witnessing without being embarrassed. If you happen to be one of the shy ones, I possibly have some advice for you. Stop stressing about when you should witness and about what exactly you must say. Do not concern yourself with what people will say or think of you. Make yourself available to God and wait until He gives you the right opportunity and the right words. Then you will discover that your embarrassment will dissolve like mist before the sun and that you will be able to easily share your faith with others.

Lord Jesus, please forgive me for finding it so hard to share my faith with others. Help me to be able to witness freely about You. Amen.

The Testimony of Philip

Andrew, Simon Peter's brother, was one of the two who heard what John had said and who had followed Jesus. The first thing Andrew did was to find his brother Simon and tell him, "We have found the Messiah" (that is, the Christ) (John 1:40-41).

Philip, one of the followers of John, was there when John the Baptist declared that Jesus is the Lamb of God. As a result of John's testimony, he decided to follow Jesus. He went after Jesus and asked where He was making His home. When Jesus invited him to come and see, he went with Him and spent the whole day with Him. After this, he went with great excitement to find his brother Peter, and told him that he had found the long awaited Savior of Israel.

Philip did more than just witness; he physically took Peter to where Jesus was. After this, both Philip and Peter were chosen by Jesus to be His disciples. And Peter, the one to whom Philip had witnessed, became, together with James and John, a member of the inner circle of Jesus. Later, when Peter in answer to Jesus' question said that He was the Christ, the Son of the Living God, Jesus said to him, "Blessed are you, Simon son of Jonah, for this was not revealed to you by man, but by my Father in heaven. And I tell you that you are Peter, and on this rock I will build My church" (see Matt. 16:17-18).

Eventually this person to whom Philip had witnessed played a far greater role in God's kingdom than Philip himself. Who knows, perhaps the same can happen to someone you witness to?

Lord, make me willing to witness to others about my relationship with You – and then use these people who have heard my testimony for the good of Your kingdom. Amen.

A Witness from Samaria

Many of the Samaritans from that town believed in Him because of the woman's testimony, "He told me everything I ever did" (John 4:39).

To me, one of the most beautiful stories of witnessing in the Bible is the one of the Samaritan woman whom Jesus met at the well. To her amazement, Jesus asked her for water. He also told her that everyone who drank of the water that He gives will never again be thirsty. When the woman said to Him that she too wanted some of that water, Jesus asked her to go and call her husband. At this, she told Him her life story and He told her that He was the long awaited Messiah.

She was so enthusiastic to tell the people in her village about the Messiah that she left her water jar at the well. And her testimony had an amazing effect: many Samaritans believed in Jesus based on the words of the woman who had witnessed. They all went to the well to meet Jesus personally. After this they asked Jesus to stay with them for a little while, and after two days many more Samaritans believed in Him. The people in the village also had a testimony, "We no longer believe just because of what you said; now we have heard for ourselves, and we know that this man really is the Savior of the world" (John 4:42).

Lord Jesus, make me as enthusiastic about telling people about You as the Samaritan woman. Thank You that I also know for certain that You are my Savior. Amen.

Peter Denies Jesus

A servant girl saw him seated there in the firelight. She looked closely at him and said, "This man was with Him." But he denied it. "Woman, I don't know Him," he said. A little later someone else saw him and said, "You also are one of them." "Man, I am not!" Peter replied. About an hour later another asserted, "Certainly this fellow was with Him, for he is a Galilean." Peter replied, "Man, I don't know what you're talking about!" (Luke 22:56-60).

The most eager of Jesus' twelve disciples, Peter failed his witnessing test – he denied Jesus. He allowed no less than three opportunities to pass him by in which he could have witnessed about his unique relationship with Jesus.

While he was denying Jesus, the cock crowed and Peter remembered the words of Jesus: that he would deny Him three times before the cock had crowed. Peter was extremely sorry about his transgression – Luke tells us that he went outside and wept bitterly (Luke 22:62).

After His resurrection, Jesus appeared to Peter and three times asked him if he loved Him (see John 19:15-19). And this time Peter was ready to testify that he loved Jesus each time. He was also willing to look after Jesus' sheep. Jesus prepared him for the things that his witnessing would require of him: "When you are old you will stretch out your hands, and someone else will lead you where you do not want to go" (John 21:18).

Are you, like Peter, prepared to care for your fellow believers and to pay whatever price your witnessing might ask of you?

Lord Jesus, like Peter, I want to testify of my love for You. Make me willing to pay the price that my witnessing requires. Amen.

The Testimony of Mary Magdalene

Mary Magdalene went to the disciples with the news: "I have seen the Lord!" And she told them that He had said these things to her (John 20:18).

Mary Magdalene had an intimate relationship with Jesus. He had in fact cast seven demons out of her (see Mark 16:9). We, however, never read that she had the boldness to personally speak to others about Jesus.

This fact changed after the resurrection of Jesus: when Jesus appeared to Mary He asked her not to touch Him but to go to His disciples and to tell them that He had risen from the dead and was ascending to His Father. Her task was now not to cling to Jesus but to go and be a witness for Him. Jesus Himself empowered her testimony. For the first time in the Bible we hear that a woman received an equal command to witness: "Go and tell them!" Jesus said to Mary. And Mary obeyed immediately. Straight away she went to the disciples with the good news that Jesus was not dead but alive, that she had seen Him with her own eyes. She also told them what Jesus had said to her.

The resurrected Jesus really wants you to be His messenger and to tell other people that He has risen from the dead. Are you willing to respond to His request?

Lord Jesus, help me to be prepared to obey Your command to witness and to tell others what You mean to me and to share with them the message of Your love for us. Amen.

Thomas Does Not Believe His Friends

So the other disciples told him, "We have seen the Lord!" But he said to them, "Unless I see the nail marks in His hands and put my finger where the nails were, and put my hand into His side, I will not believe it" (John 20:25).

Sometimes, even though you carry out your calling to be a witness, there are people who do not believe your testimony. This is exactly what happened when the ten disciples to whom Jesus appeared after His resurrection went and told Thomas what had happened to them.

When they told Thomas that they had seen Jesus, his immediate response was that he wouldn't believe it was true unless he put his own fingers into the nail marks on His hands and his own hand into the spear wound on Jesus' side. Eight days later, when Jesus appeared to the disciples again and invited Thomas to do exactly that, Thomas was ashamed about his earlier lack of faith. All that he could utter was, "My Lord and my God!" In response Jesus said that people who are able to believe without seeing are blessed (John 20:27-29).

If it ever happens to you that people doubt your testimony, do not be upset about it. God is able to bring about faith in a person's heart, and He too will make sure that the good work that you have begun through your witnessing will one day come to completion.

Lord, I am sorry that I sometimes become despondent when my testimony is not believed. Help me to persevere in my witnessing for You because I know that You Yourself will empower my testimony. Amen.

Those Who Proclaim the Gospel

Then the disciples went out and preached everywhere, and the Lord worked with them and confirmed His word by the signs that accompanied it (Mark 16:20).

After the resurrection of Jesus He gave His disciples another commission to be His witnesses, "Go into the world and preach the good news to all creation" (Mark 16:15). Jesus also told them that they would be able to cast out demons in His name, speak in other tongues, heal the sick and do all kinds of other miracles.

After this, Jesus ascended to heaven and the disciples began their task of witnessing on earth. Luke reported that they proclaimed the gospel everywhere and that God worked together with them and empowered their preaching. Because the Lord Himself was with them, many people believed in Jesus. In the book of Acts you can read more about the different ways in which they witnessed wherever they went and how many miracles actually took place when the disciples proclaimed the gospel over the whole of the then known world.

Today we can still see the results of the disciples' obedience to witness. There are millions upon millions of people on earth who believe in Jesus and it is as a direct result of the disciples' obedience to the commission Jesus gave them to be His witnesses. They went and spread the gospel and it is because of them that you and I now have the privilege of being Christians.

Lord Jesus, make me like Your disciples of old, obedient to Your commission to be Your witnesses. Thank You very much that I know that You will also empower my testimony and will help and support me when I witness. Amen.

Peter Testifies on Pentecost

When the people heard this, they were cut to the heart and said to Peter and the other apostles, "Brothers, what shall we do?" Peter replied, "Repent and be baptized, every one of you, in the name of Jesus Christ for the forgiveness of your sins. And you will receive the gift of the Holy Spirit" (Acts 2:37-38).

On the day of Pentecost, the very same Peter who denied Jesus three times, delivered a powerful testimony of the Jesus who had lived amongst them, who had been crucified and who had ascended to heaven where He is now seated at the right hand of God His Father. The people who were listening to him asked him what they could do to be saved. "Repent and be baptized in the name of Jesus Christ. And you will receive the gift of the Holy Spirit," was Peter's answer. The story of Pentecost is widely known – more than three thousand people repented and received the Holy Spirit that day.

It is probably the dream of every evangelist today to deliver a sermon that causes more than three thousand people to repent. And it was the fearful Peter who at first did not even want to acknowledge that he knew Jesus who delivered this sermon! The Spirit of God in Peter's life was the cause of an unbelievable change – it transformed him from a coward into a powerful witness. The Spirit of God can – and will – do the same for you. Ask Him to take your fear away and to help you with your task of witnessing.

Holy Spirit, I pray that You will change me, that You will bring me to the place where I can replace my fear of witnessing with faith in You. Amen.

May 19

Read Acts 4:13-20

It Is Impossible to Keep Quiet!

Peter and John replied, "Judge for yourselves whether it is right in God's sight to obey you rather than God. For we cannot help speaking about what we have seen and heard" (Acts 4:19-20).

When Peter and John healed a lame man near the temple, everyone was in an uproar. The people who had seen the miracle were amazed; the man who had been made whole praised God – and Peter and John got a golden opportunity to bear witness to Jesus who had made the miracle possible.

Peter used the opportunity to preach to the people in Solomon's colonnade and on hearing his sermon still more people came to salvation. At this, the Jewish Council and the scribes were not happy at all and they brought Peter and John before them to give account of what had happened.

When two fishermen witnessed before the Jewish Council, a second miracle took place! The council members tried in vain to silence the mouths of Peter and John because they did not want large numbers of people to run after them. But Peter and John did not take any notice of this ban regarding speaking about Jesus. They would decide for themselves what was right before God, they told the Council that they would rather obey God than them.

God has asked you to be His witness in the world and to proclaim the message of Jesus. If you truly love Jesus, it will be almost impossible for you not to talk about Him.

Lord Jesus, thank You very much that I can love You and talk to people about You. Like Peter and John, may I find it impossible not to talk about You. Amen.

Witness to Everyone

Then Peter began to speak: "I now realize how true it is that God does not show favoritism but accepts men from every nation who fear Him and do what is right" (Acts 10:34-35).

The Jews in Jesus' day did not ever mix with heathens. But God convinced Peter through a vision of unclean animals that He commanded him to kill and eat, that people should not see things as unclean which God has declared as pure and that His gospel is meant for all people.

Peter obeyed God's command and went with Cornelius who was not a Jew and his three servants to his house in Caesarea. When Peter arrived there he told them that God makes no distinction between people, but accepts people from all nations who honor Him. He also testified to them that each one who believes in Jesus will receive forgiveness for their sins. While he was still busy talking to them, the Holy Spirit came upon the people who had gathered together in Cornelius's house to listen to Peter's testimony. Then Peter baptized them.

You too should not decide that there are people you are not prepared to witness to. All people are included in God's invitation to be His children. Even those that you might not consider worthy.

Lord, forgive me for sometimes selecting the people that I want to witness to. I realize now that all people are included in Your invitation and that each one should be given a chance to hear the gospel. Amen.

The Spirit Gives Confidence

After they prayed, the place where they were meeting was shaken. And they were all filled with the Holy Spirit and spoke the word of God boldly (Acts 4:31).

From the start the chief priests and the Jewish Council did their best to prevent Peter and John from witnessing. They were afraid that too many people would listen to them and they forbade them to speak to anyone else in the name of Jesus.

After Peter and John had been released by the chief priests they went to their fellow Christians and reported back to them. After this they all prayed together that they would be allowed to proclaim the Word with boldness and that signs and wonders would take place as a result of their witnessing. After they had prayed, the place where they had gathered was shaken and all those who were there were filled with the Holy Spirit and they proclaimed the Word of God with boldness.

The shaking of the building was more than likely caused by the Holy Spirit who took possession of their lives. *The Message* says, "They were all filled with the Holy Spirit and continued to speak God's Word with fearless confidence."

To try to witness without the power of the Holy Spirit is a task that is doomed to fail. It is He who gives you the boldness and the words to talk to others about God. Without Him it is not only impossible to be a witness but your testimony will also not bear fruit.

Holy Spirit, I pray that You will give me the boldness and the right words to proclaim the Word of God. Amen.

Philip and the Ethiopian

The Spirit told Philip, "Go to that chariot and stay near it." Then Philip ran up to the chariot and heard the man reading Isaiah the prophet. "Do you understand what you are reading?" Philip asked. "How can I," he said, "unless someone explains it to me?" (Acts 8:29-31).

On a quiet road between Jerusalem and Gaza an Ethiopian was busy reading the scroll of Isaiah. The section that he was reading happened to be a prophecy about Jesus who would be led like a lamb to the slaughter. Even though the Ethiopian was a heathen, God knew that there was a hunger for Him in his heart. He sent Philip to talk to him.

When Philip asked the man if he understood what he was reading, he answered that he could not understand unless someone explained it to him. This was Philip's chance to tell the man about Jesus. When they drove past a stream of water, the man asked if Philip would baptize him.

God knows when people are seeking Him – and He always gives these people the opportunity to find Him. But God needs us to tell other people about Him. Are you, like Philip, willing to be a witness and to make the way of sanctification clear to those who do not yet understand? As He did for Philip, God will give you the right words and the right point of contact.

Lord, forgive me for being so wary of talking to other people about You. Thank You that You will Yourself give me the right words and will send opportunities across my path so that I can do so. Amen.

Paul, a Diligent Witness

Saul spent several days with the disciples in Damascus. All those who heard him were astonished and asked, "Isn't he the man who raised havoc in Jerusalem among those who call on this name?" (Acts 9:19, 21).

Paul testified that Jesus had said to him on the road to Damascus: "I have appeared to you to appoint you as a servant and as a witness of what you have seen of Me and what I will show you. Open their eyes and turn them from darkness to light, and from the power of Satan to God" (Acts 26:16).

Paul did not allow any grass to grow under his feet. When he regained his sight, he immediately began with this work of testifying which was received somewhat skeptically by the Christians in Damascus. They realized that he was the same man who had previously tried to get rid of the Christians. He had even, before his conversion, obtained letters from the High Priest that gave him the right to arrest Christians outside of the borders of Jerusalem (see Acts 9:2).

The Christians in Damascus wondered if it was not perhaps some kind of trap, but Paul simply preached all the more powerfully and many people believed in Jesus as a result of his testimony. He then returned to Jerusalem where he went around with the Christians and brought about even more conversions.

Lord, I really want to be like Paul – he never allowed any opportunity to pass him by to tell people about You. Make me, too, a diligent and enthusiastic witness so that people will come to salvation through what I say. Amen.

Be an Example of Your Faith

You became imitators of us and of the Lord. The Lord's message rang out from you not only in Macedonia and Achaia – your faith in God has become known everywhere. Therefore we do not need to say anything about it (1 Thessalonians 1:6, 8).

The first epistle that Paul wrote was directed at the church in Thessalonica. And the Thessalonians followed the example of their mentor – they too became witnesses of the good news of Jesus.

They acquitted themselves so well in this work of witnessing that other people who looked at their lives could see that something dramatic had happened to them. But these new Christians not only lived out their faith, they also testified of it. "The Lord's message rang out from you not only in Macedonia and Achaia. Your faith in God has become known everywhere. Therefore we do not need to say anything about it," Paul writes to them.

There are two things that are needed if you believe in God: that you will be willing to speak about your faith and that you will live according to the commands of God. Your life ought to be a mirror of your faith. It never helps to preach one thing and then to live another. It also does not help to live like a Christian but to keep quiet about your faith. From now on you need to be prepared to speak and live as God asks of you.

Heavenly Father, I truly want to proclaim Your message and live in such a way that people will be able to see from my actions that I am serious about my faith. Please help me to get this right. Amen.

The Message of Paul and Barnabas

When the Gentiles heard this, they were glad and honored the word of the Lord; and all who were appointed for eternal life believed. The word of the Lord spread through the whole region (Acts 13:48-49).

Paul and Barnabas were sent out by the church in Antioch on Paul's first missionary journey. During their visit to Antioch, Paul and Barnabas spoke of how they had told the residents of the cities that Jesus was sent as a light to the nations so that He could bring salvation to the farthest corners of the earth. All those who believe in Him will be set free from their sins, they testified. The heathens listened attentively to them, and many of them believed in Jesus.

The Jews in the city were definitely not happy with the large number of heathens who came to listen to Paul and Barnabas and came to faith in Jesus. But the message of Paul and Barnabas was crystal clear, "We had to speak the word of God to you first. Since you rejected it and do not consider yourselves worthy of eternal life we now turn to the Gentiles" (Acts 13:46).

The danger still exists today that you could become so used to the good news of God's salvation that you continually put off accepting it, and that people who hear this message for the first time will go ahead of you in the faith. Make sure that this is never true of you!

Lord, protect me from becoming so used to the message of salvation that I will neglect to accept it for myself. Help me to believe in You and to speak of my faith spontaneously. Amen.

Talk about the Good News!

We're Christ's representatives. God uses us to persuade men and women to drop their differences and enter into God's work of making things right between them. We're speaking for Christ Himself now: Become friends with God; He's already a friend with you (2 Corinthians 5:20, THE MESSAGE).

Witnessing was a way of life for Paul. He committed his whole life to convincing people through the proclaiming of the gospel that Jesus is the Christ. The reason why he testified was because the love of Jesus in his heart compelled him to do so. God reconciled people to Himself through Jesus and entrusted the ministry of reconciliation to us.

Paul saw himself as an ambassador of God in the world. He told the church in Corinth that God Himself was speaking to them through him. And the message that he proclaimed to them was that anyone who belongs to Christ is a brand-new person. All his previous sins are now something of the past.

God forgives sinners because Jesus paid for them on the cross. The Good News that each person ought to hear is that Jesus came to make peace between God and the world through His crucifixion. Because He died for your sins, you can be a child of God.

This is a wonderful message that every person on earth ought to hear. Make sure that you tell other people about it.

Lord Jesus, I praise You because through Your crucifixion You made it possible for me to be reconciled with God. Help me to carry out this message and not to keep it to myself. Amen.

Witnessing Among the Heathens

"Now get up and stand on your feet. I have appeared to you to appoint you as a servant and as a witness of what you have seen of Me and what I will show you. Open their eyes and turn them from darkness to light, and from the power of Satan to God" (Acts 26:16, 18).

Paul's dramatic testimony before King Agrippa still leaves us speechless even after many centuries. When he told the king of his vision on the road to Damascus, he also testified that God Himself appointed him as His witness. That He had set him apart to open the eyes of the heathen nations so that they could turn from the darkness to the light and from the power of Satan to God. He brought to them the message that if they believed in Jesus their sins would be forgiven and they would become one of God's people (see verses 16-18).

Paul's brilliant reasoning almost convinced the king to become a Christian! "Do you think that in such a short time you can persuade me to be a Christian?" he said to him. "Short time or long – I pray God that not only you but all who are listening to me today may become what I am" (verses 28-29).

Unfortunately Paul's testimony to King Agrippa did not have the desired result – the king was not prepared to change his life and to turn from the darkness to the light.

Heavenly Father, make me responsible for Your message when I hear it so that I will not be like King Agrippa who turned away from Your grace. Amen.

Testimony About an Unknown God

For as I walked around and looked carefully at your objects of worship,
I even found an altar with this inscription: TO AN UNKNOWN
GOD. Now what you worship as something unknown I am going to
proclaim to you (Acts 17:23).

When Paul was in Athens he looked for a point of contact so that he could tell the learned Athenians about God. He went and stood beside one of the city's many altars – one on which was written: "TO AN UNKNOWN GOD" and told them that it was precisely this God to whom he wanted to introduce them.

Then Paul proceeded with one of his most compelling sermons: It was this God who made the world and all that is in it, it is He who gives breath to all who live, he told them. God made all people to seek Him – He is never far away from any one of us because in Him we live and move and have our being (see verses 24-28). After this Paul told the Athenians about Jesus who rose from the dead.

Unfortunately the Athenians with their many gods were not really receptive to Paul's gripping testimony. Yet Luke tells that there were at least a few of them who became believers and who joined Paul.

Here Paul gives you a show-and-tell lesson of how a witness should set about his task. With his striking testimony he connected with the life experiences of the Athenians. When you testify before people it is a clever idea to talk about things that they can relate to.

Heavenly Father, help me, like Paul, to witness in such a way about You that people will understand my testimony and that they will open their hearts and lives to You. Amen.

Faith Causes You to Speak

It is written: "I believed; therefore I have spoken." With that same spirit of faith we also believe and therefore speak (2 Corinthians 4:13).

Paul was a zealous witness for Jesus. God Himself said to Ananias, "This man is My chosen instrument to carry My name before the Gentiles and their kings and before the peoples of Israel. I will show him how much he must suffer for My name" (Acts 9:15-16).

Shortly after his conversion Paul began with this command to bring others to repentance. We read that he immediately began preaching in the synagogues, proclaiming that Jesus is the Son of God. The surprise of the believers that the man who wanted to get rid of the followers of Jesus with great zeal, now witnessed about Jesus, did not put him off. Mark tells us that he simply preached with more fervor and brought much confusion among the Jews who lived in Damascus (see Acts 9:20-22).

In his letter to the church in Corinth Paul quoted from Psalm 116:10 where the psalmist testified that he believed and that was why he spoke. The same Spirit was at work in Paul and helped him not only to believe, but also to speak about his faith so that people would hear him and would believe in God.

The Holy Spirit is still available to you to help you testify of your faith. With his support it is possible for you to be a powerful witness for Jesus.

Holy Spirit, I praise You because You have made it possible for me to be a witness who spreads the Good News of the gospel amongst people. Amen.

Speak to Your Children

What we have heard and known, what our fathers have told us. We will not hide them from their children; we will tell the next generation the praiseworthy deeds of the LORD, His power, and the wonders He has done (Psalm 78:3-4).

Here the psalmist tells his children what God has done for their nation. Then through the rest of the psalm he presents us with a history lesson and tells in the most minute detail the wonderful things God did for His nation.

As the psalmist did here it is the duty of us as parents to tell our children about God, to share our faith with them and to ensure that each one of them also comes to the certainty of faith.

Already in Deuteronomy 6:6-7 Moses impressed it on to the hearts of the Israelites that they should carry out this work of witnessing to their children, "These commandments that I give you today are to be upon your hearts. Impress them on your children. Talk about them when you sit at home and when you walk along the road."

Make sure that your children know that you belong to God and that they also know how they can become His children too. Also tell your grandchildren of the wonderful things of God from the past so that your children and future generations can also share your faith.

Heavenly Father, thank You very much for the privilege of being able to share my faith with my children and that I can testify to them of You and Your love boldly. I pray that You will open the hearts and lives of my children. Amen.

The Power to Witness

"You will receive power when the Holy Spirit comes on you; and you will be My witnesses in Jerusalem, and in all Judea and Samaria, and to the ends of the earth" (Acts 1:8).

Jesus' command to witness is never random. When Jesus requested His disciples to make the people of the world His disciples, He also assured them that He would be with them and that all the authority in heaven and on earth had been given to Him (see Matt. 28:18-20). Also, when He told them that the Holy Spirit would come to the earth, He promised that God would work in Him with all His power and that He would make it possible for them to talk about Him – in Jerusalem, in all of Judea and Samaria, and to the farthest corners of the earth.

Therefore, you need never hold back in your work of witnessing. God promises to equip you through His Holy Spirit. Through the working of His Holy Spirit, God will provide you with the necessary power to be able to witness for Him. All that He asks of you is your willingness to put yourself at His disposal. If you agree He will send the right opportunities your way, put the right words into your mouth and touch the hearts of the people with whom you speak so that they will not only hear your testimony, but will hear the voice of God speaking through your words.

Lord Jesus, I declare myself willing to be Your witness. Thank You that You equip me through Your Holy Spirit and make me a powerful witness. Please give me the boldness to carry Your message to the farthest parts of the world. Amen.

rayer

Lord Jesus,
In the past month I have learned so much about
spreading Your Good News throughout the world.
I know that it is You who sends me, that You will be with me
and will equip me, that You will teach me what to say
so that I can be a light for the nations.
Forgive me for sometimes being embarrassed to speak about You,
and please bring about the right opportunities for me
so that other people will be able to hear about Your love.
Forgive me for sometimes feeling discouraged
when there is no fruit of my witnessing –
make me prepared to persevere as Your witness
until the hearts and lives of people open up to You.
It is impossible for me to remain silent about Your love for me!
I truly want to use every opportunity
to present Your message of salvation to others.
I also want to live in such a way that my faith will be clearly visible
through my actions, so that all those who look at me
will know that I belong to You.
Thank You for the privilege of being able to share my faith
with my children and for the joy of knowing
that they too can love and serve You.
I praise You for Your Holy Spirit who makes it possible for me
to be an enthusiastic witness and for the power
that He makes available to me
so that it becomes easy for me to proclaim Your Good News.

Amen.

June

The Secret of Happiness

A while ago I was at the airport, and as usual I was browsing in the bookshop when I discovered a book that delighted me greatly when I read it and which also made me think about the things that make me happy.

David Niven's *The 100 Simple Secrets of Happy People* contains dozens of stories about happy people and hints about how to be truly happy.

During my flight, I thanked God once again for the many things that bring joy to my life and once again realized that each one of us can choose to be happy through the things we do for others, through our thoughts and through our lifestyles.

In the month that lies ahead we are going to focus on a few personal secrets of happiness. If you apply these secrets, you will be happy for the rest of your life.

The Source of Your Joy

We also rejoice in God through our Lord Jesus Christ, through whom we have now received reconciliation (Romans 5:11).

Although we are going to be busy with Davis Niven's secrets of happiness for the rest of the month, I do want to begin with a "secret" that is not in Niven's book: If God is not the source of your joy, you will never truly know what happiness is. Only if you belong to Him will you experience unconditional joy in your life because without Him there can be no happiness.

On the days when I am feeling a bit down, I remember this saying, Jesus source of all my joy, Jesus light of my belief. Full of grace and truth, You are my Savior Lord and Chief.

With Jesus as the main source of your happiness, it is possible to approach each day with joy and to solve each crisis with joy. With God as the Source of your joy, you will be able to live with joy even though others might not see anything in your life over which to rejoice. The joy that God gives stands completely alone from all other things: it is joy *in spite of.*

In spite of your negative circumstances you will be able to bubble over with joy because your joy is not dependent on your physical circumstances but is anchored in a Person with whom you have a living relationship.

Lord Jesus, I praise You as the source of my joy. You make it possible for me to be happy in all circumstances. Thank You that You brought about my reconciliation with God. Amen.

Your Life Has a Specific Purpose

For we are God's workmanship, created in Christ Jesus to do good works, which God prepared in advance for us to do (Ephesians 2:10).

You can know that you are important to God, He loves you unconditionally and He showed this love for you by sacrificing His Son to die in your place on the cross so that your debt of sin could be paid for. You are therefore not just alive by chance; God put you in the place where you are now because He has a specific purpose in mind for you.

Niven writes that nothing would be the same if you were not there. Every place where you have ever been and every person you have ever met would be different without you. We are all connected to one another and we are all influenced through the decisions and the existence of the people around us. Therefore, always be the best person that you can be. Find out what things God has in mind for you and do them. Discover your talents and use them. Commit your life to the good things that God has planned for you.

According to Lepper, seven out of ten people feel uncertain about their lives but when they strive towards a particular goal, they feel satisfied with their lives. If you are sure that you make a positive difference in the world – you will be a happy and satisfied person.

Heavenly Father, thank You that You have especially made me to commit my life to the good deeds that You have planned for me. Please help me to discover and carry out the purpose You have in mind for me. Amen.

Accept Yourself Unconditionally

God created man in His own image, in the image of God He created him; male and female He created them. God saw all that He had made, and it was very good (Genesis 1:27, 31).

After God had created the world and man, He looked at what He had made and it was very good, reports Genesis 1:31. God made you in His image to be His representative here on earth. Yet there are very few people who are happy with how they look and who they are.

Most people strive continuously to be more beautiful, more popular, thinner and richer. Yet Jesus said that the one command equal to "love the Lord your God with all your heart" is to "love your neighbor as yourself."

If you are satisfied with yourself you will succeed in being able to love yourself and only then will you know how God wants you to love other people. Make it your task to accept yourself unconditionally with your strong and weak points. Work on the negative things in your life that you can change and make peace with the rest. Remember: God made you the way you are. Stop comparing yourself to other people and being unhappy because you are not as good or as pretty as they are. Concentrate on your good qualities and forget the negative ones. From today you are going to be happy because you are the image bearer and representative of God Himself.

Heavenly Father, please forgive me for being so dissatisfied with myself. Help me to accept myself unconditionally as Your image bearer and representative. Amen.

Believe in Yourself

I can do everything through Him who gives me strength. Yet it was good of you to share in my troubles (Philippians 4:13-14).

People who believe in themselves and in their abilities are not only happier than people who doubt their abilities, but they are also much more successful. Myers and Diener write that in spite of your age, a steadfast belief in your own abilities will cause your life satisfaction to increase by thirty percent and that people who believe that they can achieve things, are thirty percent happier both in their homes and in their work situations.

Furthermore, if you are a Christian, you never have to doubt your abilities – you know that you have the God who can do all things on your side. There is absolutely nothing that is impossible for Him, and with His help and strength you will also be able to move mountains.

"What, then, shall we say in response to this? If God is for us, who can be against us? He who did not spare His own Son, but gave Him up for us all – how will He not also along with Him, graciously give us all things?" writes Paul to the church in Rome. Underline this Scripture verse in your Bible and learn it off by heart for those days when you begin to doubt yourself (and God).

Heavenly Father, I know that I can do all things because You give me the strength to be able to move mountains; I believe that if You are for me no one can be against me. Thank You for that assurance! Amen.

Live Positively

We know that in all things God works for the good of those who love Him, who have been called according to His purpose (Romans 8:28).

When an unhappy and dissatisfied person has to interpret the happenings in the world, eight out of ten times he or she will only see the negative side of a situation. When a happy person looks at the same occurrence, eight out of ten times he or she will see the positive.

The way in which you look at your life is much more significant than the things that happen to you. Many times I have seen how positive people are able to take the best out of negative situations. One of my friends, who has Parkinson's disease, told me that it is in fact her illness that has brought her to the place of listening to the voice of God in her life again. Another friend who has cancer testifies that her illness has taught her to be grateful for health, and another one who has a child with disabilities says that this child is the greatest factor in her life that lets her live close to God each day.

If you truly want to be happy you will need to learn to see every single situation in your life in a positive way. And God will make it possible for you because He promised that He will cause all things – even the negative ones – to work out for your good in the long run.

Heavenly Father, I pray that You will give me a positive attitude. Thank You very much for the assurance that You cause all things to work out in my life for the best – even those things that hurt me and which I cannot understand. Amen.

Don't Try to Be a Problem-Solver

Cast all your anxiety on Him because He cares for you (1 Peter 5:7).

One of the biggest stealers of your joy is trying to solve your problems in your own strength. You will soon realize that this is impossible and become even more despondent and unhappy. But if you take your problems to God from the very beginning, discuss them with Him and ask Him for strength it is a whole different story.

You will discover over and over that God will give you the right solution for each problem and that when He does not do so immediately He will provide you with the strength to be able to hold on, as well as the patience to wait until He will work out a solution for you (Luke 12:22).

A survey found that people who called on other people to help them were fifty-five percent less worried, while those who tried to solve their own problems showed no improvement. Therefore, do not try to hide your problems from your friends – rather ask for help. A problem shared is a problem halved.

As soon as you realize that you do not have to wrestle with a specific problem alone, you will not only gain perspective on it but you will also be able to solve your problems more easily.

Heavenly Father, it is good to know that You are always there for me when problems happen in my life. I now want to bring them to You with the full confidence that You will care for me. Amen.

Money Cannot Buy Happiness

Do not wear yourself out to get rich; have the wisdom to show restraint. Cast but a glance at riches, and they are gone, for they will surely sprout wings and fly off to the sky like an eagle (Proverbs 23:4-5).

If we want to be honest, we must admit that we all want more money. Many people who struggle to make ends meet every month, claim that if they only had a little more money they would be happier.

Unfortunately it does not work this way. For many years my husband was a pastor in a rich suburb. In the years of his ministry we gained firsthand experience of the truth that money cannot buy happiness. (Although one of our friends jokingly says that at least it allows a person to be unhappy in comfort!) The chances are good that if you are unhappy without money, you will also be unhappy with money. David Niven claims that if money could buy happiness there would be very expensive stores on every street corner where you would be able to buy happiness.

Rather forget about constantly yearning for more money and take note of the things around you that make you happy. Count your everyday blessings and say thank You to the Lord for each one of them. Money will not make you happy, but thankfulness will. The more thankful you are, the more things you will discover to be thankful for and the happier you will be.

Heavenly Father, I am sorry that I am so focused on money and material possessions. Teach me once again that money cannot buy happiness and make me a happy and thankful child of Yours. Amen.

Do Not Be Afraid of Growing Old

*Planted in the house of the L*ORD*, they will flourish in the courts of our God. They will still bear fruit in old age, they will stay fresh and green, proclaiming, "The L*ORD *is upright; He is my Rock, and there is no wickedness in Him" (Psalm 92:13-15).*

One thing that will definitely make you unhappy is to nurture an unrealistic fear of growing old. Older people are in no way less happy than young people. With the wisdom that age brings, they have learned to look at life through different eyes and to be satisfied with less. Even though you will have to make adjustments because your strength will weaken and you will suffer from aches and pains, older people usually have a better understanding of the wonders of life and they also have more time available to enjoy life and to add quality to their lifestyles.

When a person knows that he does not have much time left in the world, he learns to live with more thankfulness and to treasure life. Therefore, make peace with the fact that you will get older – and prepare for the fact that there is a down side to it, but make a conscious decision to be a happy and well adjusted senior citizen.

Then you can count on it that you – even though you grow older – will still be happy and will be able to lead a quality life. Phil Bosmans rightly says that the last joys of life are quieter, but also fuller and deeper.

Heavenly Father, thank You that I do not have to be afraid of growing older because I know that You will still be with me when I am old and that You will make me strong. Amen.

Focus on What You Have

All man's efforts are for his mouth, yet his appetite is never satisfied. Better what the eye sees than the roving of the appetite. This too is meaningless, a chasing after the wind (Ecclesiastes 6:7, 9).

We wear ourselves to the bone for food and yet our hunger is not satisfied, says the writer of Ecclesiastes. Because we are human we are very hard to satisfy (see Eccles. 6:7). Some of the unhappiest people I know are people who always want more and are never satisfied with what they have.

Unfortunately, these kinds of people very often discover – when the things they considered as unimportant are taken away from them – that they were not grateful enough. Make sure that you do not fall into that trap. Each day you should be aware of all the good things that God gives you, even though you do not deserve them. Consciously think of these things and thank God for them. Content people are almost always happy people.

"The first gift of joy is the gratitude of the heart," says Jörg Zink. The next time you catch yourself being ungrateful, think back to where you were ten years ago and compare your situation now and the things that you have today with what you had then. Be thankful for all that you have achieved with the help of God.

In future, make lists of the things that you already have rather than lists of all the things that you would still like to get. God promises that He will provide for all your needs – therefore, be satisfied with what you have received from Him.

Heavenly Father, thank You for teaching me that what I have is far better than all the things that I still want. Make me content with what You have already given me. Amen.

Live with Integrity

I will be careful to lead a blameless life. I will walk in my house with blameless heart. I will set before my eyes no vile thing. I will have nothing to do with evil (Psalm 101:2-4).

There is nothing that dampens ambition or enthusiasm more than when someone promises something but never does it. "It is crucial in both your home life and your work life that you stay focused and committed to whatever you say you will do. Credibility is like the bottom of a ship. If it has holes, it doesn't matter whether they are big or little – they all matter," writes Niven.

Unfortunately we get very few people these days who do what they have promised or who are truly honest. Integrity has become a rare virtue. Make sure that you are different. God asks His children to live in such a way that the things you think, do and say will co-incide; that they will be righteous.

Make sure that you are a woman of your word; that you, not only in your house, but also in your workplace, act with honesty and righteousness. Then it will not be hard for you to be truly happy because people who live with integrity and fulfill their promises feel good about themselves, while people who are dishonest and unreliable are secretly unhappy with themselves and their actions.

Heavenly Father, I truly want to be a woman of my word. Please make it possible for me to live honestly and righteously, to keep my promises so that the things that I think, say and do will agree with one another. Amen.

June 11

Confusing Possessions with Success

He will take your daughters to be perfumers and cooks and bakers. He will take the best of your fields and vineyards and olive groves and give them to his attendants (1 Samuel 8:13-14).

To judge people according to their possessions or to have a low estimation of yourself because you do not have as much money or things as most of your friends is very short-sighted. Say for instance that today was to be the last day of your life – think carefully about the things that would be important to you. It will definitely not be your new car or your luxurious house, but rather the people in your life, your family and your friends; the difference that your personal contributions have made to your environment, things that have eternal value, such as relationships.

Examine what things have priority in your life and then look carefully and consider whether those things are truly worthwhile. True success is to have God with you – this was the secret of David's success. And to achieve lasting success you must be prepared to keep working at that and to give of yourself. Success is never cheap.

John Maxwell says that success means to choose to give selflessly of yourself and to act in such a manner that you will make a lasting contribution to the building up of humanity. Always remember that when you are indeed successful that it is a gift of grace from the hand of God because it is He who makes you successful.

Heavenly Father, please forgive me for so often having the wrong priorities. I'm sorry for placing such a high premium on possessions. Teach me once again that Your presence in my life is the only thing that makes it possible for me to achieve lasting success. Amen.

Your Thoughts Are Important

Stop thinking like children. In regard to evil be infants, but in your thinking be adults (1 Corinthians 14:20).

Wise people through the centuries agree with the fact that what a person thinks is far more important than what happens to you. Scientists have also proved that a person's thoughts have unbelievable power over your body.

If you think that you are sick, you will get sick before long; if you think that you are going to get something right, you are right – and if you think that you will not get something right, then you are also right! Your thoughts determine who you are, says John Maxwell. You can change yourself – and your whole outlook on life – by changing the way you think. If you can teach yourself to think happy and positive thoughts, you will more than likely be a friendlier and happier person and it will be child's play for you to be happy.

Ask that God Himself will teach you to think positively, and to focus your thoughts on "Whatever is true, whatever is noble, whatever is pure, whatever is lovely, whatever is admirable," as Paul advised the church in Philippi to do (see Phil. 4:7-8). If you succeed in doing this you will experience the peace of God that passes all understanding. It will stand guard over your heart and mind and will be present in your daily life.

Heavenly Father, I want to make my thoughts obedient to You and focus them on all things that are beautiful and good and right so that my life will reflect Your peace. Please make me happy because I have learned how to be mature in my thoughts. Amen.

Laugh More!

All the days of the oppressed are wretched, but the cheerful heart has a continual feast. A cheerful heart is good medicine, but a crushed spirit dries up the bones (Proverbs 15:15 and 17:22).

Happiness is a laughing matter," writes David Niven. The Bible has known this secret for years already – things always go badly for someone who is depressed, while a joyful person's whole life is not only a feast, but she also has the advantage of being a healthy person, says the writer of the Proverbs.

It has been scientifically proven that laughter is good for your health. The more you laugh, the less you will need to see a doctor because when you laugh the same hormones are released in your body that are prescribed by doctors for stress and depression. "The ability to laugh, whether at life itself or at a good joke, is a source of life satisfaction. Indeed, those who enjoy silly humor are one-third more likely to feel happy," asserts Niven.

Therefore, make a point of laughing more; of noticing the comic things in life and telling them to others. Collect jokes for yourself; cut out the funniest comic strips from the newspaper and put them on your fridge; remember the funniest things your grandchildren have said and retell them with relish.

In this way you will not only laugh more and so be healthier, but other people will laugh together with you so that their health can also improve!

Heavenly Father, thank You that You created people in such a way that we can see the funny things in life and laugh about them. Help me to discover the humor in every situation so that I will be joyful and laugh a lot. Amen.

Stay Busy!

Whatever your hand finds to do, do it with all your might, for in the grave, where you are going, there is neither working nor planning nor knowledge nor wisdom (Ecclesiastes 9:10).

Find something to keep you busy, because the feeling of having too much to do is much more satisfying than the feeling of having nothing to do, writes Niven. There are few things that make a person as happy as to know that she is busy with something constructive that will benefit other people. My husband and I have enjoyed our retirement immensely from day one, because both of us are busy writing and we often minister to different churches.

It is great to be busy with things that you enjoy doing rather than wasting your time in meetings. Since we retired I have clearly seen that busy people are happy people, while the retirees who have nothing to do are unhappy, grumpy old people. According to a survey undertaken by Bailey and Miller in 1998, college students enrolled in tough courses were fifteen percent more satisfied than those who had less to do. The more a person has to do, the more you seem to be able to do.

The writer of Ecclesiastes says that we should commit ourselves to doing whatever our hand finds to do. So if you want to be happy, ensure that you remain constructively busy. Because there are few things that make a person as satisfied as a task completed well.

Heavenly Father, thank You very much that I have so many things to keep me busy and that it is satisfying for me to have a busy schedule. I really desire to do everything that my hand finds to do with diligence. Amen.

June 15

Make Your Work a Calling

Obey them not only to win their favor when their eye is on you, but like slaves of Christ, doing the will of God from your heart. Serve wholeheartedly, as if you were serving the Lord, not men (Ephesians 6:6-7).

If you see your work as just another job, it will drag you away from the things that you really want to do. But if you see it as a calling it will no longer be a drag, but an expression of yourself, an integral part of who you are, writes David Niven.

I read somewhere that when you do a job that you enjoy, you will never have to do a stitch of work in your life. Paul gives an excellent recipe for work in our Scripture reading for today: he advises the slaves in Ephesus not only to work to gain the favor of other people but also to work with diligence and enthusiasm, and to do their work in the first place for God. If you follow this recipe, you will be successful in your work.

Always try to find a job that you enjoy and where you can make use of your God-given talents. If this is not possible, do your best in your workplace and work to the very best of your abilities. If you do this your work will truly become a calling to you in which you can express yourself.

Heavenly Father, thank You very much that I have the privilege of doing a job that I enjoy and that I can use the gifts that I have received from You. I pray today for all those who do not have this privilege. Amen.

Nurture Your Family

But as for me and my household, we will serve the LORD (Joshua 24:15).

With all the demands that the modern lifestyle places on people, it is a matter of fact that people have less time than ever before to spend with their families and relatives. And the intimacy and security that you find in your own family and that your family experiences by being together is precisely one of the things that brings about happiness.

A mother is only as happy as the unhappiest member of her family. One of my friends loves to say that the family is a nursery for life. Remember that your family is a gift from God. "Sons are a heritage from the LORD, children a reward from Him. Like arrows in the hands of a warrior are sons born in one's youth. Blessed is the man whose quiver is full of them" (Ps. 127:3-5).

Make sure that each one of your family members knows the Lord and loves Him. Make time to do things together as a family. Every now and then have a family gathering and invite your nearest family. Nurture your family as well as the rest of your relatives; do your best to keep the bonds between you tight, even if you no longer all live under the same roof. Pray regularly for each member of your family and make sure that they know that you love them and care about them. Then you will not only find happiness in good family relationships, but each one of them will too.

Heavenly Father, thank You very much for the privilege of being able to have a family that serves You and loves You. Help me to spend more time with my family and assure them each day of Your love and mine. Amen.

Enjoy What You Have

"I am the Lord your God, who brought you up out of Egypt. Open wide your mouth and I will fill it" (Psalm 81:10).

People who are satisfied with what they have received from life, do not worry about how their possessions compare to those of others. If you value and greatly appreciate the things that you have and not constantly yearn for what you do not have, you will be a happier person.

There are two kinds of people: those who are satisfied with what they have, and the dissatisfied who are always wanting something bigger and better. It is obvious that the former are happy people and the latter remain unhappy.

While they were wandering around in the wilderness, God provided everything for His people that they had need of, so that they never lacked anything. The psalmist then testifies that He will also still provide in abundance all that His children have need of. God wants to provide everything that is necessary for you, too – in an abundant measure. Therefore, enjoy everything that He has so lavishly given you, be prepared to share the things that you have with others who have less and forget about all the things that you do not have. Listen to the advice of the writer to the Hebrews, "Be content with what you have, because God has said, 'Never will I leave you; never will I forsake you,'" (Heb. 13:5). The more satisfied you are, the happier you will be.

Heavenly Father, I am sorry that I am still so often dissatisfied with my possessions and compare myself with people who have more than I do. Thank You that You have always provided those things that I need in abundance. Amen.

Be a Peacemaker

Make every effort to live in peace with all men and to be holy; without holiness no one will see the Lord (Hebrews 12:14).

When he prophesied the coming of the Messiah, the prophet Zachariah said that the Child who was to be born would rise like the morning sun to bring light to those who lived in darkness and in the shadow of death, and would guide our footsteps on the path of peace (see Luke 1:79). Thirty-three years after this prophecy, when Jesus was returning to His Father, He promised His disciples that He would leave His peace behind for them, "Peace I leave with you; My peace I give you. I do not give to you as the world gives. Do not let your hearts be troubled and do not be afraid," He said (John 14:27).

People who live with the peace of Jesus in their hearts are happy people because they are not characterized by the unrest and strife of the world; they also manage to live without fear. But Jesus asks more of you than to simply be a recipient of His peace. It is His will for you to be a peacemaker, someone who will bring about peace in the lives of others. "Blessed are the peacemakers, for they will be called sons of God," He promises in His Sermon on the Mount (Matt. 5:9).

Therefore, be finely tuned in to the state of mind of the people around you and be prepared to make peace if quarrels arise, because peacemakers are happy people!

Heavenly Father, thank You that I can have Your peace and tranquility in my life. Make me a peacemaker so that I too will be able to settle the differences amongst other people. Amen.

Do Not Sacrifice Your Values

Do not wear yourself out to get rich; have the wisdom to show restraint (Proverbs 23:4).

In today's world it often seems like people sacrifice their values in order to achieve their goals in life. A large number of motorists have illegal drivers' licenses that have been bought in neighboring countries; and many people manage to get jobs with false university qualifications. Corruption is the order of the day.

Telling lies has become so common that no one even raises an eyebrow over it anymore. But this is not what the Bible teaches us. God wants us to honor the guidelines that He has set for us, and He wants us to be honest and righteous and to keep His commandments. Being happy is almost synonymous with subscribing to the right values, because deceitful people are seldom happy people. Their consciences trouble them and the fact that their achievements are built on a foundation of lies also makes them unhappy. Niven reports that they are half as happy as the people who adhere to the right values.

"When traditional life values and wisdom are ignored, the loss is incalculable. From that moment on society no longer has a compass to show the way, and we do not even know which harbor we are heading for," is Edmund Burke's contribution. Therefore, make sure that your integrity is preserved and that you will never lose your sense of values.

Heavenly Father, thank You for Your Word in which You have pointed out for me the things that are truly important. Help me to never sacrifice my values or tell lies to gain earthly things. Amen.

Get Enough Sleep

I will lie down and sleep in peace, for You alone, O LORD, make me dwell in safety (Psalm 4:8).

It is extremely important to get enough sleep – at least seven to eight hours a night. People who do not get enough sleep start their day wrong and are so tired during the day that they cannot do their work properly.

Don't skimp on sleep. A full night's rest is fuel for the following day. Rested people feel they work better and are more comfortable when the day is over, says David Niven. Pilcher and Ott further state that people are eight percent less positive for every hour less than eight hours that they sleep. Unfortunately, one of the factors of the world in which we live is that people don't get enough sleep. At night we lie awake and toss and turn before we fall asleep, and then we often wake up in the middle of the night because we can't stop thinking about all the things that are worrying us.

When God is with you, it is easy to fall asleep peacefully at night. You know with certainty that He is holding you in His hand and guarantees your safety. Share your concerns with Him before you fall asleep and talk to Him when you wake up in the middle of the night. Then you will find that your sleeplessness will be something of the past.

Lord, You know how often I struggle to fall asleep because there are so many things that worry me. Make me peaceful so that I can fall asleep without a care because I know that You guarantee my safety. Amen.

Do Something Worthwhile Each Day

This is the day the LORD has made; let us rejoice and be glad in it (Psalm 118:24).

Research conducted by McGregor and Little on hundreds of college students revealed that students were at their happiest when they felt that they were working towards their goals. The group of students who could see no progress in their work were three times less satisfied than those who were actually making progress.

There are many people who go through life aimlessly. Fortunately, there are also people who make a point of doing something worthwhile each day, who make optimal use of every minute available to them because they know that time is a gift from the hand of God that can easily be wasted. If you feel that many days just pass by without anything worthwhile happening, you should make better use of your time from now on. Do something each day that you find satisfying and pleasant: read an enriching book, listen to your favorite music, go for a walk in natural surroundings, do an extra half an hour of Bible study, go and visit a sick friend or speak encouraging words to someone who is not doing well.

Ask yourself every day: What have I achieved today that has been worthwhile? If you can answer this positively, you have learned to use each day that God has given to you productively.

Heavenly Father, thank You for the 365 days every year of which I can be glad and use for the best. Please help me to do something every day that is truly worthwhile. Amen.

Carry a Pen and Notebook with You

This is the word that came to Jeremiah from the LORD: "This is what the LORD, the God of Israel, says: 'Write in a book all the words I have spoken to you'" (Jeremiah 30:1-2).

People who have learned to keep pen and paper at hand so that they can jot down a bright idea or record an interesting dream feel that they are in control of their lives, writes Niven. They are also more inclined to be happy.

Every purposeful activity contributes to your happiness while lost opportunities leave behind feelings of frustration. People who feel that their best ideas pass by unused are thirty-seven percent less inclined to be satisfied than people who write down their ideas and can recall them.

Jeremiah received an instruction from God to write down everything that God conveyed to him in a book. I am also never without a pen and notebook; I carry them around with me everywhere. When someone tells a memorable joke or if I encounter a striking quote, I immediately record in my book. Even at night if I think of a good idea, I write it down quickly before it slips away from me. Most of the ideas that I use in my books come about in this way. Your life can be greatly enriched if you learn to keep pen and paper close at hand. Also write down those things that God says to you in your quiet time, as well as your answers to them. In this way you will learn to be responsive to the voice of God.

Lord, You speak to me in so many different ways – through other people, through Your Word and through the written word. Thank You that I can write these things down so that they will not be lost. Amen.

Help Others

If it is encouraging, let him encourage; if it is contributing to the needs of others, let him give generously; if it is leadership, let him govern diligently; if it is showing mercy, let him do it cheerfully (Romans 12:8).

Julius Rosenwald writes that all the pleasures of life decrease at some or other time, but the pleasure of helping someone in need always remains the same. Perhaps this is one of the forms of the abundant life of which Jesus spoke.

To offer your help to others is a win-win situation, so be prepared to give all the help you can to people who might have need of it. "Life satisfaction was found to improve by twenty-four percent with the level of altruistic activity," writes Niven. Therefore, if you want to be happy look around to see where you can offer help. It always leaves you feeling good when you know that other people have been helped through what you have done. "Carry each other's burdens, and in this way you will fulfill the Law of Christ," writes Paul to the church in Galatia (Gal. 6:2). "Do not withhold good from those who deserve it, when it is in your power to act. Do not say to your neighbor, 'Come back later; I'll give it tomorrow' – when you now have it with you," is the contribution from the writer of Proverbs (Prov. 3:27-28). The help that you offer does not have to be complicated. So right now, why don't you take your hands out of your pockets and see if there is someone who needs your help today? God will reward you for it.

Lord, thank You that You make it possible for me to be able to help other people. I praise You because I know that You are always there for me when I need help. Amen.

Do Not Be Critical

"Why do you look at the speck of sawdust in your brother's eye and pay no attention to the plank in your own eye? You hypocrite, first take the plank out of your own eye, and then you will see clearly to remove the speck from your brother's eye" (Matthew 7:3, 5).

I have yet to meet anybody who is constantly belittling and criticizing other people and is still happy. The way in which you look at other people influences your way of life as well as how they perceive you. Therefore, think twice before you say something critical about someone else. A person's words can hurt someone very deeply, sometimes even without you realizing it.

Count your words carefully and guard your mouth, as the psalmist advises. If you must say something negative, always be constructive. Make your criticism reflect your love and respect, not your disappointment, is David Niven's advice.

In the Sermon on the Mount Jesus warns that God will judge you in the same way you judge other people. Therefore, follow His good advice and first take the log out of your own eye – remove the wrong things from your own life before you begin to criticize the wrong things that others do.

Father, I am sorry that I am such a critical person. Please forgive me for my sharp criticisms of others and help me so that from now on I will first take the log out of my own eye before I point out the splinter in someone else's eye. Amen.

Do the Things You Are Good At

I wish that all men were as I am. But each man has his own gift from God; one has this gift, another has that (1 Corinthians 7:7).

It is important for people to feel competent. Therefore, take responsibility for the areas in which you excel, whether this be cooking, gardening or bookkeeping – and ask for help if you get stuck, writes David Niven.

The people who have taken courses at university in the subjects they are good at will know that people usually achieve good results in the areas where their talents lie. If you decide to take the risk of doing something you do not like or for which you have no aptitude, the exact opposite occurs. I have struggled for years to organize meetings and bazaars like a good pastor's wife before I took a "Use Your Gifts" course and realized that these were definitely not the areas in which I shine. Since I began to do the things I have a God-given talent for, things have gone much better. To struggle with the things that even with the best intentions in the world you cannot get right, will make any optimist despondent and certainly does not lead to happiness.

There are few things that are as wonderful – and that make one as happy – as doing something that you are really good at. My mother is a topnotch flower arranger and you can see her happiness overflowing when she completes an arrangement that causes people to remark on how beautiful it is. So, from now on do the things that you excel in and your capacity for joy will increase.

Heavenly Father, thank You for the gifts and talents which I have received from Your hand. Help me to make my contribution in the areas in which I shine so that I can be happy. Amen.

Smile!

The Lord's servant must not quarrel; instead, he must be kind to everyone, able to teach, not resentful. Those who oppose him he must gently instruct, in the hope that God will grant them repentance leading them to a knowledge of the truth (2 Timothy 2:24-25).

A frown uses much more face muscles than a smile, say the scientists. Furthermore, a frown causes stress to arise – even if you just look at someone else's frown! (And above all it causes wrinkles between your eyes). If a person is happy, they definitely do not frown at others. A smile, on the other hand, has the result of making a person feel good.

If someone gives you a radiant smile you find that you spontaneously smile back and immediately feel better. To receive a smile and to give one back makes you happy. Therefore, smile more. There is an old saying that goes that if you meet someone who does not have a smile, you should give him one of yours. Make it your life's motto and share your smiles lavishly – especially among people who do not smile often.

Lundqvist and Dimberg in 1995 conducted research which found that all people have a tendency to imitate the expressions on the faces of the people around them. Sad faces bring about more sad faces while smiling faces cause other people to smile and feel happy. "Your smile makes other people happy, which in turn makes you happy," says David Niven.

Lord, I am sorry that I so often walk around with a sour face. I realize that it is Your will for me to be friendly to everyone. Help me to smile more so that I can make other people and myself happy. Amen.

Choose Right!

Who, then, is the man that fears the LORD? He will instruct him in the way chosen for him (Psalm 25:12).

Every day we are faced with choices. In the morning you choose what you will wear, what you will eat for breakfast and what you will do on that specific day. You choose what groceries you will buy and which coffee shop you will go to with your friends. These kinds of choices are not all that significant but we also face important choices in the course of our lives, such as choosing a marriage partner or a career.

When a person makes the right choices in these areas they are happy, while a wrong choice can cause much trouble and be like a rope around your neck. The motto of one of my friends who has been diagnosed with cancer three times but who has come out of the fight healthy once again is, "Happiness is a choice." She believes that each one of us can choose to be happy and get the very best out of life, or to be unhappy all day long because things do not always turn out the way we would like them to. Lana always walks around with a radiant smile because she has chosen to be happy.

If you know the Lord and love Him He will help you to make the right choices – so go ahead and ask Him to help you to make the right choices when you have important decisions to make. Choose to be happy each day.

Heavenly Father, will You please lead me each day to make the right choices when I have to make important decisions. I also want to choose from now on to be happy regardless of what things happen in my life. Please help me to do this well. Amen.

Enjoy Your Life

Go, eat your food with gladness, and drink your wine with a joyful heart, for it is now that God favors what you do. Enjoy life with your wife, whom you love, all the days of this meaningless life that God has given you under the sun (Ecclesiastes 9:7, 9).

The writer of Ecclesiastes was someone who knew how to live life to the fullest. That is why he also urges all people to enjoy life with the wife (or husband) whom they love.

Not one of us knows how long we have to live – therefore enjoy every moment of your life and make the most of it. Do not forget to have fun. You can actually do a lot to make sure that you are happy through doing things that are pleasant and enjoyable for you.

There are few things that make me as happy as discovering a new book by one of my favorite authors in the library; or better yet to buy such a book so that I can have it on my bookshelf to read whenever I want to. Other things that make me happy are to write something that flows easily from the beginning, to talk to my husband, to visit my children and grandchildren and of course to travel and eat good food!

According to David Niven people who have fun have a twenty percent chance of being happier than others. Therefore, decide right now to put aside more time in the future for the things that you enjoy and that make you happy.

Lord, I praise You for Your goodness to me – there are so many things that are wonderful that make my life worthwhile. Thank You for each one of them. Amen.

Focus on Things That Give You Hope

Hope does not disappoint us, because God has poured out His love into our hearts by the Holy Spirit, whom He has given us (Romans 5:5).

Unhappy people focus on their fears while happy people focus on potential improvements in future, according to Niven. There are things that happen around us that cause us to lose hope daily – and this should not be. Rather than focusing on things like crime and disasters everywhere, focus on the things that give you hope. There are still so many lovely things in life.

Be sensitive to the beauty around you and know that God made these things so that you could enjoy them. Listen to your favorite music, go for a walk in nature, do enjoyable things together with the people you love and know that even though negative things do happen in the world and you will necessarily be confronted with hurts and difficulties, you can still cling to hope. "May the God of hope fill you with all joy and peace as you trust in Him, so that you may overflow with hope by the power of the Holy Spirit," is Paul's wish for the church in Rome (Rom. 15:13). It is also my wish for you today – that you will be able to look away from all the burdens and focus on God who is the source of your hope. Then you can't help but be happy!

Heavenly Father, please make it possible for me to focus on the things that give me hope and to look away from the things that scare me. Amen.

The Best Is Yet to Come!

We fix our eyes not on what is seen, but on what is unseen. For what is seen is temporary, but what is unseen is eternal (2 Corinthians 4:18).

Researchers have conducted a long-term study of Northern Californians. Over a period of thirty years they've asked citizens when they were the happiest in their lives. Each time, eight out of ten of the people answered, "We are now at our happiest."

People who have learned the secret of living each moment to the fullest and are aware of each one of their blessings are people who are happy. Therefore, stop yearning for the past or thinking that you will be happier tomorrow; just enjoy every day to the fullest. Christians actually have the assurance that the best still lies ahead of them because we know that heaven still awaits us! Even if you are experiencing difficulties and cannot succeed in being happy, you can know that true happiness awaits you. "Therefore we do not lose heart. Though outwardly we are wasting away, yet inwardly we are being renewed day by day. For our light and momentary troubles are achieving for us an eternal glory that far outweighs them all" (2 Cor. 4:16-17). Be happy about the heavenly glory that awaits you in the future!

Lord, You know that sometimes I struggle to be happy. I praise You for the promise that the best is yet to come – that heaven is waiting for me in my future. Amen.

Prayer

Heavenly Father,
I praise You as the Source of my joy.
Please help me to discover my purpose in life;
to accept myself unconditionally, to believe in myself
and to live each day with a positive outlook.
Forgive me for all the times that I have tried to solve
my problems on my own, for the fact
that I am so focused on money and possessions.
Help me to be satisfied with what I have.
Thank You that I do not have to fear growing older
because I know that You will always be with me.
I really want to live with integrity –
and to fulfill each of my promises to You and others.
Teach me to purify my thoughts
so that my life will reflect Your peace.
Help me to laugh more and to help others laugh;
to view my work as a calling and to do it as for You;
to nurture my family and make enough time for them.
Make me a peacemaker so that I can help
to restore broken relationships.
Show me again how important the right values are to You.
From now on I am going to be happier by
doing something each day that is important,
offering more help to others; doing those things at which
I excel and sharing a smile with everyone I meet.
I now choose to be happy and to make other people happy
because I know for certain that the best
still lies ahead of me – heaven – because I know You.

Amen.

July

Focusing on Prayer

I have read dozens of books about prayer – and I have even written one about it – and yet I continue to struggle with my own prayer life. The more a person reads about prayer, the more you realize that every Christian struggles to pray.

We do not always have the right words to talk to God. We wonder if our prayers ever help. And yet people are the only creatures on earth who can engage in a conversation with God. Prayer is therefore, a formidable responsibility which every Christian should take seriously. But just because it is so deceptively easy to pray, we sell prayer short of its real value. Yet if it is so easy why do we struggle so much with it?

This month we are going to focus on prayer. It is my prayer that your own prayer life will have received a positive injection by the end of the month that will last for the rest of your life.

July 1

Blueprint for Prayer

"When you pray, go into your room, close the door and pray to your Father, who is unseen. Then your Father, who sees what is done in secret, will reward you" (Matthew 6:6).

When the disciples of Jesus came to Him to seek help and asked Him if He could teach them to pray, He told them in detail how to go about it. In Jesus' day the Jews often used to pray alongside the streets so that they could be seen by other people. Jesus taught His disciples that this is not right.

The first requirement for prayer is that you should find a place where you can be alone with God, as Jesus so often did. *The Message* translation's blueprint for prayer sets it out in such a way that even a child can understand it:

* Find a quiet, secluded place so you won't be tempted to role-play before God.
* Just be there as simply and honestly as you can manage.
* This is your Father you are dealing with, and He knows better than you what you need.

After this Jesus gave His disciples the Lord's Prayer as a model prayer that they could use whenever they prayed. If you do not know it off by heart yet, it is a good idea to learn it now and repeat the words of Jesus in those times when you are struggling to pray.

Lord Jesus, thank You for Your blueprint for prayer. I know that You are with me when I seek You in my inner room and that I do not have to pray long prayers because You know me so well that You already know everything that I want to ask You. Amen.

Ask and It Will Be Given to You

"Ask and it will be given to you; seek and you will find; knock and the door will be opened to you" (Matthew 7:7).

When you do not know how to pray or cannot find the right words to say you can simply ask God to teach you to pray. This is assuredly the one prayer request that is completely in line with His will and that He will be delighted to answer.

In the Sermon on the Mount Jesus promised that those people who ask will receive the things they ask for. In the corresponding Scripture passage in Luke 11, Jesus says, "If you then, though you are evil, know how to give good gifts to your children, how much more will your Father in heaven give the Holy Spirit to those who ask Him!" (Luke 11:13). And it is indeed the Holy Spirit who teaches you to pray, and who better yet, will pray for you when you struggle to find the right words. "The Spirit helps us in our weakness. We do not know what we ought to pray for, but the Spirit Himself intercedes for us with groans that words cannot express," Paul assured the church in Rome (Rom. 8:26).

If you really want to learn how to be a true prayer and intercessor, all that you need to do is to ask the Holy Spirit to be your Prayer Master.

Holy Spirit You know how I struggle to pray. Will You please teach me to pray according to the will of God? And when I do not manage to get it right, please pray in my place. Amen.

Prayer Is Confession

If we claim to be without sin, we deceive ourselves and the truth is not in us. If we confess our sins, He is faithful and just and will forgive us our sins and purify us from all unrighteousness (1 John 1:8-9).

There is no person on earth who is righteous. We are all sinners from the moment we are born and that is why we continuously sin. We ought to bring our sins to the throne of God's grace and confess them before Him.

The Norwegian theologian Ole Hallesby writes, "Only he who is helpless can pray." Philip Yancey agrees with this when he says that prayer is our declaration of dependence on God. When we prayer we must be well aware that we are sinners who are engaging in conversation with a holy God, that we are completely helpless and can do nothing to change our sinful condition. It is, therefore, necessary that we confess before God just how loveless, sinful, proud and selfish we are – even though no one knows it better than He does.

Before you start praying it is necessary for you to realize who you are and who God is. He is the Almighty Creator God and you are a worthless creature of dust. At the same time you should be aware of your own inabilities. Jesus said, "Without Me you can do nothing." When you pray, you should declare your dependence on God. Only then can you pray with the certain knowledge that God will listen to you, that He will be merciful to you and that He will forgive your sins.

Father, I stand helpless before You – You are so immeasurably great and I am so unworthy and sinful. It is incomprehensible to me that You are actually prepared to listen to my prayers. I come and confess my sins before You – please forgive me. Amen.

Bring Your Doubts to God

"Why are you troubled, and why do doubts rise in your minds? Look at My hands and My feet. It is I Myself! Touch Me and see; a ghost does not have flesh and bones, as you see I have" (Luke 24:38-39).

When I was young we always sang the Hallelujah hymns in town at Pentecost. One of my favorites was *All my doubts I bring to Jesus.* There is probably not a Christian who has never had doubts about God.

Luke tells us that the disciples were absolutely terrified and doubtful when Jesus appeared to them after His resurrection. But Jesus did not judge them; He knew that they were only human and He gave them visible proof that it was really Him. When Thomas – surely the most well-known skeptic in the Bible – expressed his doubt verbally and declared that he would not believe unless he could see with his own eyes that Jesus had risen from the dead. Jesus appeared to him and invited him to, "Put your finger here; see My hands. Reach out your hand and put it into My side. Stop doubting and believe" (John 20:27).

Prayer means that you can freely bring your doubts to Jesus and discuss them with Him. When Jesus was on the earth He had great sympathy for doubters and He was always prepared to reach out to them with grace. He still wants to do that for you.

Lord Jesus, please forgive me because I still often doubt. Teach me to bring my questions of doubt to You and please strengthen my weak faith. Amen.

Be Honest When You Pray

O LORD, You have searched me and You know me. You know when I sit and when I rise; You perceive my thoughts from afar. Your eyes saw my unformed body. All the days ordained for me were written in Your book before one of them came to be (Psalm 139:1-2, 16).

When we pray honesty must be one of the primary requirements. It does not help to hide things from God – in any case He already knows everything about us, even those things that we hide from other people.

C. S. Lewis declares that we must lay before Him what is in us, not what ought to be in us. Habitual prayers prevent you from really laying yourself bare before God. You can do so peacefully because God knows all there is to know about you anyway. Sometimes we are a bit afraid that God will be disappointed in us and so we present the same front when we pray that we do when we are dealing with people.

You are allowed to complain to God when your prayers are not answered, remind Him of His promises if they have not come to pass. You can also share the things with Him that you feel ashamed of: your selfishness, lack of love, bitterness and jealousy – all those negative emotions that you struggle with so badly. It is amazing to think that God still loves you even though He knows about all your sins.

As long as you expose your negative emotions before God He can help you change for the better into the person He desires you to be.

Heavenly Father, will You please help me to share with You all the things that are in my heart when I pray? Thank You that You already know about all my sins and yet still love me. Amen.

The Paradox of God's Love

For as high as the heavens are above the earth, so great is His love for those who fear Him. For He knows how we are formed, He remembers that we are dust (Psalm 103:11, 14).

When we pray we must never lose sight of God. From our limited human perspective God remains a paradox that we will never be able to grasp. He simultaneously controls millions of galaxies of stars and planets and keeps them all in their orbits, yet He knows about each sparrow, and He loves you. Philip Yancey says that in one hand we hold the truth of God's vastness, and in the other hand we hold the truth of God's desire for intimacy.

It remains completely incomprehensible to me that the Almighty Creator God who holds millions of solar systems in His hand, loves sinful humans; that He is prepared to listen to my prayers; that He is interested in me; that He desires to be in a relationship with me and longs for me to engage in conversation with Him. In fact, it does not seem to make any sense, and yet it is wonderfully true!

Before you begin to pray think of everything that God has made and sustains each day, and when you have finished with this, focus on the incomprehensible love of God for you. This love caused Him to sacrifice His only Son so that your sins could be forgiven and that you could be His child.

Heavenly Father, the miracle that You, the Almighty Creator God, am interested in me and desire to have a relationship with me takes my breath away. I cannot understand it, Lord, but I revel in the love You have for me. Amen.

July 7

A Page from Jesus' Book

"He longed to fill his stomach with the pods that the pigs were eating, but no one gave him anything" (Luke 15:16).

For Jesus, prayer was of the utmost importance. Often, in spite of His busy program, He made time to be alone with His Father. Luke writes that Jesus went off to isolated places to go and pray and Matthew reports that after the first miracle of the bread and fish He sent the people away, "When He had sent the multitudes away, He went up into a mountain apart to pray: and when the evening came, He was there alone" (Matt. 14:23).

Jesus would never have been able to keep up with His busy program on earth if He had not regularly gone to His Father to find strength by setting aside time to pray alone. Apart from His daily times of prayer with His Father He also, in every crisis situation, turned to God. He turned to God before He chose His disciples, after He was tempted by the Devil and also before He was crucified. You can readily take a page out of Jesus' Book: make time every day to be alone with God so that He can give you the strength and inspiration to fulfill your daily responsibilities. Also go and seek Him for help when things get too much for you, and in times of crisis separate yourself to be alone with God.

The busier you are, the more prayer time you need. Alone with God you will, every time, receive the necessary strength and inspiration that you need.

Heavenly Father, it is wonderful that I can spend time with You and that every time I pray I discover that You bless me and give me the strength to be able to succeed in everything that is expected of me. Amen.

You Have a Mediator

He is not a man like me that I might answer Him, that we might confront each other in court. If only there were someone to arbitrate between us, to lay his hand upon us both, someone to remove God's rod from me, so that His terror would frighten me no more (Job 9:32-34).

Job struggled to reach God. His friends could not understand him at all, which is why he wanted to speak to God himself so that he could explain his personal situation to Him. He expressed the desire that he really wanted to have a mediator – someone who could be a go-between between God and him; someone who could present his case to God.

Fortunately, we live *after* the cross and we are, therefore, in a much better position than Job. We no longer need to struggle to get through to God. You already have an intercessor who stands between you and God. When Jesus came into the world to pay for your sins, He undertook to be your go-between. "For this reason Christ is the mediator of a new covenant that those who are called may receive the promised eternal inheritance – now that He has died as a ransom to set them free from the sins committed under the first covenant," reports the writer to the Hebrews (Heb. 9:15). This Mediator sits at the right hand of God and He is always busy praying for you.

Lord Jesus, I praise You because You are my Mediator, because You intercede for me before God and present my case to Him. Thank You that I can now freely approach God because You earned that privilege for me on the cross. Amen.

To Know God

I want to know Christ and the power of His resurrection and the fellowship of sharing in His sufferings, becoming like Him in His death (Philippians 3:10).

In his letter to the Philippians, Paul wrote that for him to know Jesus surpasses the value of all other things. With the word "know" he doesn't mean a superficial acquaintance but a personal, intimate relationship. He lived so close to Jesus that he truly experienced the power of His resurrection and shared in His suffering.

"The main purpose of prayer is not to make life easier, nor to gain magical powers, but to know God," writes C. S. Lewis. When you have discovered this truth, prayer becomes a voyage of discovery. On this journey you will learn more and more about God, get to know Him a little better day by day, and fall more and more in love with Him. You will realize how wonderful He is and how much He loves you. The better you know God, the more you will want to spend time with Him and the more enjoyable it will be for you to converse with Him.

Make sure that your own prayer time will deepen your relationship with God and that you will never simply pray to tell God everything that He should do for you or that you really want. Do not pray only in times of crisis, but make prayer an integral part of your life; a crucial part of being a Christian.

Lord Jesus, help me to learn to know You better and more intimately each day. Let me, like Paul, experience the power of Your resurrection and share in Your suffering. Amen.

God Knows What You Have Need Of

"When you pray, do not keep on babbling like pagans, for they think they will be heard because of their many words" (Matthew 6:7).

When Jesus taught His disciples how to pray He said that they need not use a lot of words when they speak to God because God already knows what they need. Perhaps you have wondered if it even makes sense to pray if God already knows what you want to say to Him. Tim Stafford says that we do not pray to tell God what He does not know, nor to remind Him of things He has forgotten. He already cares for the things we pray about ... He has simply been waiting for us to care with Him about these things. When we pray, we stand next to God and look toward those people and problems we want to give to Him.

When we pray we agree with God about the people and problems in our lives, and He really wants us to communicate with Him even though He already knows everything about us.

When you pray you need not try to impress God with your beautiful prayers. You also do not need to feel bad if your prayers are not long and complicated. All that God asks of you when you talk to Him is that your relationship with Him will be right and that you will share with Him the things that are on your mind.

Heavenly Father, thank You that I never have to try to impress You with my prayers because You already know what I have need of even before I ask You for it. Amen.

July 11

The Main Reason for Prayer

"I pray for them. I am not praying for the world, but for those You have given Me, for they are Yours. All I have is Yours, and all You have is Mine. And glory has come to Me through them" (John 17:9-10).

The simplest answer to the question "Why pray?" is because Jesus did, writes Philip Yancey. Jesus often spoke to His Father. Interestingly enough only one of the prayers of Jesus has been recorded where He asked something for Himself, and that is His prayer in Gethsemane when He pleaded with God to take the cup of suffering away from Him.

In the beautiful High Priestly prayer in John 17 Jesus lifted up His disciples before His Father as well as all the people who will believe in Him in the future. He prayed that God would make them one, that they would have His joy and love in them and that they would be surrendered to God. On the cross He asked His Father to forgive the people who had crucified Him.

The prayers of Jesus are never centered on His own needs, but are conversations with His Father in which He asks for things for other people. What do your prayers look like? Do you also use them to communicate with God, to praise and thank Him and to intercede for others, or do your prayers revolve around yourself and your own selfish requests?

You should not pray only because Jesus prayed, but you should also pray the way Jesus prayed.

Lord Jesus, please teach me to pray in the same way You prayed so that I will truly communicate with You when I pray and not simply ask You to do things for me. Amen.

Jesus' Prayer for Peter

"Simon, Simon, Satan has asked to sift you as wheat. But I have prayed for you, Simon, that your faith may not fail. And when you have turned back, strengthen your brothers" (Luke 22:31-32).

If we read a little further, it would seem as if the prayer Jesus prayed for Peter was not answered. And yet Jesus prayed for him in any case – even though He well knew (and even said so to Peter) – before the rooster crowed that day, that Peter would have denied Him three times. Peter vehemently denied this fact – he assured Jesus that he was prepared to be arrested with Him and even to die with Him.

Because we know the Bible we know that Peter did in fact deny Jesus three times before the crucifixion. When Peter discovered that Jesus' prediction was true, he went outside and wept bitterly. But when Peter confessed his sin, he did indeed become the rock on which the first church was built. Furthermore, after His resurrection Jesus gave Peter the chance to confess his love for Him and he also received the command from Jesus Himself to care for His sheep three times (see John 21:15-19).

Although Peter did deny Jesus, the result of Jesus' prayer for him was that he would present a powerful sermon on the first Day of Pentecost and also be a powerful witness for Jesus the rest of his life.

Lord Jesus, thank You very much for the privilege of being able to know that You not only prayed for Peter, but that You now sit at the right hand of God and intercede for me! Amen.

Jesus Prays for Us

Because Jesus lives forever, He has a permanent priesthood. Therefore He is able to save completely those who come to God through Him, because He always lives to intercede for them (Hebrews 7:24-25).

The writer to the Hebrews shares a wonderful truth with us: unlike the priests in the Old Testament who regularly had to be succeeded by others, Jesus is the Priest forever. Also, unlike them, He does not have to bring sacrifices to God so that the sins of the people can be forgiven – His once-and-for-all sacrifice on the cross was enough to forgive all our sins and to set us free forever.

If we come to God through Jesus He will personally pray for us and present our case before God. Jesus is at this moment permanently busy interceding for you before God. This promise is almost too good to be true. And He does not pray alone for you. The Holy Spirit helps Him to do so. In Romans 8:26-27 Paul assured the church in Rome that the Holy Spirit Himself prays for us "with groans that words cannot express" when we do not know what to pray.

Above all, the prayers of the Holy Spirit are in line with the will of God. You can, therefore, know for sure that Jesus and the Holy Spirit are interceding before God for you.

Lord Jesus, it is such a comfort for me to know that You are constantly presenting my case before God and that the Holy Spirit prays together with You for me. I really want to hold fast to this promise of Yours. Amen.

Conversations with God

The Sovereign Lord *has given me an instructed tongue, to know the word that sustains the weary. He wakens me morning by morning, wakens my ear to listen like one being taught. The Sovereign* Lord *has opened my ears, and I have not been rebellious; I have not drawn back (Isaiah 50:4-5).*

There are few things as irritating as someone who does not give others a chance to speak. A conversation in fact means that there will be communication between people from both sides.

Prayer must never become a monologue where you are the only one speaking. Rosalind Rinker, the American writer who wrote the first book about conversational prayer, says that prayer is always a conversation between two people who love each other.

Mother Teresa who was a true prayer giant was eager to share her prayer secret, "My secret is a very simple one: I pray. Prayer is simply talking to God. He speaks to us: we listen. We speak to Him: He listens. A two-way process: speaking *and* listening."

If you struggle to pray take a close look at your prayers and see if perhaps – even without your being aware of it – your prayers have deteriorated into a monologue. Learn to tune in and listen to the voice of God once again, ask Him to teach you to listen and also to give you the right words to use. Only after you have listened carefully can you answer Him with your prayers.

Heavenly Father, I see now that my prayers have not been conversations but monologues. Please forgive me, give me the right words to use and teach me to listen to Your voice and to answer You with my prayers. Amen.

Remind God of His Promises

I have posted watchmen on your walls, O Jerusalem; they will never be silent day or night. You who call on the Lord, give yourselves no rest (Isaiah 62:6).

In Isaiah 62 God assures His people that He loves them and that He will care for them. He encourages them to remind Him of His promises to them. But during the time of these beautiful promises, the people were still taken into exile and the promises of God were not coming true for them.

Sometimes God asks His children to wait for a long time before His promises come to pass in their lives. Prayer giants such as Moses, Jeremiah, Job and David were actually never embarrassed to point out to God if His promises were not coming to pass for them. Martin Luther tells how he did exactly that when his sick friend, Phillip Melancton, in spite of his repeated prayers did not get better. "This time I besought the Almighty with great vigor," he writes. "I attacked Him with His own weapons, quoting from Scripture all the promises I could remember, that prayers should be granted, and said that He must grant my prayer, if I was henceforth to put my faith in His promises."

If you become despondent because your prayers are not being answered, you can remind God of the promises in His Word. Make sure that you know your favorite promises off by heart so that you can repeat them back to God even if you do not have your Bible close at hand.

Heavenly Father, I praise You for the hundreds of promises that are recorded in Your Word that I can take for myself and in which I can trust. It is wonderful that You do not mind being reminded of Your promises. Amen.

It Is Possible to Reason with God!

Whenever the Israelites planted their crops, the Midianites, Amalekites and other eastern peoples invaded the country. Gideon replied, "If now I have found favor in Your eyes, give me a sign that it is really You talking to me" (Judges 6:3, 17).

Some of the characters in the Scriptures dared to reason with God and even presented conditions to Him, and God is so merciful that He accepted this! My favorite story is that of Gideon. When the angel of God appeared to him and told him that the Lord was with him, Gideon was absolutely not convinced. With his humble, "Excuse me, Sir" he wanted to know from the angel why God had allowed them to be oppressed by the Midianites if this were true. He was indeed audacious enough to ask for a miracle from the Lord as proof that it was really Him.

At this the Lord asked him to prepare a kid goat and a loaf of bread and to bring them before Him. When He touched the bread and meat, a fire flared up from the rock and consumed the food. Only then did Gideon believe that it was truly God who was speaking to him and that He would do as He had promised.

God knows that you are only human and that times of doubt might arise in your life. That is why you can, like Gideon, reason with Him to present your case. His grace is sufficient to overcome your doubt.

Heavenly Father, thank You so much that I can reason with You when I pray because Your grace is sufficient to overcome my doubt. Amen.

Answer to Prayer

In those days Hezekiah became ill and was at the point of death. He prayed to the LORD, who answered him and gave him a miraculous sign. But Hezekiah's heart was proud and he did not respond to the kindness shown him; therefore the LORD's wrath was on him (2 Chronicles 32:24-25).

In his book *Miracles* C. S. Lewis writes about prayer. He says that someone who can scientifically prove that something occurs because of his prayers will feel like a magician. The chances are good that he will become proud.

This is exactly what happened to King Hezekiah. When the Lord answered his prayer and brought about a miraculous healing (see 2 Kings 20) Hezekiah was not grateful – the Bible records that he became impressed with himself so that the wrath of the Lord was on him and Judah.

It is better to believe that everything that happens is an answer to prayer, whether it is our requests that are granted or refused. "All prayers are heard, although not all prayers are granted," writes Lewis. Perhaps you too have received miraculous answers to your prayers – so you should never boast about it. God is sovereign and all-knowing. He knows what the very best answer to your prayer is, even when this answer is vastly different from the one you expect.

Know that God hears each one of your prayers – even though there are many that He does not grant to the letter.

Heavenly Father, I know You listen to each one of my prayers and I know too that You answer each one in the very best way possible. Please forgive me for sometimes wondering why You do not always give me everything that I really want. Amen.

God Wants to Show You Mercy

Yet the Lord *longs to be gracious to you; He rises to show you compassion. How gracious He will be when you cry for help! As soon as He hears, He will answer you (Isaiah 30:18-19).*

The more I read and think about prayer, the bigger a mystery it becomes to me. I have personally experienced that miracles occur when people pray. No person who prays doubts that his prayer is being heard, and yet it often happens that our prayer requests are not granted. "When I pray, coincidences happen, when I don't, they don't," says archbishop William Temple.

Even though we cannot twist God's arm with our prayers, God is so merciful that He does sometimes grant our human desires after He has decided about a situation already. When Abraham asked for Sodom to be spared if they could find fifty righteous people in the city, God agreed, although He had already decided to destroy the city. He was even willing to spare the city for the sake of forty, thirty, twenty and even ten believers (see Gen. 18:24-32).

God is still the same merciful God of Abraham's day. You can, therefore, plead with God if there is a special prayer request that is lying very heavily on your heart, with the certain knowledge that He will do His best to grant that request if it is in line with His will.

Heavenly Father, it is incomprehensible that Your grace is so great towards me. Thank You very much that You hear and answer the prayers of Your children as soon as You hear them. I know that You will grant my requests as long as they are best for me. Amen.

July 19

Pray *and* Work

What good is it, my brothers, if a man claims to have faith but has no deeds? Can such faith save him? As the body without the spirit is dead, so faith without deeds is dead (James 2:14, 26).

When a person prays for someone else, or if you intercede with God about a certain matter, you are often reminded by the Holy Spirit that you can perhaps make a difference by becoming involved yourself.

Philip Yancey tells how when he prays for his neighbor, who is a single mother, the Holy Spirit often causes him to wonder when last he had taken her son to go skiing with him. God answers us when we ask Him things in prayer, but He expects more from us than just requests. Before Queen Esther went to address the king in an attempt to save the lives of her people she and the people of Israel prayed and fasted for three days. Only after that did she have enough courage to confront the king. God answered the prayer of the courageous queen because not only did she pray, but she was also prepared to do something so that her prayer request could be answered.

If you believe and bring prayer requests to the throne of God's grace, you need to be prepared to do something so that your prayer can be answered. Sir Thomas More's well-known prayer says, "The things, good Lord, that we pray for, give us the grace to work for."

As soon as you discover the secret of prayer *and* work you will also discover that God will answer your prayers.

Heavenly Father, make me prepared not to only ask things of You but also to have the right motives so that my prayer requests will be granted. Amen.

Can God Change His Mind?

Let man and beast be covered with sackcloth. Let everyone call urgently on God. Let them give up their evil ways and their violence. Who knows? God may yet relent and with compassion turn from his fierce anger so that we will not perish (Jonah 3:8-9).

When the disobedient Jonah eventually arrived in Nineveh and confronted the people with the message of judgment that he had received from God, the people immediately listened to him. They repented of their wrongdoings in the hope that God would not destroy them. This retuning to God did in fact make Him change His original plans to destroy them.

Through the centuries the prayers of believers have caused God to change His plans. When Abraham begged God to spare Sodom and Gomorrah if only fifty righteous people could be found in the city, God agreed. He was even prepared to spare the city if there were only forty, thirty, twenty and eventually even ten believers in the city. Also when Moses prayed that the Lord would not destroy the people in the wilderness, but still go with them, God listened. (see Gen. 18:23-33 and Exod. 32:11-14).

God still listens to the prayers of His believing children. Through your prayers people can be saved and the mercy of God can be spread through the world. God never makes a declaration of punishment without adding a little bit of grace to it. If you want it, the grace of God is available to you.

Heavenly Father, it is amazing that through my prayers I can have You change Your plans! I pray that Your grace will increase, that all over the world people will repent and turn to You so that many more people will be saved. Amen.

Discipline and Prayer

Be joyful in hope, patient in affliction, faithful in prayer (Romans 12:12).

If you want to learn to pray, there is only one way to get it right and that is to pray with perseverance. The more time you spend praying the easier it will be for you to get it right, the more natural it will become for you to talk to God. But discipline is necessary for prayer. It does not just happen by itself. You will have to make extra time for prayer; organize a special time and place for yourself where you can talk to God unhindered.

Even when you have done that you will more than likely still struggle to find the right words with which to honor God, and thank Him and with which you can make your prayer requests heard. In *Prayer* Philip Yancey tells how he once could not manage to pray for a year. So he simply just read prayers out of a prayer book and asked the Lord to accept them as his own prayers.

If you struggle to pray you too can take a piece from the Bible and repeat it back to the Lord. When you pray your relationship with the Lord is far more important than your prayer technique. Ask that God Himself will help you to pray, and that He will give you the right words to communicate with Him. Believe then that He listens to you, even when it does not feel like it.

Heavenly Father, I truly want to set aside extra time for prayer. Please help me with the right words to talk to You. Thank You that I can know for certain that You listen to every word when I pray. Amen.

A Practical Lesson in Prayer

"Listen to me, O house of Jacob, all you who remain of the house of Israel, you whom I have upheld since you were conceived, and have carried since your birth" (Isaiah 46:3).

The next time you struggle to pray, take a few Scripture verses and read it through attentively. Then write down the Scripture verse or verses that spoke to you the most and think about what exactly that Scripture verse wants to say to you on that specific day. Remember that it is God Himself who wants to speak to you. If you have lingered long enough in the Word of God, it is now your turn to answer Him. Do that through your prayers.

The message of the Scripture passage for me for today is that God has cared for me even before I was born; that He has held me close since I was very little. That He still promises to be my God through my whole life and will carry me when I am very old. After I meditated on these wonderful promises, I remembered the many times when God has undertaken for me in the past and I thanked Him for that. I also take His promise that He will be with me in the future and will carry me even when I am very old.

When I looked at my watch again, half an hour had already passed – a wonderful blessed half an hour in which I could feel the presence of God with me and could hear His voice speaking to me.

Heavenly Father, how wonderful it is that You speak to me personally through Your Word, and that I can respond to You through the Word. Teach me to spend time with You in this way and to hear Your voice speaking to me personally. Amen.

When Believers Pray Together

"Again, I tell you that if two of you on earth agree about anything you ask for, it will be done for you by My Father in heaven. For where two or three come together in My name, there am I with them" (Matthew 18:19-20).

It is not easy for some people to pray in front of others. I remember very well how many years ago when I was still a very young pastor's wife how I almost sweated blood when I was asked to close the proceedings with prayer at a very formal prayer meeting. I am afraid that I did not take in one word of the message of the rest of the proceedings; I was just too scared about the prayer that I was to say at the end.

It is not necessary to stress when you have to pray in front of others, writes Rosalind Rinker in her book *Communicating Love through Prayer*.

There is a four-step formula that you can apply very successfully:

1. Jesus is here (Matt. 18:19-20)
2. Help me, Lord (James 5: 13-16)
3. Thank You, Lord (Phil. 4:4-7)
4. Help my brother (Mark 11:22-25).

The next time you are asked to pray in public, focus on the fact that Jesus is there and that He has promised to hear your prayer requests and to answer them. Then make your needs known to Him, thank Him and intercede for others. With this formula you cannot go wrong.

Lord Jesus, please forgive me for being scared when I have to pray in front of other people. Make me calm and aware of Your presence so that I can freely and without fear talk to You. Amen.

Pray without Ceasing

Pray continually; give thanks in all circumstances, for this is God's will for you in Christ Jesus (1 Thessalonians 5:17-18).

Although there are many instructions, examples and formulas for prayer, they are only aids and not one of them needs to be followed slavishly. We are all different and we do not need to pray like Mother Teresa or Martin Luther. You can of course use written prayers and benefit from them in those times when your own words dry up and it is hard for you to express your feelings.

It is not necessary for you to pray like someone else. What Jesus taught us about prayer can be summarized in three points, writes Philip Yancey:

1. Keep it honest
2. Keep it simple
3. Keep it up.

Do not ever give up praying. And when you pray, be honest, keep your prayers simple and keep on praying. Your prayers do not even always need to have words – when you come before God in quietness and kneel before Him in worship, words are not at all necessary. Being still before God is probably the kind of prayer God takes the most pleasure in. When you have been still before the throne of God's grace for a while, then you can talk to Him as a child does to his dad, with the certain knowledge that He loves you and cares for you. Therefore, you know that He will listen to your prayers and will answer each one in the very best way possible.

Lord Jesus please teach me to be completely honest when I engage in conversation with You and to keep my prayers simple. Help me to be prepared to pray without ceasing. Amen.

Sometimes God Answers Differently

During the days of Jesus' life on earth, He offered up prayers and petitions with loud cries and tears to the one who could save Him from death, and He was heard because of His reverent submission (Hebrews 5:7).

In the Bible we read that God sometimes did not grant answers to the prayers of His children. I have often thought how difficult it must have been for God not to have granted Jesus' prayer in Gethsemane.

A while ago I discovered a Scripture verse in Hebrews that says that God did in fact answer this prayer of Jesus through not rescuing Him from death, but rather through taking away His anxiety about dying (Heb. 5:7, NLT).

After Jesus had wrestled in prayer in Gethsemane He was calm and peaceful. He went to meet His death on the cross with courage. There was no longer any sign of the anxiety that had caused His drops of sweat to fall to the ground like blood (see Luke 22:44). We also never again hear Him ask His Father to remove the cup of suffering from Him. Instead, He prays that His enemies would be forgiven.

Sometimes God will also answer your payers in ways other than what you expected. Perhaps He will not heal you, but He might teach you a precious life lesson through your illness. Perhaps you do not get the job you have prayed for, but later you find out that it was actually for your best. God's answer is always the best one for you.

Heavenly Father, I am sorry that I have been dissatisfied when You have not answered my prayers to the letter. Teach me once again that Your answer is the very best one for me. Amen.

Get Rid of Prayer Hindrances

Let us then approach the throne of grace with confidence, so that we may receive mercy and find grace to help us in our time of need (Hebrews 4:16).

Martin Luther complained that as soon as he started to pray a hundred thousand hindrances came up. Why is it that the minute you kneel down to pray your telephone rings, your husband wants his shirt to be ironed right then or many thoughts flash through your mind, so much so that even with the best will in the world you cannot concentrate on your prayer?

I have often found that when I wake up an hour earlier than usual in the morning and decide to spend an extra hour in prayer, my thoughts begin to wander – I begin thinking about what I will cook for dinner, about the car that needs to be serviced – or right there on my knees – I fall fast asleep.

Because I found it hard to concentrate I have found that it helps to wash your face with cold water and keep a pen and paper close at hand to write down all the things that keep your thoughts away from your prayers so that they do not hinder you.

It is also a good idea to switch off all electronic appliances while you are busy with your quiet time and to teach your children that you are not to be disturbed. Finally you can ask the Lord to help you to keep your thoughts focused on Him.

Heavenly Father, I am sorry that I struggle to concentrate on You when I pray. Please take away all those things that draw my attention away from You so that I can talk to You without interruptions. Amen.

When God Looks Away

How long must I wrestle with my thoughts and every day have sorrow in my heart? How long will my enemy triumph over me? My enemy will say, "I have overcome him," and my foes will rejoice when I fall (Psalm 13:2, 4).

In this psalm David asks why God keeps forgetting him, why He looks away from him. He wants to know if it will be like this forever. And yet in verse six of this psalm he testifies that he still clings to God's faithful love and that his heart rejoices over the outcome that he expects from God.

Like David, every Christian experiences dry times in her prayer life. In these times it feels as if the Lord has forgotten about her, as if her prayers are not heard and as if God no longer listens to her or answers her prayers.

If it feels like God is keeping quiet, that is not really the case, says Teresa of Avila. It is only us who are deaf! Teresa herself wrestled for almost twenty years with a prayer drought like this before she came through the battle as a master of prayer.

These deserts in your prayer life can have two outcomes: they can make you depressed and leave you feeling guilty because you cannot reach God, or they can make God a greater reality to you simply because the silence that you experience from God's side compels you to set aside more time for Him and to learn to know Him so much better than you ever did before. The choice is yours.

Heavenly Father, I praise You for the assurance that You will never forget about me, that You are always prepared to listen to my prayers. Thank You that, like the psalmist, I can cling to Your love and that I can find hope in the outcomes which You bring. Amen.

Look at Your Life

Dear friends, if our hearts do not condemn us, we have confidence before God (1 John 3:21).

We will receive the things that we ask of God in prayer, but there is a condition, writes John in his epistle: we must obey His commands and do what pleases Him.

Your way of living has a direct connection with the way in which God will answer your prayers – or not answer them. He gives His children what they ask for because they keep His commands and obey His instructions. But He also withholds answers to your prayers when He can see that you are not relying on Him. When God grew tired of the unfaithfulness of His people He said to them, "When you spread out your hands in prayer, I will hide My eyes from you; even if you offer many prayers, I will not listen" (Isa. 1:15).

Next time you pray and nothing happens, carefully consider if there is not possibly some unconfessed sin in your life. Sin has always resulted in a wall that separates you from God, a wall that hinders God from responding to your prayer requests.

So get rid of this hindrance so that you can communicate spontaneously with God again and experience His love and grace in your life. "If I had cherished sin in my heart, the Lord would not have listened; but God has surely listened and heard my voice in prayer" (see Ps. 66:18).

Heavenly Father, I see now that You have not answered my prayers because of my unconfessed sin. Please forgive me for my sins so that the communication channel between us can be opened up again. Amen.

Waiting Time

Out of the depths I cry to You, O LORD; O Lord, hear my voice. Let Your ears be attentive to my cry for mercy. I wait for the LORD, my soul waits, and in His word I put my hope (Psalm 130:1-2, 5).

In Psalm 130 the psalmist testifies that he called to God from the depths of his crisis. That he put his faith in God, trusted in Him and waited for the fulfillment of His Word. David is prepared to wait for God's answer.

When Jesus was on earth, one hundred and eighty three times trick questions were asked of Him and He only gave a direct answer to these questions on three occasions. The rest of the time He responded with another question, a parable or an example from which the answer could be deduced. He wanted people to work out the right answer for themselves using the guidelines according to which He lived and to apply the lessons that He had taught them.

In *Prayer* Philip Yancey writes that he views the times when he is struggling to pray and it feels to him as if the Lord is not listening as times of waiting. We are all in fact willing to wait – in a queue at the post office or shopping center or at the airport when a plane is delayed. When God delays in answering your prayers, you should, like the psalmist, be willing to wait for His answer. He will in His perfect time give you exactly the right answer.

Heavenly Father, I am sorry that sometimes I am so impatient when You do not answer my prayers immediately. Make me willing to fix my trust on You and be prepared to wait for Your answers. Amen.

Selfish Prayers

You want something but don't get it. You kill and covet, but you cannot have what you want. You quarrel and fight. You do not have, because you do not ask God. When you ask, you do not receive, because you ask with wrong motives, that you may spend what you get on your pleasures (James 4:2-3).

Years ago my husband entered a competition where he won a car. When we shared the wonderful news with my mother, she was not excited in the least. She quite calmly informed us that she had known all along that it would happen because she had prayed for us to win!

The more we told her that a person cannot ask the Lord to make them win a competition, the more she insisted that we needed the car more than any of the other people who had entered the competition!

There are some prayers that a person should quite simply never pray. If everyone who took part in a rugby or cricket match was to pray that their team should come through the match as victors, it would be impossible for all those prayers to be answered.

God does not answer prayers that revolve around yourself and your own advantage. When you pray you should always make sure that your prayers do not contain selfish elements and that you never pray "against" someone else. Also make sure that your prayers are honoring to God, that your relationship with Him is right and that He is the one who will get the glory when your prayer requests are granted.

Heavenly Father, please teach me to pray according to Your will, so that my prayers will never be selfish. Help me too, when You do answer my prayers, to always give You the honor. Amen.

God Knows Best

You have made known to me the path of life; You will fill me with joy in Your presence, with eternal pleasures at Your right hand (Psalm 16:11).

During the American Civil War Christians from both the north and the south were absolutely certain that God was on their side. In one of his best-known speeches, the American president, Abraham Lincoln, warned them that they should rather make sure that they were on God's side. He later requested the American people to use the traumatic time that followed the war to confess their sins and to make their relationship with Him right.

If God were to answer every little prayer that is directed at Him as the prayer thinks it should be answered, the whole world would be plunged into unprecedented chaos. Fortunately, God always knows best. He is omniscient and completely righteous and He answers your prayers in the way that benefits you most, even though His answer differs vastly from the answer that you really wanted.

For this reason it is necessary to accept God's answers to your prayers. It does not help to expect Him to give you answers about why He did not prevent a natural disaster or why – in spite of your prayers – He did not bring an end to the rampant crime in a country. God has a greater purpose in mind. And what He gives you as an answer to your prayers is always the best answer for you.

Heavenly Father, I praise You because You are omniscient and all-wise and that You always answer each one of my prayer requests in the very best way for me. Help me to accept Your answers because I believe that You know best. Amen.

rayer

Lord Jesus,
Teach me to pray in accordance with Your will,
just as You did so long ago for Your disciples.
I want to confess my many sins before You – please forgive me
so that the channels of communication between us can be opened.
I confess my absolute dependence on You
because without You I can do nothing.
Please forgive me for sometimes doubting You.
Thank You that I can know that You listen to each
one of my prayers, even though You do not answer
every single one the way I want.
Keep me so close to You that I will never be dissatisfied with
Your answers because I know for sure that Your answers to my prayers
are always for my best even when they differ vastly
from what I have asked You.
Make me willing to wait for Your answers
and teach me to get to know You better in the waiting times.
Keep me from praying selfish prayers and help me not only to ask
You for things but also to be willing to act.
I know that You are all-wise and absolutely righteous –
forgive me for sometimes questioning
Your wisdom because You do not always give me
what I ask; because You permit disasters
and tragedies and crime in the world.
Thank You for the assurance that You always know
best and that Your answers to my prayers
are the best answers for me.

Amen.

August

The Story of Two Sisters

This month we are going to focus on two women from the Bible whom every woman can identify with. Decide for yourself which one of the two you are most like: Are you a Mary who desired to spend time at the feet of Jesus, or a Martha who is continuously busy and on the go.

Somewhere between these two women lies the perfect balance which every woman should strive for in her life. The more you get to know Mary and Martha, the easier it will be for you to achieve this balance in your own life.

By the end of this month may you be better equipped and happier than ever before. May you be a woman who has learned to spend more time with Jesus, who prioritizes properly; a woman who chooses the best. I pray that you might be such a woman and that no one will ever take that away from you.

Two Sisters

As Jesus and His disciples were on their way, He came to a village where a woman named Martha opened her home to Him. She had a sister called Mary, who sat at the Lord's feet listening to what He said (Luke 10:38-39).

Jesus and His disciples often went to visit His friends Mary and Martha and their brother Lazarus in Bethany. When that happened, the whole house was all hustle and bustle – and the differences between the two sisters became clearly evident.

Martha, the homekeeping body, was extremely busy preparing for all the extra guests while her sister, Mary, calmly went and sat at the feet of Jesus and listened to Him. She made no effort to help the busy Martha. Martha was – understandably – not happy with this state of affairs. She complained to Jesus that He should order Mary to help her. But Jesus said, "Martha, Martha, you are worried and upset about many things, but only one thing is needed. Mary has chosen what is better, and it will not be taken away from her" (Luke 10:41-42).

While Martha was so concerned about unnecessary things, Mary had realized what was truly important. For her, fellowship with Jesus was much more important than providing for the needs of the distinguished guests.

What about you? Do the needs of the people in your house come first or are you like Mary, completely content at the feet of Jesus?

Lord, sometimes I wish that I had more time to spend at Your feet. Help me to be like Mary and each time choose what is best by making time to listen to Your voice. Amen.

Meet Mary

She had a sister called Mary, who sat at the Lord's feet listening to what He said (Luke 10:39).

In the story of Jesus' visit to Bethany Luke describes Mary with a few strokes of the pen. Mary was a dreamer. She did something unheard of for the time in which she lived: she risked sitting in the company of men to listen to Jesus. Ordinary women would never have done something like that – they, like Martha, would have been busy in the kitchen making sure everything was ready.

But Mary did not bother herself with the traditions of the time. She so desperately wanted to know and learn from Jesus that she simply made herself comfortable at His feet and listened to Him.

Perhaps she knew that Martha needed help, but chose to be still before Jesus. And Jesus – in contrast to what we or the other guests would have expected – approved of Mary. She was the one who chose what was better, He said.

What do you do when you are asked to choose between your busy schedule and your quiet time? Women of today are almost all as super busy as Martha. We not only have our households to manage, but also a husband and children who demand our time and more than likely a career outside the home.

All of us have need of the calm and peace that only Jesus can give us. The invitation in Matthew 11:28-29 is still addressed to you. Make ready use of it!

Lord Jesus, thank You for inviting me to come to You when I am tired and overburdened and that You offer me Your rest. I now want to accept Your invitation. Amen.

The Restless Martha

As Jesus and His disciples were on their way, He came to a village where a woman named Martha opened her home to Him. But Martha was distracted by all the preparations that had to be made (Luke 10:38, 40).

Martha was rushing around – she had a whole house full of important guests for whom she needed to prepare. And her lazy sister, Mary, was sitting with Jesus instead of helping her! There were so many things to be done – and so little time to do it all! With her request, Martha was trying to force Jesus to reprimand Mary, but He did not. Instead He acknowledged that Martha was busy and worried; He understood her problem but He knew that she was trying to do too many things too fast. It was not the things that Martha did that were the problem, but the way she did them.

Most women will probably see themselves in Martha's actions rather than in Mary's. Women of today have more to do than ever before in history. Most of us just do not have more time in our busy day for the things that really matter.

Like Martha we also often do not understand Jesus' way of doing things. We reckon He ought to be on our side and then discover that Jesus sets a higher premium on rest than on being busy.

Become still before Jesus. He knows you like He knew Martha. He knows how busy you are and how many things are expected from you – He wants to help you to do it all.

Lord Jesus, thank You very much for knowing all about me – also how rushed my life is. Make me restful; change my priorities so that I can spend more time with You. Amen.

Lord, Does It Not Bother You?

Martha was distracted by all the preparations that had to be made. She came to Him and asked, "Lord, don't You care that my sister has left me to do the work by myself? Tell her to help me!" (Luke 10:40).

Martha could not believe that Jesus did not care about her rushing around to get everything ready while her lazy sister just sat and listened to Him. It seemed to her as if Jesus did not care about her at all and yet all her busyness was actually for Him.

We sometimes think that the Lord does not notice everything we do for Him. We also like to question God as Martha did when things arise in our lives that we cannot understand. Like Job we try to get answers from God. At the end Job admitted that it had in fact been his portion of hardship that had caused him to see God in a different light.

When you are stressed and worried, it sometimes seems as if God does not really care about you. That it does not concern Him that you are going through such difficulties, that you are so sick, that you have to drag so many worries and responsibilities with you. Perhaps you too have asked God if He does not care that you are going through such difficulties. The answer to this question is a definite "Yes!" God cares for you so much that He was even willing to let His Son die so that You could have a relationship with Him.

Heavenly Father, I confess that like Martha I have also thought that my circumstances have left You cold. Thank You for Your assurance that You love me unconditionally. Amen.

Jesus Reaches a Conclusion

"Martha, Martha," the Lord answered, "you are worried and upset about many things, but only one thing is needed. Mary has chosen what is better, and it will not be taken away from her" (Luke 10:41-42).

Martha most likely thought that Jesus would approve of her actions, and for this reason she risked complaining to Him. But Jesus did not look at the fact that Mary was possibly trying to get out of work. He noticed her hungry heart. She had made a choice between being busy and spending time with Him. She did not worry about a lot of things, like her busy sister. There at Jesus' feet she got rid of her worries by listening to His wisdom and through working on her relationship with Him.

This story is not about doing (Martha) and being (Mary), but about the difference between the sisters, and the many things that put a demand on a woman's time and the one thing that is truly important.

Martha was busy with many things – and in the process she sacrificed the one thing (Jesus) that really mattered. Be careful that you do not become so occupied with your busy daily program that you let the best thing of all fall by the wayside.

Time with Jesus is always the best choice. If you present your day to Him early every morning and pray about the things that need to be done, He will time and time again give you the right solutions and also provide you with the strength for all that you need to do.

Heavenly Father, thank You that I can make time every morning to discuss my busy day's program with You and that every day I can experience the strength that You will give me and which I need to get through the day. Amen.

Fear and Worry

What I feared has come upon me; what I dreaded has happened to me.
I have no peace, no quietness; I have no rest, but only turmoil (Job
3:25-26).

When one calamity after another hit Job, he was shattered and confessed that all the things that he feared had happened to him.

If you are not careful, your many worries can become fears and these fears can later drain all peace from your life. We are also worried about many things: the rampant unrest and violence, inflation, children who are working overseas, old age that looms ahead with all the infirmities that go along with it.

One of my friends recently admitted how desperately she worries about her children – about the world in which they are growing up and all the things that could happen to them. But worries are fruitless. It would be so much better for you if you put all those worries down at Jesus' feet. "Cast all your anxiety on Him because He cares for you" is Peter's advice (1 Pet. 5:7).

Leave your worries and concerns right there at the feet of Jesus. Listen to how He speaks to you through His Word and talk to Him when you pray. It is unnecessary to stumble through life worried and trapped by fear. After all, you have the promise that He will care for you – even during the times of great danger – and that you are safe with Him. Furthermore, the future is not such a bad place when you love Him. Rather learn to trust in God right from the start.

Heavenly Father, thank You that I can bring each one of my concerns to You and can be sure that You will care for me in the future. Amen.

Let Go of Your Fears

There is no fear in love. But perfect love drives out fear, because fear has to do with punishment. The one who fears is not made perfect in love (1 John 4:18).

John says that the love of God drives out all fear. To just let go of your fears is perhaps easier said than done. Unfortunately, it does not always work like that. Yet there are more than three hundred and fifty Scripture verses in the Bible that say that the children of God do not need to be afraid.

While Karl Barth was preaching on 1 John 4:18 during the Second World War, bombs were dropped all around his small church. "If we enter the space of God's love, all fears are driven to the outside," he said in his sermon on that specific day.

If you continue to brood over your worries, they will definitely hatch into a batch of fears and worries. Most of us suffer from unnecessary fears because we do not put sufficient trust in God. I am guilty of this. While I was writing about how you should handle your fears, I was actually stressing about all sorts of unnecessary things! My husband always says that it is impossible for a person to both fear and have faith, but believe me, I manage to do that without even trying!

Martha probably had other fears apart from not managing to get all the work done on her own. It would be best for you if you could instead get used to exchanging your fears for time at the feet of Jesus.

Lord Jesus, I am sorry that I still so often stress about unnecessary things, that I am afraid of so many things that will most probably never happen. From now on I want to exchange my problems for time with You. Amen.

Advice for Your Worries!

Do not be anxious about anything, but in everything, by prayer and petition, with thanksgiving, present your requests to God. And the peace of God, which transcends all understanding, will guard your hearts and your minds in Christ Jesus (Philippians 4:6-7).

God knows your thoughts. He knows exactly what you are worried about even before you tell Him. According to statistics, you can do nothing about seventy percent of the things you are worried about. A recent American survey about women's worries have found that forty percent of the things we worry about will never happen; thirty percent of our worries are about the past which we can do nothing about; twelve percent of our worries are about the criticisms of other people which are mostly untrue. Only eight percent of all worries are about real problems that can be satisfactorily solved.

There are three steps that you can follow to avoid worry :

1. Do not worry about anything
2. Pray about everything
3. Be thankful for all things.

The only way in which you can carry out the first step is to let go of your worries – you can do this by obeying the second step – by praying about them. Nothing is too big or too small to take to God. Change each one of your worries into prayers and experience the peace of God in your life. Lastly, you need to be thankful: Before you start worrying again, rather count your blessings.

With these three steps your worries should soon become something of the past!

Heavenly Father, I come to You about each one of my concerns and express my thankfulness to You. Amen.

Go Ahead and Ask!

The watchman replies, "Morning is coming, but also the night. If you would ask, then ask; and come back yet again" (Isaiah 21:12).

In this passage the prophet Isaiah is busy with a ruling from the Lord against Edom (Both Duma and Seir are regions within Edom). Someone asked the night watchman when the night would be over. At that moment it was still night, and it was the task of the watchman to announce the arrival of the dawn. The watchman answered that the morning was coming even though it was still night at the moment.

Martha wanted to know if Jesus did not care about her. We too sometimes have questions that we want to ask God. Go ahead and ask; God will answer your questions, but in His own time and in His own way. More than likely He will give you a different answer from the one you expected. If you sometimes wonder why at times things seem to go so completely wrong for you, you will not find any answers by pulling away in unbelief or by becoming angry with God. Rather find your answers by studying the Word, sitting at His feet and listening to His voice as Mary did, by spending quality time with Jesus.

God is still Immanuel, God with us, even though we know that life is not always fair. Therefore, let go of your doubts and fears and discover how much He really cares for you.

Heavenly Father, thank You very much for the invitation that I can bring all my doubts to You. It is wonderful to know that each time I can come and ask You again, until You give me the right answer at the right time. Amen.

Battling to Sleep

I lie down and sleep; I wake again, because the Lord *sustains me. I will not fear the tens of thousands drawn up against me on every side (Psalm 3:5-6).*

The older I get, the more uneasily I sleep. These days I wake up a few times in the middle of the night, and then cannot for anything in the world, fall asleep again. I catch myself using this time of wakefulness to think about my worries. If you are in the same boat, you can – as I now do – readily follow the advice of Psalm 3: You can sleep peacefully at night with the knowledge that God is with you; and that He is protecting you. He will answer your prayers and will guarantee you a peaceful night's rest and a tranquil awakening.

Remember that the Lord is always available – He does not slumber or sleep, writes the psalmist (see Psalm 121:3-4). Go ahead and talk to Him the next time you struggle to fall asleep. If you belong to God, you need never lie awake at night and worry about dozens of things that you can in any case do nothing about.

Be at rest with the Lord when you go to bed. And if you, like Job, find that the things you fear do indeed seem to happen, it is not the end of the world. God is still with you and undertakes to care for you. He really wants you to take each one of your worries to Him.

Heavenly Father, I praise You for the promise that I can sleep peacefully at night with the sure knowledge that You are with me, that You will care for me and will take each one of my concerns on Your shoulders. Amen.

Peace for You

The peace of God, which transcends all understanding, will guard your hearts and your minds in Christ Jesus. Whatever you have learned or received or heard from me, or seen in me – put it into practice. And the God of peace will be with you (Philippians 4:7, 9).

If you bring your problems to Jesus at night, lay them at His feet, pray for them and thank Him for every blessing; He will not only give you a good night's rest, but He will also offer you His peace. As soon as you accept the peace of God into your life, your thoughts will automatically begin to line up – then you will no longer think about your many worries, but will be at peace because you know that God will take care of you.

If you long for this peace in your own life, follow the advice of Paul in Philippians 4:8. Focus your thoughts on the right things. From now on you need not only learn to do what is right, but also to think what is right. In Isaiah 26:3 it is written, "You will keep in perfect peace him whose mind is steadfast, because he trusts in You."

Do not any longer use your imagination to give substance to your worries, but focus on God. He loves you; He offers you His peace. He is Almighty and completely in control. The next time your peace is threatened by your fears, meditate on the promises of God that are recorded in His Word. Then calmly sit back and experience first hand how God's peace washes over your life.

Heavenly Father, thank You for the promise that Your peace will fill my life and will stand guard over my heart and mind. Please give me the peace and prosperity that You have promised, because I trust in You. Amen.

Only One Thing Is Needed

"Martha, Martha," the Lord answered, "you are worried and upset about many things, but only one thing is needed. Mary has chosen what is better, and it will not be taken away from her" (Luke 10:41-42).

In biblical times, women were not exactly regarded as spiritual beings – they were busy with house work and taking care of their families full time. The "one thing" that is needed and which Jesus speaks of, is not in fact cooking or cleaning the house – but knowing God and listening to His voice.

We do not know exactly what Martha did after she heard these words from Jesus – perhaps she carried on with her work, or maybe she went and sat next to Mary and listened to Jesus so that she could receive that one thing that she still lacked. I tend to think that she went on with getting all the work finished – she was not the type of person who would let her guests look after themselves.

On a later occasion when we read about Mary and Martha again, she is still busy being "serving Martha" and Mary is still spending time with Jesus – this time by washing His feet with expensive ointment and drying them with her hair (see John 12:2-7).

If you are a busy housewife like Martha, make sure that you get your priorities straight. Make sure that you always set aside enough time for the one thing that is really necessary – learning to know God better.

Heavenly Father, I know that time with You is more necessary for me than managing my household. Please help me never to neglect You because I have too much to do. Amen.

Are You Busy Listening?

Indeed, to them you are nothing more than one who sings love songs with a beautiful voice and plays an instrument well, for they hear your words but do not put them into practice. When all this comes true – and it surely will – then they will know that a prophet has been among them (Ezekiel 33:32-33).

It does not help if you – like Mary – set aside special time to sit at the feet of Jesus, but you are not prepared to listen to what He has to say to you. And even listening is not actually enough – you need to be prepared to do the things that God asks you to do.

The Lord was not at all happy with the Israelites in Ezekiel's time who listened to the prophet but did nothing of what they were asked to do. The prophet who delivered the message of God to them was like someone with a beautiful voice singing songs full of desire.

It is important for you to make time for God, to listen to His voice and to obey His commands before the message of Jesus will take root in your life.

Martha was eventually prepared to listen to Jesus. When we read of her again it is clear that she has experienced a spiritual deepening. She is still practicing her talent – hospitality – but this time in a far more relaxed way. And this time she does not try to convince Mary to come and help her.

Heavenly Father, please forgive me for listening to Your voice but then not obeying Your commands. Help me to listen and obey You. Amen.

Give Your Day to God

Commit to the LORD whatever you do, and your plans will succeed.
In his heart a man plans his course, but the LORD determines his steps
(Proverbs 16:3, 9).

The reason why the overwhelming majority of women today are so tired and overburdened is because we try to do too many things at once. Each woman has received personal gifts from God and the things that you ought to be doing for Him will always fall into the area of your gifts. If you really do not like cooking, but love arranging flowers, it is not necessary to help your congregation with the catering. Rather offer to arrange flowers for the church.

Be careful not to overstrain yourself – you do not have to do all the work yourself. It is possible to be so busy with the work of the Lord that the Lord Himself is neglected because you do not have enough time left to spend with Him.

One thing is necessary, said Jesus to Martha: Yield all that you do to the Lord and allow Him to guide you in these things. Each morning present your agenda to God piece by piece and listen diligently to His voice when you read the Bible. Plan your day with God beside you and don't attempt to do a dozen things at the same time any longer – first finish one thing before you begin the next one. God will clearly show you what His will is for you on a specific day.

Lord, I now want to give the day ahead of me to You and ask You to help me with everything that I need to do today. Please show me what Your will is for my day. Amen.

A Spirit-Controlled Life

So I say, live by the Spirit, and you will not gratify the desires of the sinful nature. Since we live by the Spirit, let us keep in step with the Spirit (Galatians 5:16, 25).

In *Having a Mary heart in a Martha World* Joanna Weaver writes that Jesus was not concerned about Martha's external gifts; it was her internal flaws that He wondered about. The dark corners of pride and prejudice, the spiritual handicap of busyness that left her unable to enjoy the intimacy of His presence.

You do not need to prove yourself to inherit the kingdom of God, you also do not need to tackle the work of God in your own strength. He will give you the strength so that you will be able to do all the things that He asks of you. But there is also "one thing" necessary for you – that you surrender your whole life to the control of the Spirit. No one can do everything, but it is completely within your power to do the things that God has committed to you.

If you are prepared to do so you can spend the rest of your days under the blanket of God's love and feel how that love enfolds you moment by moment (see Ps. 32:10).

Heavenly Father, I no longer want to try to live the life that You have asked me to on my own – I am prepared to surrender my life to the control of Your Spirit so that in future He can determine my actions. Amen.

At Home with God

"If anyone loves Me, he will obey My teaching. My Father will love him, and We will come to him and make Our home with him" (John 14:23).

God really desires to make Himself at home in your life. In *The Great House of God* Max Lucado writes that, "God has no interest in being a weekend getaway or a Sunday bungalow or a summer cottage. Don't consider using God as a vacation cabin or eventual retirement home. He wants you under His roof now and always. He wants to be your mailing address, your point of reference; He wants to be your home."

Martha was rushing around in a frenzy in an attempt to please Jesus but Jesus was more pleased with Mary who sat at His feet. Sometimes we miss an encounter with Jesus because we are too busy. If you do not, like Mary, make time to listen to His voice, if you are not willing to sit at His feet, He will speak to you less and less. Rather follow the example of Mary and set aside special time to be with Him each morning. Even if you are extremely busy you will get more done after you have spent time with Jesus than ever before.

God longs for you to feel as comfortable as Mary did with Him – and even more, He also wants to feel at home in your house and your life. Jesus wants to meet with you every day in your inner room so that you can get to know Him better and better, because He loves you very much. Do not let Him wait for you in vain.

Lord Jesus, thank You that You want to make Your home with me – help me to make enough time for You in my busy program. Amen.

Do Your Housework for the Lord

Whatever you do, whether in word or deed, do it all in the name of the Lord Jesus, giving thanks to God the Father through Him (Colossians 3:17).

Brother Lawrence was a French monk who lived in the seventeenth century. He hated working in the kitchens of the monastery. Yet gradually Brother Lawrence discovered that he could serve God just as well behind the pots and pans as in the monastery itself. When his attitude toward his work changed, it became a joy to him. After his death his letters were published in a small book entitled *The Practice of the Presence of God.* In it he wrote that the things that we usually do for ourselves should from now on be done for God.

Jesus did not reprimand Martha because she was working, but because her work was irritating her. For this reason most housewives are usually more sympathetic with the busy Martha than with Mary who sat at the feet of Jesus and listened to Him.

Like Martha, we also wonder why we have to do the work and why no one will help us prepare the food, clean up or wash the dishes. Like Martha, we also sometimes become annoyed in front of the stove when the rest of the family are sitting and chatting comfortably in the living room. However, if you, in the future, do the housework that irritates you for God, you can transform your household drudgery into an act of worship so that your housework will no longer be a cross to you, but a daily joy in which you can experience the presence of God.

Lord, from now on I want to work for You so that even burdensome chores will become a joy for me. Amen.

He Who Loves You

Now a man named Lazarus was sick. He was from Bethany, the village of Mary and her sister Martha. So the sisters sent word to Jesus, "Lord, the one you love is sick" (John 11:1, 3).

The lives of the two sisters and their brother, Lazarus, definitely changed from the time that Jesus came into their house. A strong friendship developed among them. Then Lazarus fell ill. More than likely it was the worried Martha who sent for Jesus, full of faith that He would quickly come and heal her beloved brother. She sent a message to Jesus, "He whom you love is sick," and then confidently waited for Jesus to arrive to heal her brother.

But Jesus lingered – and Lazarus became sicker. The initial confidence of the sisters had now possibly turned to confusion – they could not understand why Jesus did not come. And then Lazarus died, and Mary and Martha's house of cards tumbled to the ground. They had trusted Jesus to make everything right, but it did not happen. Women in Jesus' time could not easily manage without the care of a man. Martha and Mary had now not only lost their beloved brother and caregiver, but also possibly their faith and trust in Jesus.

When disasters come knocking on your front door, your faith can so easily slip out of the back door. Jesus does not always respond the way you expect Him to. If this should happen to you, make sure that doubt does not overwhelm you and that you do not blame Jesus for it.

Lord, sometimes like Martha and Mary, I cannot understand why You do not act as I expect You to. Teach me to never doubt You. Amen.

When Jesus Delays

Jesus loved Martha and her sister and Lazarus. Yet when He heard that Lazarus was sick, He stayed where He was two more days (John 11:5-6).

The expectation of Jesus' disciples was doubtless the same as that of Martha and Mary. They knew that Jesus placed a high premium on friendship and they had absolutely no doubt that He would immediately set out for Bethany to go and heal Lazarus. But they were also confused by Jesus' response to the message, "This sickness will not end in death. No, it is for God's glory so that God's Son may be glorified through it" (John 11:4).

Jesus remained where He was for two more days before He left for Bethany (see John 11:5). And yet He insisted that He loved Lazarus and his sisters. This does not look like the actions of someone who loves. When Jesus eventually arrived in Bethany, Lazarus was already dead and buried.

Sometimes we wonder why God did not prevent the Fall that messed up so many things in our world. But Jesus always leaves the choice up to us about whether we want to obey Him or the Devil. The latter still creates chaos in our lives, even though we belong to God.

We find it hard to understand the plan of God for our lives. Through hardship, however, His plan becomes clearer to us piece by piece as time goes by.

Lord, sometimes I struggle to understand Your plan for my life. Help me to be prepared to wait when You delay and do not answer my prayers immediately. Amen.

The Chisel of Pain

If you suffer for doing good and you endure it, this is commendable before God. To this you were called, because Christ suffered for you, leaving you an example, that you should follow in His steps (1 Peter 2:20-21).

You should never doubt the fact that Jesus loves you, but He looks ahead to the full picture of your life and is aware of things that you cannot see. In this way it is often the things that are the hardest for you to accept that in the long run bring about the greatest spiritual blessings in your life: It is precisely the things that you do not understand that reveal the glory of God in your life.

The next time you struggle to understand the actions of God, when you cannot see why He has interwoven so many threads of suffering into your life's pattern, you can still trust Him. He knows best. The momentary portion of hardship will eventually lead to His glory. Jesus had a far greater plan for Lazarus in mind than simple healing.

God always has a plan even if it often differs vastly from our plans – even if it sometimes makes us question the love of God for us. We too are confused when God acts differently from the way we expect Him to. Hold fast to the love Jesus has for you; it is the things that you cannot understand that God uses as His instrument to form you into the image of His Son. The pain in your life always works like a chisel to make you even more like Jesus.

Lord Jesus, thank You for the assurance that my momentary pain will lead to Your glory because it will make me more like You. Amen.

The New Martha

"Lord," Martha said to Jesus, "if You had been here, my brother would not have died. But I know that even now God will give You whatever You ask" (John 11:21-22).

Like on the previous occasion when we met Martha, she has a house full of people. Bethany was very close to Jerusalem and many Jews went to Martha and Mary to comfort them about the passing away of their brother (see verse 19).

This time, it is actually Mary who stays in the house and Martha who forgot her guests and went out to meet Jesus. She did not try to hide her heartache from Jesus but told Him straight, "Lord, if You had been here, my brother would not have died." The deepening that Martha had experienced in her faith is clearly audible in her declaration, "But I know that even now God will give You whatever You ask."

Martha accepted the promise of Jesus that Lazarus would rise from the dead but she did not clearly understand what Jesus was actually saying to her. She thought that this resurrection would in fact take place much later – that she would see the promise of Jesus fulfilled that same day had not even entered her mind. And yet her words were a confession: She believed that Jesus could do what needed to be done and she also believed that He was the long awaited Messiah.

Martha could only have gained this new insight into the person and work of Jesus if her relationship with Him had grown as intimate as that of Mary's.

Lord Jesus, like Martha, I want to work on my relationship with You and set aside more time for You. Amen.

Jesus – the Resurrection and the Life

Jesus said to her, "I am the resurrection and the life. He who believes in Me will live, even though he dies; and whoever lives and believes in Me will never die. Do you believe this?" (John 11:25-26).

Martha rightfully says to Jesus that Lazarus would not have died if He had come on time. She had most probably often seen Him heal sick people. She also understood that people would one day rise from the dead to be with Jesus forever. But what Jesus planned to do was completely outside her field of experience – and also outside the experience of the people who were gathered in her house.

Jesus promised that everyone who believed in Him would live forever. This promise is still valid for each one of us today. The end of a believer's life is actually the beginning of his true life. When they experienced the meaning of the words of Jesus first hand, Martha and Mary were in for a huge surprise – they saw with their own eyes how Lazarus literally rose from the dead. And all the mourners who had gathered at their house were witnesses of this miracle. Many of them believed in Jesus after this.

It is and will always be hard to lose someone you love; but we know that one day Christians will see each other again in heaven. You will suffer hardships on earth, you still need to walk through the valley of the shadow of death, but you can believe with great certainty that the glory of the resurrection waits for you on the other side of that dark valley (see 1 Cor. 15:55).

Lord Jesus, I praise You that You came to take the sting out of death so that because I believe in You I need never die. Amen.

August 23

Mary and Jesus

After she had said this, she went back and called her sister Mary aside. "The Teacher is here," she said, "and is asking for you" (John 11:28).

When she had finished speaking to Jesus, Martha went and called her sister and told her that Jesus wanted to see her. It is interesting to note that this time it was Martha who went out to meet Jesus and Mary who stayed inside the house.

As was her habit, Mary knelt at Jesus' feet. Like her sister, she also did not hide her heartache from Jesus but confessed, "Lord, if You had been here, my brother would not have died" (John 11:32).

Mary knew only too well that it was irrevocably too late to heal Lazarus. There was absolutely no doubt that he was dead. It was humanly impossible that Jesus could at this point still make any difference. But Mary was wrong! Jesus was not just any person, He was God Himself – that very God for whom nothing is impossible. When Jesus saw the sincerity of Mary's heart He was deeply moved and He wept with her. The words "Jesus wept" highlights for us the intense involvement Jesus has with the pain of His children (see John 11:35).

When you are going through hardships, Jesus still weeps with you. He really cares for His children. But He also expects you to do the same; to be prepared to mourn with other Christians who are grieving (Rom. 12:12).

Lord Jesus, it is a comfort for me to know that You share in my heartache when I grieve. Help me to have the same kind of sympathy with other Christians. Amen.

Jesus Knows about Your Hardships

For we do not have a high priest who is unable to sympathize with our weaknesses, but we have one who has been tempted in every way, just as we are – yet was without sin (Hebrews 4:15).

Jesus is familiar with all our earthly sufferings. He knew that Mary and Martha were very sad about the death of their beloved brother, and He was so involved in their grieving that He wept with them.

Because Jesus was Himself human just like us, He personally experienced the whole spectrum of human emotions. He often experienced hardships, He knew poverty, He had to endure temptations ... He grew weary of the large number of people who crowded around Him, He became angry when His Father's house was used as a marketplace. He also experienced human emotions: His disciples disappointed Him, the people whom He had come to save rejected Him and allowed Him to be crucified. He experienced heartache and fear in Gethsemane as well as complete loneliness on the cross when even His Father who had until then always been with Him, forsook Him.

When these kinds of emotions cross your life, Jesus knows exactly how you feel, and He promises to be with you and to help you stay standing, to never leave you. Even when you have to go through the valley of the shadow of death He will still walk with you – and one day He will be the first one to welcome you into heaven!

Lord Jesus, thank You so much that You experienced every human emotion and thus know exactly how I feel when I am sad or go through hard times. I praise You for the promise that You will always be with me in these situations. Amen.

Jesus at the Tomb of Lazarus

"Take away the stone," He said. "But, Lord," said Martha, the sister of the dead man, "by this time there is a bad odor, for he has been there four days." Then Jesus said, "Did I not tell you that if you believed, you would see the glory of God?" (John 11:39-40).

Lazarus had already been dead and buried for four days. It was humanly impossible for him to be alive again. Palestine is a very hot country, therefore the bodies of people who had died were already decomposing after four days. This was also the spontaneous response from the practical Martha when she heard Jesus ask for the grave to be opened, "Lord, by this time there is a bad odor, for he has been there four days."

Martha had faith for what could have been; "If you had been here, my brother would not have died" (see John 11:21). Martha had faith for what would be, "I know he will rise again" (John 11:24). What Martha needed was faith for what was happening now, writes Joanne Weaver in her book *Having a Mary Heart in a Martha World*.

Martha did not even consider the possibility that Jesus could raise her brother from the dead. When that happened she experienced the revelation of the power of God first hand. For the rest of her life she – and all the people who were present at the grave – would never again doubt the omnipotence of Jesus.

Lord Jesus, I worship You as the God who can do miracles. Please help me in those areas where I am still sometimes an unbeliever. Amen.

Jesus' Prayer

So they took away the stone. Then Jesus looked up and said, "Father, I thank You that You have heard Me. I knew that You always hear Me, but I said this for the benefit of the people standing here, that they may believe that You sent Me" (John 11:41-42).

Here Jesus is doing exactly what Paul advises the church in Philippi to do, "In everything, by prayer and petition with thanksgiving, present your requests to God" (Phil. 4:6). He had absolutely no doubt that Lazarus would rise from the dead. He believed so completely that His Father would answer His prayer that He thanked Him for answering His prayer even before it had actually happened! And God brought about a mighty miracle in answer to His Son's prayer. Before the eyes of the amazed spectators, Lazarus came walking out of the tomb with the grave clothes still wrapped around him. I can just imagine how joyful Martha and Mary were and how their faith and trust in Jesus had been strengthened through this miracle. They would never doubt Him again.

In the future try to pray as Jesus did – take God at His word – He knows exactly what you have need of, and He undertakes to give it to you as long as it is in line with His will for your life. Learn to trust Him so completely that you thank Him for answering your prayers even before they come to pass.

Heavenly Father, thank You that You know exactly what I need before I ask You for it. Help me to place my trust so firmly in You that I too will thank You even before You have answered my prayer. Amen.

God Knows What You Need

"So do not worry, saying, 'What shall we eat?' or 'What shall we drink?' or 'What shall we wear?' For the pagans run after all these things, and your heavenly Father knows that you need them" (Matthew 6:31-32).

When the disciples of Jesus urged Him to teach them to pray, He told them that they did not need to use a flood of words in their prayers. God knew exactly what they had need of even before they could ask Him for it (see Matt. 6:8).

For this reason you do not have to be worried about tomorrow and wonder if you will have enough to eat or to wear. Your heavenly Father already knows that you need all these things. In the Sermon on the Mount Jesus said that the people should look at the birds and the lilies of the field – the birds did not sow or reap but God still cared for them. We admire the beauty of the lilies – but not even Solomon in all his majesty was clothed like one of them. If God cares so well for the flowers and the animals He will do so much more for the people who love Him.

You cannot add even one day to your life by worrying. Therefore, from now on seek the kingdom of God and His will first and then He will give you all the other things that you have need of.

Lord Jesus, I praise You because You know exactly what I need and that You care for me so well each day. I now want to seek Your kingdom first and Your will, believing that You will give me all the other things that I need. Amen.

Planning Jesus' Death

Therefore many of the Jews who had come to visit Mary, and had seen what Jesus did, put their faith in him. But the chief priests and Pharisees had given orders that if anyone found out where Jesus was, he should report it so that they might arrest Him (John 11:45, 57).

The people who had gathered together at Mary's house all saw how Jesus caused a dead man to live once again. It is understandable that the actual experience of such a miracle caused people to come to faith in Jesus. The chief priests and the Pharisees were not impressed with the fact that even more people now believed in Jesus. Caiaphas the high priest explained to the Jewish Council that it would be to their advantage if one man was allowed to die for the people. From that day on they were determined to kill Jesus and they began to plan how they could bring about His death.

It is ironic that it was as a result of the miracles of Jesus that the leaders wanted to kill Him, because they were afraid that He would gain too much influence with the people. The solution Caiaphas offered – that One person should die for the whole nation – was exactly why Jesus had come into the world. Another result was that the people of God who were spread across the world were brought together as one through the crucifixion of Jesus.

Jesus' crucifixion makes it possible for you to belong to God. Because He died in your place you can now be a child of God.

Lord Jesus, thank You so much that You were willing to die in my place so that the penalty for my sins has been paid for through Your death. Amen.

Mary's Extravagant Gift

Mary took about a pint of pure nard, an expensive perfume; she poured it on Jesus' feet and wiped His feet with her hair. And the house was filled with the fragrance of the perfume (John 12:3).

Here we meet Martha and Mary once again. Martha is as usual busy serving her guests, but this time she is calm and focused and has discovered her true calling as a hostess. Mary is still sitting at the feet of Jesus and listening to His voice – she is finely tuned in to Him and realizes that He is concerned about the path of suffering that lies ahead of Him. She does her best to comfort Him and to assure Him of her sympathy. She was prepared to give her best to Jesus.

She poured half a liter of very expensive nard over His feet and dried it with her hair. This was no ordinary little flask of perfume that Mary threw over the feet of Jesus. The value of the perfume was more than the wages of an average worker per year. Jesus could not help but see her love for Him and He said that she had anointed Him in advance for His burial.

Are you prepared to sacrifice your very best for Jesus? Like Mary you should be finely tuned to the voice of God. Listen to Him and be prepared to do the specific things for which He has placed you on the earth. Gather your gifts together and surrender them to God. In this way you will succeed in living out your calling.

Lord Jesus, from now on I want to be as finely tuned in to You as Mary was; I want to listen to Your voice and come to offer You my all. Amen.

Judas's Agenda

One of His disciples, Judas Iscariot, who was later to betray Him, objected, "Why wasn't this perfume sold and the money given to the poor? It was worth a year's wages." He did not say this because he cared about the poor but because he was a thief; as keeper of the money bag, he used to help himself to what was put into it (John 12:4-6).

This time it was Judas who had a problem with Mary. He was shocked that she had wasted so much money and suggested that the very expensive perfume should have been sold and the money given to the poor. And it seems as if the rest of the disciples agreed with him ... More than likely Judas made his decision to betray Jesus straight after this incident. He could see that Jesus was not planning on becoming the king of the Jews who would free the people from the rule of the Romans. Therefore, he devised his own plan to get hold of something more for himself (Mark 14:10-11).

The thirty pieces of silver – that Judas asked for as a reward for betraying Jesus – was the cost of a slave. It was less than half the amount of money that Mary had so extravagantly poured over the feet of Jesus. "Where your treasure is, there your heart will be also," said Jesus in His Sermon on the Mount (Matt. 6:21). It is clear that Mary's heart was with Jesus – she was prepared to give everything to Him. Judas, on the other hand, was the one who looked after the disciples' money and John tells that he took some of the contributions for himself.

Judas's end was horrific. When he could not undo his deed he committed suicide.

Heavenly Father, help me to think about my own possessions and money in the right way so that it will never become more important to me than You. Amen.

Mary Will Be Remembered

"Leave her alone," Jesus replied. "It was intended that she should save this perfume for the day of My burial. You will always have the poor among you, but you will not always have Me" (John 12:7-8).

Through Mary's unselfish giving of herself, Jesus clearly understood that she was the only one who had noticed His anguish. His disciples who had worked with Him every day for three years had not seen how tense He was over His approaching crucifixion.

But Mary realized that Jesus was not Himself, and with her act of love she anointed Him ahead of time for His burial. Jesus was now standing at the beginning of His path of suffering. After this came His wrestling in prayer in Gethsemane, His torment by the soldiers, His trial and finally His crucifixion.

With her unselfish act Mary made the way of suffering for Jesus a little easier. She also ensured through this that she would be remembered forever wherever the message of Jesus is preached. Jesus Himself testified, "When she poured this perfume on my body, she did it to prepare Me for burial. I tell you the truth, wherever this gospel is preached throughout the world, what she has done will also be told, in memory of her" (Matt. 26:12-13).

Mary will always be remembered for what she did for Jesus to make His last days on earth easier. Her act of love continues to remind us that the first command – to love God above all else – really is the first command.

Heavenly Father, help me to show my love for You through the things that I do for You. I really want to live in such a way that people will see that I love You above all else, like Mary did. Amen.

Prayer

Lord Jesus,
thank You that this month I got to walk
in the footsteps of Martha and Mary.
I realize that I need to make more time to sit at Your feet
and listen to Your voice. You know that I am busy,
but please help me to get my priorities straight
and to choose the one thing that is truly important –
spending time with You
and learning to know You better.
From now on I really want to do the chores that frustrate
me as if I am doing them for You. Sometimes I, like Martha,
think that You do not notice my hardships,
but now I realize that You know about all my fears and worries
and that I can freely bring them to You.
Please give me Your peace and help me be prepared to obey You.
I really want to present my day to You and ask for Your help.
I want to surrender the control of my life
to Your Spirit. When it feels as if You are delaying
in answering my prayers help me be prepared
to wait for Your answer.
Thank You that You are also the resurrection and the life;
that I have Your assurance that I will one day
live with You forever;
that You are my comfort when I'm sad and that You know
exactly what I have need of.
Make me extravagant in my love for You
so that from now on I will be prepared
to offer my whole life to You.

Amen.

September

Spiritual Growth

In South Africa spring comes in September and always brings new growth.

Whatever month you celebrate spring in, it always offers an opportunity to examine our own growth as Christians. Christians should not stay the same – it is necessary for us to grow daily in our faith and become stronger.

Paul gave the church in Colosse a flop-proof recipe for spiritual growth, "So then, just as you received Christ Jesus as Lord, continue to live in Him, rooted and built up in Him, strengthened in the faith as you were taught, and overflowing with thankfulness" (Col 2:6-7).

True spiritual growth results in real improvement in one's lifestyle. It is in fact spiritual growth because it includes the fruit of the Spirit, the difficult values such as patience and self-control that take a lifetime to develop. The experience can take place in a moment, but living it out takes much time and effort.

Return to the Lord

At the king's command, couriers went throughout Israel and Judah with letters from the king and from his officials, which read: "People of Israel, return to the Lord, the God of Abraham, Isaac and Israel, that He may return to you. For the Lord your God is gracious and compassionate. He will not turn His face from you if you return to Him" (2 Chronicles 30:6, 9).

King Hezekiah appealed to the unfaithful people of God to return to Him. If they were prepared to do this, God would also return to them, he said. And the people were willing to listen to the king: The result of Hezekiah's appeal was that the people of Israel renewed their covenant with God. They broke down the heathen altars where in the past sacrifices had been made to idols and once again brought their sacrifices to God. The feast of unleavened bread was celebrated for fourteen days and the whole nation praised God (verses 21-22). The relationship between God and His covenant people was eventually restored. The priests and Levites declared a blessing over the people and they were all filled with joy. "The priests and the Levites stood to bless the people, and God heard them, for their prayer reached heaven, His holy dwelling place" (verse 27).

The very first step to spiritual growth is for you to turn back to God because a restored relationship with God always results in growth. Draw close to God and He will draw near to you, promises James (James 4:7). Do not delay any longer!

Heavenly Father, I want to come back to You and restore my re-lationship with You so that in this month I will grow spiritually and become stronger. Amen.

A Glorious Promise

"For I know the plans I have for you," declares the Lord, *"plans to prosper you and not to harm you, plans to give you hope and a future. Then you will call upon Me and come and pray to Me, and I will listen to you. You will seek Me and find Me when you seek Me with all your heart. I will be found by you," declares the* Lord *(Jeremiah 29:11-14).*

Through the mouth of the prophet Jeremiah, God delivers a beautiful message to His people who were in exile. If they were willing to return to Him, He would give them a hope for the future. He would answer their prayers. The people would then know His will and would meet with Him, if they sought Him with their whole heart.

Jeremiah's beautiful promise is still meant for you today. If you are willing to make a U-turn back to God today (and that is precisely what is meant by repentance) He will be there for you. In fact, He is already waiting impatiently to show His mercy to you. He wants to give you new hope; He is planning only the best for you: to prosper you and not to harm you. He wants to offer you a new future, one to be eagerly anticipated! Do not wait any longer to walk away from your wrong way of life, and to turn to God. He has never yet turned anyone away who has turned to Him. Accept God's invitation right now.

Lord God, I want to turn back to You now. Thank You for the prosperity that You have planned for me, for the heavenly future that You have prepared for me. I now want to accept Your invitation and invite You into my life. Amen.

A New Person

To be made new in the attitude of your minds; and to put on the new self, created to be like God in true righteousness and holiness (Ephesians 4:23-24).

Nature renews itself in spring and for you to be renewed you need to stop living according to your old life. "You were taught, with regard to your former way of life, to put off your old self, which is being corrupted by its deceitful desires," is the advice Paul gives to the church in Ephesus (Eph. 4:22). *The Message* says, "Everything – and I do mean everything – connected to the old way of life has to go. It's rotten through and through. Get rid of it! And then take on an entirely new way of life – a God-fashioned life, a life renewed from the inside and working itself into your conduct as God accurately reproduces His character in you."

People who have put on the new self are people who have undergone a change of heart and from this it is only natural that a change in lifestyle will flow. A person who is made new no longer lives as he wants to live, but subjects his own desires and interests to what God is asking of him.

You will more than likely find it hard to break with your old way of life. It is not easy to distance yourself from old bad habits, but it is possible and God promises to give you the strength you need to do so.

Heavenly Father, I now come to You to take off my old, sinful nature. Please make it possible for me to undergo a complete change of attitude, so that I can become new like the new growth of spring. Amen.

Guidelines for the New Self

Be imitators of God, therefore, as dearly loved children and live a life of love, just as Christ loved us and gave Himself up for us as a fragrant offering and sacrifice to God (Ephesians 5:1-2).

People who have been made new and who have put on the new self do not only need new clothes, but also new guidelines. Our new life should make us look more and more like God; we should from now on surrender ourselves completely to Him. In his letter to the Ephesians, Paul sets out clear guidelines according to which people in Christ ought to behave: they need to speak the truth; they may not remain angry; thieves need to stop stealing and make an honest living, no bad language is to be used and people ought not be bitter, volatile or irate.

We should also no longer grieve the Holy Spirit who lives in us, but should treat one another well as Christians and deal properly with one another. We should also overlook the faults people make, just as God does with us.

Make a list of all the guidelines that are mentioned here that are still lacking in your own life and then set to work to obey them. If you are willing to allow the searchlight of this portion of Scripture to fall on your own life and get rid of all the things that are mentioned here, you will not be able to help but become spiritually stronger each day.

Lord, I truly want to live like a new person. Please show me the things in my life that I still need to get rid of, and then please give me the strength to do it. Amen.

Children of Light

You were once darkness, but now you are light in the Lord. Live as children of light (for the fruit of the light consists in all goodness, righteousness and truth) (Ephesians 5:8-9).

The children of light whom Paul is talking about here are the people who have left the dark life of sin behind them and have crossed over into a new life in the light of the Lord. These people ought not to continue in their old, troubled relationships any longer. From now on they are children of the light who ought to live like people of the light and do all things openly. What this means, Paul explains at length in verse 10-11, "Find out what pleases the Lord. Have nothing to do with the fruitless deeds of darkness, but rather expose them." Children of light should live carefully, make the best use of their opportunities and time, and should be filled with the Holy Spirit. Furthermore, children of light are prepared to work at the troubled relationships in their lives – not only on their relationship with God, but also their relationships with their fellow human beings. Children of light should be thankful at all times.

After Paul had written down the guidelines for a new life in Christ for the people of Ephesus (see Eph. 4:25-5:5) he highlighted three relationships in which children of light should be living differently than before. We will focus on each of these in the next few days.

Lord, make me into a child of the light who will from now on do all that is good and right and true: Help me to expose sin and be willing to work on my relationships with other people. Amen.

Live Differently in Your Marriage

Submit to one another out of reverence for Christ. Wives, submit to your husbands as to the Lord. Husbands, love your wives, just as Christ loved the church and gave Himself up for her (Ephesians 5:21-22, 25).

Spiritual growth always takes place in our relationships with other people. One of the most important relationships that we ought to focus on is our marriage relationship. The very first area then in which the new self should come to the fore, is in marriage. Marriage partners first need to be submitted to God and then to one another. Submission does not mean the rulership of one over the other, but rather a sense of being there for one another.

Christian women need to submit to their husbands through willingly honoring the role of leadership that God Himself has awarded to men. Husbands are also reminded that they need to love their wives with the same kind of unselfish, sacrificial love that Christ showed to His church. The purpose of this kind of love is always to bring glory to God.

How are things going with your marriage? Are you and your husband both submitted to God? Can you honestly say that you support your husband's leadership role in your marriage, even with regard to your children? The two most important building blocks in a marriage are love and honesty towards one another. This love and honesty must be based on the love and honesty between Christ and His church.

Lord, thank You so much that You have given me a husband whom I can love – make me willing to support him in the leadership role that You have awarded to him. Amen.

Live Differently within Your Family

Children, obey your parents in the Lord, for this is right. Fathers, do not exasperate your children; instead, bring them up in the training and instruction of the Lord (Ephesians 6:1, 4).

One of the most difficult areas in which to live out your faith is within your family. Paul here exhorts the children of Christian parents to be obedient to their parents. He quotes the fifth commandment as his motivation, "'Honor your father and mother' – which is the first command with a promise – 'that it may go well with you and that you may enjoy long life on the earth'" (verses 2-3).

After this, he requests fathers, the men to whom God has given the role of leadership within the family: that they should be His representatives in their families and will behave in a reasonable way towards their children. Christian parents should nurture their children with the right discipline "in the Lord" and this nurturing should always take place in an environment of love.

God established the family system as part of His creation so that any member of a family can feel safe within it and can be prepared for life. So for true help in life we cannot loosen the family from the grip of God. Jesus Christ needs to rule in the family before it can function as an effective life unit. Make sure that your relationships with the members of your family always follow biblical guidelines. Ask the Lord to make you the kind of parent who will raise your children for Him.

Heavenly Father, thank You very much for the privilege of having a family that I can love. I pray that You will help me to be Your representative in my own family so that I can bring my children up according to the guidelines found in Your Word. Amen.

Live Differently in Your Workplace

Slaves, obey your earthly masters with respect and fear. Serve whole-heartedly, as if you were serving the Lord, not men. And masters, treat your slaves in the same way (Ephesians 6:5, 7, 9).

To a person who has put on the new self the usual borders between people that have been erected by things such as race and status are no longer applicable. All that should matter to us is Christ. Christians from all nations and churches can take hands and walk a path together. Paul first talks to the slaves. There are, of course, no longer slaves in the time in which we live, but there are employees. These people are encouraged to work for their employers as if they are doing their work for God Himself. The authority of the employer should be recognized by the employees and they ought always to do their work to the best of their ability.

For the owners (employers) Paul's message is that they need to handle their slaves (employees) with great responsibility, that they will always remember that they in turn are responsible to God and that all people are equal before Him.

If you are an employee, the message for you is that you need to do your work to the very best of your ability as if you are doing it for God. And if you are an employer, you must never exploit your employees. Treat them as you would like to be treated. Also always remember that you will eventually have to give an account to God.

Heavenly Father, thank You that You have given me a job through which I can earn my livelihood. Please help me to always do my work to the best of my abilities as if I am doing it for You. Amen.

Growth Comes from God

He has lost connection with the Head, from whom the whole body, supported and held together by its ligaments and sinews, grows as God causes it to grow (Colossians 2:19).

In spring we water our gardens, fertilize and plant the prettiest flower seeds, but we cannot make the plants grow, only God can bring the seeds to life. In the same way, it is also God who can awaken spiritual growth in His children.

"I planted the seed, Apollos watered it, but God made it grow" writes Paul to the church in Corinth (1 Cor. 3:6-7). The work that we do for God only gains meaning when He Himself blesses that work and when He causes the seedlings that we plant to grow.

To grow suggests that you will change. When you plant your flower bulbs in the autumn they are hard brown knobs. But when they push up their heads in spring they are at first green sprouts and later become beautiful, colorful flowers. If you want to grow spiritually, you will need to be prepared to change more and more until you eventually reveal the characteristics of Christ in your life. Only then will you "reach unity in the faith and in the knowledge of the Son of God and become mature, attaining to the whole measure of the fullness of Christ" (see Eph. 4:13).

Heavenly Father, while I watch the reawakening of nature outside, I pray that You will help me to grow spiritually, that I will change and will become more and more like Jesus. Amen.

The Right Root System

So then, just as you received Christ Jesus as Lord, continue to live in Him, rooted and built up in Him, strengthened in the faith as you were taught, and overflowing with thankfulness (Colossians 2:6-7).

Here Paul compares spiritual growth to a tree that grows vigorously because its roots are firmly planted in the soil. It gets the nutrients it needs in order to grow from the soil.

Spiritual growth in your own life is impossible if you are not connected to Christ. Just like an electric light cannot burn if it is not connected to a power source, a Christian cannot grow if he is not attached to Jesus. *The Message* states it well, "Let your roots go down into and draw up nourishment from Him."

The quickest way to cause a tree to die is to damage its root system. To grow spiritually and become stronger you need to be rooted in Jesus and to build on Him. Jesus Himself says in John 15 that no branch can bear fruit of its own if it does not stay connected to the vine, and so too with us if we do not remain in Him (see John 15:4).

A tree cannot grow if its roots are not strong and are unable to take sufficient food out of the earth. Without God you cannot grow and neither can you bear fruit.

Lord Jesus, I want to live very close to You. I want to be rooted in You and established in You so that I can receive sufficient food from You and so that You can cause me to grow. Amen.

Things of Eternal Value

Since, then, you have been raised with Christ, set your hearts on things above, where Christ is seated at the right hand of God (Colossians 3:1).

In this paragraph to the Christians in Colosse Paul is trying to change their way of thinking. It is his desire that they will be turned away from an obsession with the things of the world and move in the direction of a truly Christian outlook. With the "things above" he means things that have an eternal value. Every person is by nature sinful and earthbound. The things of this world remain very important to us and we place great value on them. In the Sermon on the Mount Jesus asked us to exchange our treasures on earth for heavenly treasures. In 1 Timothy 6:18 Paul expands on this, "Command them to do good, to be rich in good deeds, and to be generous and willing to share."

If you want to grow spiritually, you will need to commit yourself to consciously begin living a new kind of life, to get a brand-new value system. Paul testifies that he now regards as worthless those things that were once important to him (see Phil. 3:8). What things are particularly valuable to you? Think carefully about whether they are all truly things that will bring you closer to God. If not, make an effort from today on to live according to God's guidelines in His Word, to obey His will and to follow in the footsteps of Jesus every day.

Lord Jesus, from now on I want to act like someone who lives only for You. I want to reach for those things that are above, where You are, so that one day I will have sufficient treasure in heaven. Amen.

Learn to Think Right

*Set your minds on things above, not on earthly things. For you died,
and your life is now hidden with Christ in God (Colossians 3:2).*

Thoughts play an extremely important role in your life. No one does
or plans to do anything before he has first thought through the issue.
That is why the life of the person made new begins in the realm of
your thoughts. New people are those who have learned to think in
new ways. "Do not conform any longer to the pattern of this world,
but be transformed by the renewing of your mind. Then you will be
able to test and approve what God's will is – His good, pleasing and
perfect will" Paul advises the church in Rome (Rom. 12:2).

To the Ephesians Paul says, "be made new in the attitude of your
minds; and to put on the new self, created to be like God in true
righteousness and holiness" (Eph. 4:23-24). The secret is to consciously and deliberately fill your mind with thoughts of God; to
meditate on His attributes, His love for you, His wonders of creation.
If we bring our thoughts back to the Triune God again and again, we
will gradually give Him the central place not only in our inner most
being but also in our practical, everyday life.

Are you willing to let God change your way of thinking, so that
you will know what His will is? If so, then you can pray together
with the psalmist, "May the words of my mouth and the meditation
of my heart be pleasing in your sight" (Ps. 19:16).

*Heavenly Father, please teach me how to change my thoughts, how to
make them new so that I will not only be a new person but will also
think in a new way. Amen.*

Put to Death Earthly Things

Put to death, therefore, whatever belongs to your earthly nature: sexual immorality, impurity, lust, evil desires and greed, which is idolatry. Because of these, the wrath of God is coming (Colossians 3:5-6).

Paul admonishes the Colossians to get rid of the sinful practices that were still to be found amongst them. Because they had chosen Christ, they should now get rid of everything that did not line up with their new status as believers. It is interesting to see that he writes here of Christians and yet does not hesitate to mention by name the things that belong to their "earthly nature." It sounds weird that Christians could still be dissolute, impure, lustful and greedy. That there is anger, hate, envy and swearing to be found in their lives. Unfortunately it is true that no Christian is without sin. Spiritually stronger, we strive to be sinless because we want to be more like Jesus.

Go and spend some time thinking carefully about whether there are similar sins that you need to get rid of. Look at Galatians 5:22-23 to see what the life of a Spirit-filled Christian ought to look like. See the Word of God as a mirror and look at yourself through His eyes. What do your temper, your thought life and your relationships with other people look like? God expects you to break ties with the sin in your life and to live only for Him from now on.

Lord, I still fall so far short when I measure myself against Your standards. Please help me to recognize the wrong things in my life and to let go of them. Amen.

Live New!

Do not lie to each other, since you have taken off your old self with its practices and have put on the new self, which is being renewed in knowledge in the image of its Creator (Colossians 3:9-10).

The reason Christians need to get rid of their sinful habits from their pre-conversion time is because when they were born again they purposefully chose to live for Christ. This conversion process is not something that lasts for just a few days and then it's all over; it is a long process that will continue for the rest of your life. Day by day you are renewed more and more into the image of God. You are gradually becoming a "Paradise person", as God created Adam and Eve to be before the Fall. You are becoming more and more like Jesus, who is the perfect image of God. "The Son is the radiance of God's glory and the exact representation of His being" testifies the writer to the Hebrews (Heb. 1:3).

The more you become like Jesus the more you will reflect His glory in your own life. "We, who with unveiled faces all reflect the Lord's glory, are being transformed into His likeness with ever-increasing glory, which comes from the Lord, who is the Spirit" writes Paul (2 Cor. 3:18). Make sure that this will be true of you if you are willing to begin to live a new life.

Lord Jesus, I really want to break with my old, sinful habits and from now on live the life of a new person, who will be more like You every day. Please help me from now on to radiate Your glory. Amen.

Blueprint of the New Person

Therefore, as God's chosen people, holy and dearly loved, clothe yourselves with compassion, kindness, humility, gentleness and patience. Bear with each other and forgive whatever grievances you may have against one another. Forgive as the Lord forgave you (Colossians 3:12-13).

The Message beautifully describes what this new person, who is the end product of our spiritual growth, ought to look like:

You should "dress in the wardrobe God picked out for you: compassion, kindness, humility, quiet strength, discipline. Be even-tempered, content with second place, quick to forgive an offense. Forgive as quickly and completely as the Master forgave you. And regardless of what else you put on, wear love. It's your basic, all-purpose garment. Never be without it. Let the peace of Christ keep you in tune with each other, in step with each other. None of this going off and doing your own thing. And cultivate thankfulness. Let the Word of Christ – the Message – have the run of the house. Give it plenty of room in your lives. Instruct and direct one another using good common sense. And sing, sing your hearts out to God! Let every detail in your lives – words, actions, whatever – be done in the name of the Master, Jesus, thanking God the Father every step of the way" (see Col. 3:12-16).

Build your new life according to this plan, you can't go wrong!

Lord Jesus, thank You for the blueprint that You have given me according to which I can build my life. Please help me to have each of the qualities mentioned here in my own life. Amen.

The Bond That Keeps You Together

And over all these virtues put on love, which binds them all together in perfect unity (Colossians 3:14).

As a part of his blueprint for the person made new in Christ, Paul describes love as the bond that will bind believers together in perfect unity. Without this love we will never be able to be one like Jesus prayed for in His High Priestly prayer. Love for one another keeps believers close to each other. Christian love requires absolute loyalty to your fellow Christians: As children of God we need to remember the things that Jesus taught and apply them to our lives, we need to care for one another and be prepared to carry one another's burdens. And our love for one another should be modeled on the unconditional love Jesus has for us.

Love is the one distinguishing factor by which Christians can be identified. Without love in our lives we will never be able to make God smile. "Dear friends, let us love one another, for love comes from God. Everyone who loves has been born of God and knows God. Whoever does not love does not know God, because God is love," writes John (1 John 4:7-8). John further tells us in what way we should be living out the love of God, "Dear children, let us not love with words or tongue but with actions and in truth" (1 John 3:18).

Of all the Christian values, love is the most important. Spiritual growth cannot take place in the loneliness of your inner room. To live out your love, you need to be with other Christians.

Lord Jesus, I praise You because You first loved me. Please make it possible for me to live out Your love towards others. Amen.

In the Service of Christ

Since you know that you will receive an inheritance from the Lord as a reward. It is the Lord Christ you are serving (Colossians 3:24).

Here Paul is speaking to slaves who have repented. They should no longer work for their masters, but for the Lord. We too are in the service of Jesus if we belong to Him.

It was a very special experience for me to meet Henry Blackaby, the very well-known writer of the best-seller *Experiencing God*, at a book show in Johannesburg in August 2002. The absolute humility of this venerable writer struck me immediately. At this gathering we received two of his books as a gift and we asked him to sign them for us. Above his signature, he wrote, *His servant*.

Other distinguishing features of the renewed self are humility and the willingness to serve. You should be willing to be in the service of Jesus and do everything that you do as if you were doing it for Him. Offer the talents that He has given you in His service and do not always expect to be served, but rather be willing to serve others, as Jesus was. Make His credo your own, "Even the Son of Man did not come to be served, but to serve, and to give His life as a ransom for many" (Mark 10:45).

Heavenly Father, I want to prove my love for You and others through being humble and willing to serve. From now on I want to come and report for duty with You! Please show me where You need me in Your kingdom. Amen.

Walk with God

After he became the father of Methuselah, Enoch walked with God 300 years and had other sons and daughters. Enoch walked with God; then he was no more, because God took him away (Genesis 5:22, 24).

The life story of Enoch reads like a fairy tale. He was a God-fearing man who lived close to God. Day by day he walked on his road through life together with God, and then suddenly Enoch was not there any more because God had taken him away to be with Him.

Enoch lived so close to God that one day God simply came and took him away to heaven. And I am sure that Enoch is still walking together with God there on those golden streets!

In the first verse of Psalm 119 the psalmist says, "Blessed are they whose ways are blameless, who walk according to the law of the LORD." To walk with the Lord is a slow and continual journey.

When you wander with God you cannot remain in the same place. Therefore spiritual growth is a daily wandering together with God – not only when you have your quiet time but all through the course of the day. Make sure that you walk with God every day so that you can learn to know Him better and will love Him even more.

Heavenly Father, like Enoch of old, I want to walk with You every day so that I will learn to know You better and will be able to make progress on the highway of holiness day by day. Amen.

September 19

Be Obedient!

This is love for God: to obey His commands. And His commands are not burdensome, for everyone born of God overcomes the world. This is the victory that has overcome the world, even our faith (1 John 5:3-4).

Oswald Chambers liked to say that the golden rule for understanding spiritual things is not intellect but obedience. "Those who obey this command live in Him, and He in them" writes John (1 John 3:24). If you really want to grow spiritually you will need to be prepared to obey the commandments of God. God places a high premium on the obedience of His children. "Does the Lord delight in burnt offerings and sacrifices as much as in obeying the voice of the Lord? To obey is better than sacrifice, and to heed is better than the fat of rams" says Samuel to Saul in 1 Samuel 15:22. Because Saul refused to obey God and followed his own way, his kingdom was taken away from him.

Regeneration – general regeneration as well as personal regeneration – has always had much to do with obedience. According to Norman Grubb revival is "a clean-cut breakthrough of the Spirit, a sweep of Holy Ghost power bending the hearts of hardened sinners as the wheat before the wind, breaking up the fountains of the great deep, sweeping the whole range of emotions, as the master hand moves across the harp strings, from the tears and cries of the penitent to the holy laughter and triumphant joy of the cleansed." If you want to grow spiritually in this month of spring, you need to decide once more to obey God. Your own obedience to God is proof of your love for Him. Right now make a decision of your will to be absolutely obedient to God from now on.

Heavenly Father, I really want to prove my love for You through being obedient to You because I know the One who obeys Your commands remains in You, and You in Him. Amen.

Three Principles for New People

I consider everything a loss compared to the surpassing greatness of knowing Christ Jesus my Lord. I want to know Christ and the power of His resurrection and the fellowship of sharing in His sufferings, becoming like Him in His death (Philippians 3:8, 10).

Cindi McMenamin wrote in an article in the *Discipleship Journal* of December/January 2002 that there are three principles that Christians should follow if they want to deepen their relationship with God: First, tell God – share anything that happens to you with God first of all; your greatest heartaches but also your greatest joys, an insurmountable problem or a great challenge. When you do this, it shows that He is the most important person in your life.

Secondly, regard God as more important than anything else – your priorities should be the things that He requires from you and you must let go of the things that He forbids. Make sure that nothing steals the time set aside to nurture your relationship with God.

Lastly, trust absolutely in God. Sometimes God asks things of you or He allows things to happen in your life that you cannot understand or cannot reconcile with His love. It does not matter what happens to you, you must never allow anything or anyone to come between you and God. Take your fears and problems directly to Him and trust Him for the solutions.

If you follow Cindi's three principles, God will become a greater reality in your life each day and you will draw even closer to Him.

Lord Jesus, You are the most important person in my life – from now on I want to focus on the things that You desire from me and trust in You completely. Amen.

Keep on Growing!

He has lost connection with the Head, from whom the whole body, supported and held together by its ligaments and sinews, grows as God causes it to grow (Colossians 2:19).

Paul did not agree with the Jewish practices and rules that strictly prescribed how people ought to live. The various feasts that they celebrated and the rules that they obeyed were only a shadow of Christ, he writes. The body grows from Him. The church receives everything it needs to grow from Christ. He is the head of this body and without Him there can be no question of any real growth. Paul used the image of a body here because he wanted to emphasize the connectedness of a congregation. Just as the different parts of the body grow together as a person gets older, so too should the body of Christ grow together and become stronger.

Without Jesus in your life you will never be able to grow. Spiritual growth always requires an active response from your side. It is also easy to be so satisfied with your own growth that bit by bit – without even being aware of it – you stop growing. If you want to become spiritually stronger you will have to set aside time to spend with God: time for Bible study, prayer, witnessing and attending church. This process of spiritual growth will never be complete in your lifetime on earth – the purpose of it is, after all, that you will one day be as complete and mature as Christ (Eph. 4:13).

Lord Jesus, please make it possible for me to grow spiritually each day because I am connected to You. Amen.

Remain Enthusiastic

Never be lacking in zeal, but keep your spiritual fervor, serving the Lord (Romans 12:11).

In Romans 12:9-12 Paul provides various guidelines for the Christian life. These guidelines directly follow the portion of Scripture in which he asks Christians to offer themselves as living sacrifices to God so that He can change them and make their thoughts and lives new (see Rom. 12:1-8).

If you really feel passionate about an issue, it is almost a given that you will be successful in it. It is therefore imperative that you remain passionate about your spiritual growth, and do not slack off in your commitment after a while. If you, like the Laodician church of old (see Rev. 3:14-22), are an unenthusiastic and lukewarm Christian you will get nowhere in your spiritual growth. Without enthusiasm there will be no progress in the world, said the well-known American president Woodrow Wilson. And I want to add to that: Without enthusiasm there will not be any spiritual progress among Christians.

Enthusiasm is exactly the right word here – in fact it should be written Enthusiasm because it is only the Holy Spirit who can ensure that a Christian will remain enthusiastic about the growth of his faith right to the end. Do not slack off in your perseverance, exhorts Paul. Some Christians are all too ready to throw in the towel when time after time they find they cannot make it on their own and they end up doing those things that they fully resolved not to do. Rather you should keep on keeping on – ask the Holy Spirit to keep you enthusiastic all the time – and serve the Lord!

Lord Jesus, I am sorry that I am so often an unenthusiastic and luke-warm Christian. Please forgive me and make me enthusiastic about my faith and my spiritual growth. Amen.

Live with Commitment

Have nothing to do with godless myths and old wives' tales; rather, train yourself to be godly. For physical training is of some value, but godliness has value for all things, holding promise for both the present life and the life to come (1 Timothy 4:7-8).

Absolute surrender to God is vital for spiritual growth. After his transgression with Bathsheba, David found that his life lacked commitment. "Save me from bloodguilt, O God, the God who saves me, and my tongue will sing of Your righteousness" he asks in Psalm 51:14.

To stay committed, it is necessary for you to remain spiritually fit, for you to establish a disciplined routine in your spiritual life – exactly as you do for a physical exercise program. This spiritual fitness program has far greater value than a physical one, because it benefits you both in this life and the life to come, writes Paul to Timothy.

Without real surrender to God you will not manage to become spiritually stronger. Sincere surrender will demand endurance and perseverance from you. If you are serious about this, you will need to learn the will of God by studying His Word; you will need to talk to Him regularly and listen to Him. You can readily follow the advice of Paul to Timothy if you want to be successful in this, "Pursue righteousness, godliness, faith, love, endurance and gentleness. Fight the good fight of faith. Take hold of the eternal life to which you were called when you made your good confession in the presence of many witnesses" (1 Tim. 6:11-12)

Heavenly Father, please help me to serve You with absolute commitment from now on. Give me the strength of mind and the ability to persevere so that I maintain my spiritual exercise program right to the end. Amen.

Listen to Your Conscience!

Holding on to faith and a good conscience. Some have rejected these and so have shipwrecked their faith (1 Timothy 1:19).

People often think that a particular sin cannot really be all that bad if "everyone is doing it." Many people today also maintain that a person will go to heaven just as long as they believe – it does not matter whether they believe in Jesus or in Allah or in Buddha. And then we Christians usually remain silent – we do not after all want to be the only ones who are continuously going against the current. It is so much easier just to go with the flow.

If the modern way of thinking and living is becoming all the more acceptable to you, if crude language and a degenerate lifestyle bothers you less and less, if you no longer risk saying something when people go against the guidelines of the Word of God, you should be seeing the flicker of warning lights. As you should too when you no longer think it necessary to listen to that stubborn little voice that whispers that a child of God should not be watching this movie, reading this book or being around these kinds of friends.

People who want to grow in their faith "must distinguish between the holy and the common, between the unclean and the clean" declares Leviticus 10:10. Pray that the Holy Spirit will give you discernment so that your faith will not in the long run be shipwrecked because you refused to listen to your conscience.

Lord, I am sorry that I too sometimes remain silent when I should speak up. Make me sensitive to the voice of my conscience and prepared to obey it so that I will not keep quiet about my convictions of faith. Amen.

It Is Necessary to Change!

We, who with unveiled faces all reflect the Lord's glory, are being transformed into His likeness with ever-increasing glory, which comes from the Lord, who is the Spirit (2 Corinthians 3:18).

Israel was often hindered by the veil of unbelief from recognizing the work of God. Change is necessary before the image of Christ can be seen in people. Only when this veil is removed can people be seen to be formed into the image of Jesus, and the glory that radiates from them will increase, writes Paul to the church in Corinth.

The new life of spring brings complete and absolute change. The dry, brown branches of trees are covered with blossoms and tiny new green leaves, and everywhere in the garden the bulbs begin to show their heads until every garden is transformed into a feast of color.

If you want to be transformed into the image of Jesus you too will need to change and begin to show His characteristics in your life. The glory that is a reflection of God's glory should reflect through your life. And this glory should increase day by day. Unfortunately, you will never be able to get this right on your own, but the Holy Spirit who lives in you will Himself make sure that the process of positive change that God has begun in your life will ultimately come to completion. "This is what the Lord who is the Spirit does," writes Paul to the people of Corinth. Are you willing to let the Holy Spirit make you new so that you will radiate the glory of God?

Lord Jesus, I really want to change and radiate Your glory so that I will become even more like You. Amen.

The Eternal Image of Jesus

For those God foreknew He also predestined to be conformed to the likeness of His Son, that He might be the firstborn among many brothers (Romans 8:29).

It was God's intention that every person whom He has chosen to belong to Him will eventually look like Jesus. *The Message* says that God "decided from the outset to shape the lives of those who love Him along the same lines as the life of His Son. We see the original and intended Shape of our lives there in Him" (Rom. 8:24).

Can people who look at you already see Jesus reflected in your life? If you want to know exactly how Jesus lived and behaved, read the four gospels through like a storybook and study the way in which Jesus lived. If you want to live like Jesus today, it will require of you to, like Him, be obedient to God in all things; for you to love other people more than yourself and to always be prepared to help them. It will also require that you always put the will of God first.

If you are prepared to do this, the promise in Philippians 1:6 will come true in your life. "Being confident of this, that He who began a good work in you will carry it on to completion until the day of Christ Jesus" writes Paul. On that day you will indeed be conformed to the image of Jesus.

Lord Jesus, it is wonderful that God has destined me to be the very image of You one day, when You come again! Please transform me until Your characteristics can be clearly seen in my life. Amen.

Wait on the Lord

Be still before the L<small>ORD</small> *and wait patiently for Him; do not fret when men succeed in their ways, when they carry out their wicked schemes. Refrain from anger and turn from wrath; do not fret – it leads only to evil (Psalm 37:7-8).*

Change does not just happen overnight. Time is needed for a winter garden to be transformed into a sea of flowers; for an ugly brown pupa to change into a dainty, colorful butterfly. Therefore you need to be prepared to wait until the promises of God become a reality in your life.

Chawl is a very interesting Hebrew word that is translated as "trust". It actually means to wait patiently (for Him), the kind of waiting that hurts, a difficult period of waiting.

Sometimes God allows such a difficult time of waiting in your life. Perhaps it is an illness that lingers, or problems that just do not want to go away. We do not immediately (or ever) receive those things that we really truly want. Yet the lessons that can be learned during these periods of waiting are very precious and should never be exchanged for anything because they always result in a deepening of your relationship with God.

Two of my friends who have cancer testify that this "waiting on the Lord" during their illness strengthened their faith remarkably. Only remember that it requires faith and patience to continue believing in His promises. "But if we hope for what we do not yet have, we wait for it patiently," writes Paul (Rom. 8:25).

Heavenly Father I am sorry that I so often complain about my current difficult waiting period. Please help me to be prepared to wait patiently until Your promises are fulfilled. Amen.

The Lord Is Waiting for You!

Yet the LORD *longs to be gracious to you; He rises to show you compassion. For the* LORD *is a God of justice. Blessed are all who wait for Him! (Isaiah 30:18).*

God really wants to see a positive change in the lives of His children. And He is prepared to wait for that change.

Israel put the patience of God to the test time after time and yet God was prepared each time to forgive them and to give them another chance to renew their covenant with Him.

God still has all the patience in the world for you today. He is always prepared to give you another chance just as He did for His disobedient people.

This is, after all, the reason that the return of Jesus has not yet taken place, writes Peter. "The Lord is not slow in keeping His promise, as some understand slowness. He is patient with you, not wanting anyone to perish, but everyone to come to repentance" (2 Pet. 3:9). It is the heartfelt desire of God to be merciful to you. Surrender your life to Him so that He can make you into a new person, a person who will be transformed more and more into the image of His Son.

Heavenly Father, thank You very much for Your patience with me. I now want to surrender my life to You. Please forgive all my sins and make me new so that from now on I will live only for You. Amen.

Come to Complete Spiritual Ripeness

Because you know that the testing of your faith develops perseverance. Perseverance must finish its work so that you may be mature and complete, not lacking anything (James 1:3-4).

The bad things that happen to you are God's way of testing your faith – they teach you to trust in Him more fiercely and live closer to Him. That is why God sends negative things across your path through life; because He wants to teach you to persevere through them. And if you can manage to persist in this perseverance right to the end you will eventually become the person that God intends you to be; spiritually ripe and without any defects.

This month's devotions have dealt with spiritual growth. And if God now, for the sake of your personal spiritual growth, allows problems and disasters to come over your path through life you must be prepared to cling tightly to your faith, to persevere until the promises of God become true in your life. If you do not know how to respond in difficult times, you can pray for wisdom and God will give this wisdom to you, writes James (see James 1:5). There is however a condition: You need to pray in faith without doubting because someone who doubts God will receive nothing from Him.

Heavenly Father, thank You for the problems of life that You allow into my life to teach me perseverance so that I will eventually be spiritually ripe. Please give me the wisdom that I need to be able to handle my problems. Amen.

On the Road of God

Because we know that this extraordinary day is just ahead, we pray for you all the time – pray that our God will make you fit for what He's called you to be, pray that He'll fill your good ideas and acts of faith with His own energy so that it all amounts to something (2 Thessalonians 1:11 THE MESSAGE).

During spring we can almost see how the plants in our gardens grow and get bigger each day. God wants your spiritual growth to be just as clear so that everyone will see it. And this is only possible if you continue to walk on the road of God each day and live as He asks you to. God also undertakes to provide you with the strength you need for this through the working of the Holy Spirit.

If you see your way clear to doing this, God will personally ensure that great things happen in your life. Through His power which is at work in you, He will Himself cause your love for what is good and your faith to increase each day. Paul tells the church in Thessalonica exactly what he means by this, "The word has gotten around. Your lives are echoing the Master's Word, not only in the provinces but all the place. The news of your faith in God is out. We don't even have to say anything anymore – *you're* the message! People come up and tell us how you received us with open arms, how you deserted the dead idols of your old life so you could embrace and serve God, the true God. They marvel at how expectantly you await the arrival of His Son, whom He raised from the dead – Jesus, who rescued us from certain doom (1 Thess. 1:12).

It is my prayer for you that you will reflect the glory of Jesus in such a way that everyone who looks at you will see how great and wonderful He is.

Lord Jesus, You are so great and wonderful. Help me from now on to reflect Your glory in a crystal clear way. Amen.

Prayer

Lord Jesus,
I pray that I will learn how to grow spiritually
as I watch the growth around me in springtime.
From now on I really want to live connected to You –
rooted in You and built up on You.
Thank You for the promise that You want to give me a new future;
that You want to make me a new person.
One who will become more like
You each day and who will reflect Your glory.
Help me to live in a new way in my marriage,
family and workplace; from now on to concentrate on those things
that have an eternal value and to get rid of
all the wrong things in my life.
Make me sympathetic, humble, well disposed
to others, tolerant and forgiving.
Make sure that Your love will be seen in my life each day.
I want to be in Your service full time, Lord,
and live completely for You;
I want to be obedient to You and remain enthusiastic about my faith.
I want to surrender my whole life to You
and be finely tuned to the voice of my conscience.
I want to change for the better day by day
so that I will radiate Your glory.
I want to wait on You in the difficult times and continue to walk
on Your road each day until I eventually
come to full spiritual ripeness;
complete and without any defects, just like Jesus.
Please make this possible for me.
I ask this in Your name.

Amen.

October

Characteristics of God's Children

The Bible teaches us that there are various distinguishing features that God wants to see developed in the lives of His children.

Some of them can only be given to you by God, others depend to a large extent on your own attitude and outlook on life – the better you know God, the closer you live to Him, the more clearly these characteristics will be seen in your life. Each one of them is then also a distinguishing feature that was clearly evident in the life of Jesus.

Each day of the month that lies ahead, meditate on one of these distinguishing features. If there are some of these that are not yet visible in your life – do your best to acquire them. Perhaps you will need to work on some of these features – if you manage to incorporate them into your life with the help of God you will find that you will reap the positive fruit of them for the rest of your life.

October 1

Read 2 Timothy 1:6-14

Trust in God

That is why I am suffering as I am. Yet I am not ashamed, because I know whom I have believed, and am convinced that He is able to guard what I have entrusted to Him for that day (2 Timothy 1:12).

It seems as if Timothy's zeal was cooling down. He was no longer as enthusiastic about proclaiming the gospel as he had been in the beginning. In his letter, Paul encourages him to once again stir up the gifts that he had received from God and to work through the difficulties with the strength that God provides. Paul wrote this letter while he was in prison, but in spite of the troubles that he had to endure he knew the One in whom he trusted and was convinced that God is mighty enough to care for him until Jesus returns.

God wants you to trust Him at all times; to yield your whole life to Him with the certain knowledge that He will undertake on your behalf. Trust in God is a way of life. And no one who has completely trusted in God has ever been disappointed.

If you are prepared to put your trust in God, you will be able to make the beautiful promise in Psalm 37:3-5 your own, "Trust in the Lord and do good; dwell in the land and enjoy safe pasture. Delight yourself in the LORD and He will give you the desires of your heart. Commit your way to the LORD; trust in Him and He will do this."

Heavenly Father, I praise You that You are the One in whom I can trust. I now want to take Your promise for myself: Thank You that You will make my heart's desires a reality and will care for me always. Amen.

Have Faith

Faith is being sure of what we hope for and certain of what we do not see. This is what the ancients were commended for (Hebrews 11:1).

Faith and trust lie very close to each other. Faith is, after all, a steadfast trusting in the things we hope for; the evidence of the things that we cannot yet see, according to the writer of the book of Hebrews. And if we do not have this faith in our hearts, it is impossible for us to please God.

If you sometimes struggle to believe, look at the faith of a child. Children believe without insisting on proof, simply because they love their heavenly Father and trust Him. Faith is not knowing what the future holds, but knowing Who holds the future. Faith has very little to do with feelings: It asks you to make the promises of God your own, even if they have not yet come to pass in your life. It is impossible to believe from within yourself, because it is only God who can establish faith in your heart. The Scripture verse that sums up faith so well comes from Mark 9:23-24, "Everything is possible for him who believes," Jesus said to the father of the son who was possessed by evil spirits. The father of the boy called out immediately "Help me overcome my unbelief."

If you believe, all things will be possible for you, and God Himself will help you in the areas where you still doubt.

Heavenly Father, sometimes I struggle to believe – thank You that everything is possible for the one who believes. Please strengthen my faith. Amen.

Obedience

In the way of righteousness there is life; along that path is immortality
(Proverbs 12:28).

Faith and obedience are closely linked. The person who obeys God also trusts in Him. The person who has no faith also has no works and the one who has no works, has no faith says the writer of Hebrews. Dietrich Bonhoeffer declares frankly, "He who is not obedient cannot believe."

How obedient are you? God asks for and expects obedience from His children. But unfortunately we are not always prepared to give Him this absolute obedience – we are far too fond of getting our own way and following our own direction. Do you see your way clear to obeying the commands of God without questioning and without counting the cost if you do obey? Jesus is the perfect example for us of someone who was absolutely obedient. He was even willing to leave heaven and come down to earth as an ordinary person, to die on a cross because His Father asked Him to. In Philippians 2:8 Paul writes, "Being found in appearance as a man, He humbled Himself and became obedient to death – even death on a cross."

If you are prepared to obey the commandments and guidelines that God gives you in His Word, the promise in Exodus 19:5 is addressed to you, "If you obey Me fully and keep My covenant, then out of all nations you will be My treasured possession."

Heavenly Father, please forgive me for my stubborn disobedience and help me from now on to be absolutely obedient to You. Amen.

Love for God

Jesus replied: "'Love the Lord your God with all your heart and with all your soul and with all your mind.' This is the first and greatest commandment" (Matthew 22:37-38).

When one of the teachers of the law wanted to know from Jesus what the greatest commandment in the law was, Jesus immediately had an answer ready: To love the Lord your God with all your heart and with all your soul and with all your mind – this is the first and greatest commandment, He told him. Jesus clearly indicated that no exceptions can be made here: It is imperative that love for God must be the most important thing in your life.

"To love God with the strength of the understanding, the strength of the emotions and the strength of the will – this forms the foundation for a true Christian and a truly balanced and strong character," writes Stanley Jones.

This love for God is again linked to obedience, "This is how we know that we love the children of God: by loving God and carrying out His commands. This is love for God: to obey His commands" (see 1 John 5:2-3).

How much do you love God? Can you honestly say that you love God with all that you are? That there is absolutely nothing in your life that is as important as He is? If so, you will be obedient to Him and your love for Him will be seen in the things that you do for Him.

Heavenly Father, I truly want to love You with my whole heart, my whole soul and my whole mind. Help me to show my love for You through the things that I do for You. Amen.

Love for One Another

"A new command I give you: Love one another. As I have loved you, so you must love one another. By this all men will know that you are My disciples, if you love one another" (John 13:34-35).

When Jesus answered the trick question of an expert of the law about the most important commandment, He added something else after He had said that we should love God with all our heart and our soul and our strength. "And the second is like it: 'Love your neighbor as yourself.' All the Law and the Prophets hang on these two commandments" (Matt. 22:39-40).

"The love of God is meaningless if it is not crowned with love for your fellow human beings," writes Martin Buber. Jesus issued a command to His disciples in today's Scripture verse: they were to love one another in the same way He loved them. And He was prepared to give His life for them.

This command of Jesus is still valid today. The only way in which other people can see that you belong to God is when you love all people unconditionally, just as Jesus did. Love has always been the distinguishing mark of Christians. John puts it very clearly: "If anyone has material possessions and sees his brother in need but has no pity on him, how can the love of God be in him?" (1 John 3:17).

Whether you love other people as much as God asks you to can be seen from the things that you are prepared to do for others. Love is never a feeling but a sacrificial attitude; of being prepared to wash the feet of others, just as Jesus did.

Lord Jesus, teach me to love other people with the same unconditional, sacrificial love with which You love me. Amen.

Creativity

A wife of noble character who can find? She is worth far more than rubies. In her hand she holds the distaff and grasps the spindle with her fingers. She makes coverings for her bed; she is clothed in fine linen and purple. She makes linen garments and sells them, and supplies the merchants with sashes (Proverbs 31:10, 19, 22, 24).

Creativity comes from God because He is the Creator God. In the beginning God created the universe, the world and all that is in it out of nothing – and He also gives His children talents and abilities so that they can be creative. Every person is an artist in his own right. Unfortunately, most of us lose much of this creativity as we grow older simply because we care too much about what others think.

In 2 Chronicles 2:14 the master craftsman Hiram's exceptional creativity is described, "He is trained to work in gold and silver, bronze and iron, stone and wood, and with purple and blue and crimson yarn and fine linen. He is experienced in all kinds of engraving." When the writer of Proverbs gives us one of the most complete prototypes of a wife, her creativity is an important aspect of her character. This woman is capable with her hands, she can make things and create articles out of linen and wool.

God gave you creative talents with which you can serve Him. How creative are you? Consider carefully whether or not you have done everything in your ability to develop your creativity; to be able to look at things with different eyes. It is only when you are prepared to work on your creativity that God will bless it. Do not hesitate any longer!

Lord, thank You that You have made me a creative person. Help me to develop my talents and to build them up so that I can use them in Your service. Amen.

Knowledge

His God instructs him and teaches him the right way. All this also comes from the LORD Almighty, wonderful in counsel and magnificent in wisdom (Isaiah 28:26, 29).

Knowledge and wisdom to be able to do the right thing at the right time comes from the Lord, says the prophet Isaiah to the leaders of Jerusalem. Only God can help us to live right and to do the right things. People who refuse to listen to Him are heading for disaster. In the book of Proverbs knowledge is very highly esteemed, "My son, pay attention to my wisdom, listen well to my words of insight, that you may maintain discretion and your lips may preserve knowledge" (Prov. 5:1-2). "Whoever loves discipline loves knowledge, but he who hates correction is stupid" (Prov. 12:1).

Although knowledge comes from God, you can do much to sharpen your own knowledge of God and His Word. There are many ways to broaden your spiritual knowledge: Acquire a single volume Bible commentary for yourself and use it when you do Bible study. Invest in a library of spiritual books about various topics that interest you. The Internet also contains information about any subject you can think of.

The more you read the more you will learn and the more knowledge you will gather. And the more knowledge of God you have, the more you will realize exactly how wonderful He is.

Heavenly Father, thank You that there are so many resources available to me through which I can broaden my knowledge of You. Help me to use my knowledge to structure my life according to Your will. Amen.

Wisdom

The fear of the LORD is the beginning of wisdom, and knowledge of the Holy One is understanding. For through me your days will be many, and years will be added to your life (Proverbs 9:10-11).

There is a very fine distinction between knowledge and wisdom. Wisdom means to know how to correctly use the knowledge you have at your disposal. Knowledge is to know why the sea is dangerous in certain places, wisdom is the insight to not go and swim in that particular place.

Like knowledge, wisdom also comes from God. Unlike knowledge, wisdom usually only comes with the passing of time. An intelligent child can have more knowledge than an old person, but the latter will reveal more wisdom. I like Thomas Watson's definition, "Wisdom is the power that puts us in the position to be able to apply knowledge to our advantage and to the advantage of others."

The wisdom that the Bible speaks of can be found through studying the Word of God and through living close to God. You will need to work to gain knowledge about various subjects while you can pray to God for wisdom, "If any of you lacks wisdom, he should ask God, who gives generously without finding fault" (James 1:5). If you need more wisdom in your own life so that you can better discern between right and wrong, you can ask God to give you that wisdom. He will do so willingly.

Heavenly Father, I know that wisdom begins with serving You. Please give me wisdom in my life so that I can discern between right and wrong. Amen.

Humor

I know that there is nothing better for men than to be happy and do good while they live (Ecclesiastes 3:12).

Of all the things that God created, it is only human beings to whom He has given a sense of humor. And without this sense of humor we would have been insipid, joyless beings! It has often been said that humor makes the dark side of life a little lighter. It helps you to put things in perspective and brings people closer together. It not only feels good to laugh – it has been scientifically proven that it is good for you.

A sense of humor makes it possible for you to tackle most of your problems with a smile, it helps you to handle the crises in your life with greater ease and it allows you to be aware of the bright side of life at all times. Furthermore, it relieves stress and tension. When you are sick or feel bad, laughing from your belly will help you feel much better. People who have a well-developed sense of humor are always popular, because we like people who make us laugh.

A humorous person is also able to laugh at himself. No wonder the writer of Proverbs came to the conclusion that things always go badly for a despondent person, but that a cheerful person's whole life is a feast (see Prov. 15:15).

Heavenly Father, thank You very much for the gift of humor and the enjoyment of a good laugh. Teach me not to take life so seriously and to be aware of the comic side of life and to share it with others. Amen.

Perseverance

You need to persevere so that when you have done the will of God, you will receive what He has promised (Hebrews 10:36).

There is a wonderful story of a snail that started climbing up an apple tree one cold winter's day. While he was creeping up the bottom of the trunk, a worm stuck its head out of a hole in the bark, "You're wasting your time, there is not one single apple up there," he said. "By the time I get there, there will be," answered the snail. Perseverance means that you are prepared to endure right to the end, in spite of your circumstances.

There are quite a few places in the Bible where believers are encouraged to persevere. In Matthew 10:22, Jesus warns His followers about the persecution that lay ahead, but at the same time He promised, "He who stands firm to the end will be saved." James writes, "The testing of your faith develops perseverance. Perseverance must finish its work so that you may be mature and complete, not lacking anything" (James 1:3-4).

Is perseverance a value that is evident in your life? Usually it is difficulties that nurture perseverance and the test of perseverance usually comes when things start going wrong for you. With the strength of God at your disposal He will truly make it possible for you to be able to continue and persevere – to be able to endure to the end, so that you will be able to do the will of God and receive the things that He has promised.

Heavenly Father, I pray that You will help me to endure to the end, to persevere until each one of Your promises comes to pass in my life, and that I can receive the heavenly prize that You have promised. Amen.

Thankfulness

Give thanks in all circumstances, for this is God's will for you in Christ Jesus (1 Thessalonians 5:18).

Thankfulness ought to be a distinguishing characteristic of every Christian. We know that everything we have is thanks to God; everything that we are and own comes from Him. And that is why we should never stop thanking Him. "Be thankful," writes Paul to the church in Colosse, "Let the word of Christ dwell in you richly as you teach and admonish one another with all wisdom, and as you sing psalms, hymns and spiritual songs with gratitude in your hearts to God" (Col. 3:16).

Most of us manage to be thankful without great struggle when things are going well for us. But when we are sick or confronted with problems or if disasters occur in our lives, it is much more difficult. "One act of thanksgiving when things go wrong is worth a thousand thanks when things go right," says John of Avila.

And yet God can make it possible for you to remain thankful in all situations. No matter how badly things are going for you, you still know that God is with you, that He will carry you through adversity and will protect you in dangerous situations. Therefore, when you are tempted to doubt God's love in times of hardship, remember that He is in control; He will ultimately work all things out for your good!

Heavenly Father, I am sorry that my gratitude is sometimes shipwrecked when things do not go that well for me. Make me thankful in all things because that is what You expect from me. Amen.

Willingness to Serve

Brothers, each man, as responsible to God, should remain in the situation God called him to (1 Corinthians 7:24).

True ministry implies being willing to be of service to God and others without receiving any acknowledgement for it. Jesus came to teach us exactly what is meant by being willing to serve. "Whoever wants to become great among you must be your servant, and whoever wants to be first must be your slave – just as the Son of Man did not come to be served, but to serve, and to give His life as a ransom for many," He said to James and John when they came to ask Him if they could sit one on either side of Him in His kingdom (Matt. 20: 26-28).

Paul impresses on the hearts of the church in Corinth that God has already placed each one of us in the exact place where He wants us to serve Him. Therefore you need never go and find a different place to serve God. Rather be prepared to serve in your own town and in your own community: Be available for other people, take note of their needs and do something about them.

God is Almighty but He works on earth through His children. It is with your hands that He does His work here and with the money in your purse His kingdom is extended. Therefore, report for service in His kingdom and see how He will use you for His honor.

Lord Jesus, please prepare me to serve You and other people in the place where You have set me. Thank You that I can be Your hands and feet and purse in this world. Amen.

Hospitality

Do not forget to entertain strangers, for by so doing some people have entertained angels without knowing it (Hebrews 13:2).

It is rather pertinent that Bible characters were extremely hospitable. Abraham actually did entertain angels through his hospitality (see Gen. 18:1-8) and in the New Testament Christians are frequently urged to be hospitable. Peter writes that we should be hospitable without complaining about it (1 Pet. 4:9) and Paul singles out hospitality as one of the guidelines for Christian behavior (Rom. 12:13).

Unfortunately, it is rather dangerous to offer your hospitality to just anyone who knocks on your front door these days. But God still expects His children to reach out to others, and to be hospitable to other Christians.

Hospitality cannot be learned, you do not learn it from books. It is a deeply rooted, inward attitude of openness and liberality. Perhaps our hospitality in the busy world in which we live has suffered because we put too much effort into it.

It is not necessary to go to all sorts of trouble when you invite people for a meal. In winter, soup and bread would be enough because hospitality is not about how smart the host is or about how wonderful the food tastes – it is about the art of letting people feel welcome and at home in your home and opening your house to them.

Do not hold back from being hospitable to others.

Lord, forgive me for so often being reluctant to receive other people into my home. Please give me an attitude of true hospitality. Amen.

Worship

A time is coming and has now come when the true worshipers will worship the Father in spirit and truth, for they are the kind of worshipers the Father seeks. God is spirit, and His worshipers must worship in spirit and in truth" (John 4:23-24).

God takes pleasure in His children coming to kneel before Him in worship. Worship is more than simple prayer. Rick Warren explains it very well, "Worship is far more than praise, singing and praying to God. Worship is a lifestyle of finding delight in God, loving Him and giving ourselves to Him so that we can be used for His purposes. When you yield your life to seeing God glorified, everything that you do becomes an act of worship."

It is wonderful to communicate with God through prayer in your quiet time. But your worship should not end when you get up from your knees – it must continue through your busy day so that you will be connected to God: when you are driving to work, at work, in your interaction with other people, when you admire the beauties of nature, when you are busy doing housework ... In everything that you do, say and think, you should be worshiping God.

The more you learn to know God and the more time you set aside for Him, the easier it will become for you to worship Him. Ask the Holy Spirit to teach you to learn to worship God in Spirit and in truth.

Holy Spirit, teach me the secret of worship: to acknowledge the greatness of God every moment of my life and to praise Him for that. Amen.

Unity

I appeal to you, brothers, in the name of our Lord Jesus Christ, that all of you agree with one another so that there may be no divisions among you and that you may be perfectly united in mind and thought (1 Corinthians 1:10).

One of the distinguishing features that God expects to see in us and with which Christians struggle the most is unity. We just can't get it right to be truly one, and the reason for this is our inherent stubbornness and selfishness.

Each one of us wants to follow our own lead and expects that the rest of the community should fall in with us. When Jesus prayed for His disciples, He asked, "Father, just as You are in Me and I am in You. May they also be in Us so that the world may believe that You have sent Me" (John 17:21).

Our faith in Jesus requires that we, as His children, should be one; that we would, like the first church described in the book of Acts 2:44, be of one mind. Oneness in Christ does not require of us to all think the same and be exactly the same, but for unity to appear in our actions because we do what He asks of us and are obedient to Him.

Like God's team in this world we need to follow God's pattern and have the same goal in mind when we play the game of life. This is, after all, what Jesus did. Are you willing to be one with your brothers and sisters in the faith?

Lord Jesus, I pray that You will make me prepared to let go of my inflexibility and become one with the rest of my church community, just as You and the Father are one. Amen.

Simplicity

Better to be lowly in spirit and among the oppressed than to share plunder with the proud (Proverbs 16:19).

Any experienced traveler will know that the less baggage you take with you the easier and more satisfying the journey will be. This is also true of your journey through life.

Unfortunately, most people in the world today have become so attached to their earthly possessions that very few of us are satisfied with simplicity. We want everything that our neighbors have and we buy everything that our eyes see, whether we can afford it or not. In the process we forget that we are the actual losers because our possessions demand all our time, energy and money; to such an extent that sometimes we forget to be happy because we are so absorbed by gathering things. Rather follow the example of Jesus; He had very few possessions and He did not even have a place to lay down His head.

Perhaps the time has come for us to focus on simplicity and get rid of all the things that we do not really need: those clothes that you wore years ago, the "time saving" gadgets that fill your kitchen and never get used ... The older people get the more they realize that people can live quite happily with half the number of possessions.

Make a point of simplifying your life by channeling the excess things that complicate your life to the people who really need them. Then you will once again discover how simplicity will set you free to be happy.

Lord, please forgive me for being like a magpie who hoards attractive things. Teach me how to live a simple life. Amen.

Humility

For this is what the high and lofty One says – He who lives forever, whose name is holy: "I live in a high and holy place, but also with him who is contrite and lowly in spirit, to revive the spirit of the lowly and to revive the heart of the contrite" (Isaiah 57:15).

God is always on the side of people who have learned to be humble. In different places in the Bible we hear about how the arrogant and proud will fall while the humble will receive mercy.

Humility is thus also one of the characteristics that is specific to Christians, "Be submissive to those who are older. All of you, clothe yourselves with humility toward one another, because, 'God opposes the proud but gives grace to the humble.' Humble yourselves, therefore, under God's mighty hand, that He may lift you up in due time" (1 Pet. 5:5-6).

Jesus Himself was absolutely humble, even though He is the greatest King of all times. "Learn from Me, for I am gentle and humble in heart," He testifies in Matthew 11:29. "God made the world out of nothing and as long as we are nothing He can make something out of us," writes Martin Luther.

As soon as you realize your own limitations and acknowledge your dependence on God; as soon as you discover that you can succeed at nothing on your own because all that we have comes from God, it is not that hard to be humble.

Are you managing to be humble; to put other people first and are you prepared to put yourself second?

Lord Jesus, I am sorry that I struggle to be humble sometimes; that my pride and selfishness raise their heads time and time again. Make me humble so that others will be more important than myself. Amen.

Honesty

The righteous man leads a blameless life; blessed are his children after him. Even a child is known by his actions, by whether his conduct is pure and right (Proverbs 20:7, 11).

Honesty has been a very rare value throughout the centuries – but I wonder if it was ever as scarce as it is now in the twenty-first century. These days it is indeed a rarity to leave your handbag lying somewhere and to get it back – with everything still in it.

Most people have forgotten the value of honesty and being upright. Even in business transactions and the paying of income taxes – and this includes Christians! – it is too easy to find excuses about why it is impossible to be completely honest. In the late twentieth century the Institute of Motivational Behavior found that ninety-seven percent of all people tell lies – and that each one does so about a thousand times a year.

And it seems like this dishonesty comes a long way. Just listen to what the prophet Isaiah said thousands of years ago, "No one calls for justice; no one pleads his case with integrity. They rely on empty arguments and speak lies; they conceive trouble" (Isa. 59:4).

If you are serious about your Christianity you will need to learn to be honest and to live with integrity. Christians are supposed to be different; honest in their business transactions and money matters as well as in the things that they say. If you have not yet been able to get this right, ask God to help you with it.

Lord, I realize now that I do not always act honestly. Please show me the areas where I need more integrity and make it possible for me to be honest and upright at all times. Amen.

Courage

"The LORD *Himself goes before you and will be with you; He will never leave you nor forsake you. Do not be afraid; do not be discouraged"* (Deuteronomy 31:8).

When Joshua was appointed as Moses' successor, Moses made him a beautiful promise: There is no reason to ever be discouraged or afraid. God Himself would go before Joshua and would be with Him. He would never let him down or leave him alone. "I will refresh the weary and satisfy the faint" (Jer. 31:25).

You and I can still depend on that same promise today, even though there are currently a whole lot of reasons to feel discouraged. If we consult the media, watch the news on TV or take our own situations into consideration, it looks like there will never be an end to the raging spiral of violence and crime. And yet the children of God ought not to get discouraged for the simple reason that God is with us; that He Himself undertakes to make us courageous.

"Courage is not a permanent condition of the human spirit but a gift that people need to and will receive – if they have learned to look up at heaven," writes Johan Heyns. If you ever find yourself in the Slough of Despondency you simply need to remember the promise that is written in Isaiah 35:4, "To those with fearful hearts, 'Be strong, do not fear; your God will come.' "

Heavenly Father, thank You for the promise that You will give courage to those who have become discouraged. Please do this for me today. Amen.

Forgiveness

In Him we have redemption through His blood, the forgiveness of sins, in accordance with the riches of God's grace that He lavished on us with all wisdom and understanding (Ephesians 1:7-8).

When the blood of Jesus flowed on the cross, He made it possible for God to forgive your sins and mine. Not only the sins that we have committed in the past, but also sin that we are committing now and sin that we are still going to commit in the future. God is always prepared to forgive us on the grounds of the work of reconciliation of His Son. And God forgives us because He is merciful. We have to do nothing ourselves other than confess our sins in order to receive God's forgiveness.

And yet the forgiveness of God lays a great responsibility on us. When Paul gave the Ephesians a number of guidelines for new believers in Christ, he writes, "Be kind and compassionate to one another, forgiving each other, just as in Christ God forgave you" (Eph. 4:32). If you have found it difficult to forgive other people in the past, read what Jesus said in the Sermon on the Mount about forgiveness, "If you forgive men when they sin against you, your heavenly Father will also forgive you. But if you do not forgive men their sins, your Father will not forgive your sins" (Matt. 6:14-15).

Ask God to help you to forgive other people with your whole heart just as He is prepared to do for you.

Lord Jesus, I praise You because You died on the cross so that my sins could be forgiven. Help me to wholeheartedly forgive other people who have offended me. Amen.

October 21

Joy

*Sing to God, sing praise to His name, extol Him who rides on the clouds –
His name is the* Lord *– and rejoice before Him (Psalm 68:4).*

God is the source of all true joy. If we do not know Him we do
not yet know what it means to be happy. "God cannot give us a
happiness and peace apart from Himself, because it is not there.
There is no such thing," writes C. S. Lewis.

Joy ought then to be a distinguishing feature of the children of
God. If you love God you will not be able to help but be a joyful
person: After all, you know that you have been saved, that God is
always with you, that He will always cause things to work out for
your best and that heaven awaits you.

Christians can even manage to testify as Habakkuk did, "Though
the fig tree does not bud and there are no grapes on the vines, though
the olive crop fails and the fields produce no food, though there are
no sheep in the pen and no cattle in the stalls, yet I will rejoice in the
Lord, I will be joyful in God my Savior" (Hab. 3:17-18).

If your flame of joy is burning low at the moment, you can do
something about it. True joy is contagious – if you make someone
else happy, you will also share in the joy that that person experiences.

God really wants to share His joy with you – stay close to Him
and make other people happy, then you will be able to live each day
in the sunshine of His joy.

*Heavenly Father, I praise You for the joy that I experience because
You are with me, and because I know You. Help me to convey this joy
to every other person who crosses my path. Amen.*

Truth

"These are the things you are to do: Speak the truth to each other, and render true and sound judgment in your courts. And do not love to swear falsely. I hate all this," declares the LORD (Zechariah 8:16-17).

The prophet Zechariah spoke to the people about the way they were acting towards others and asked them to always speak the truth to one another and to behave righteously. In this way, service to others becomes service to God. My social life becomes the place where I practice my faith.

Through the way you speak and behave it is easy for other people to know if you are twisting the truth or if you speak the truth at all times. When you always speak it, you are trustworthy. Then other people can rely on what you say; they will know that you are dependable.

Unfortunately, there are far too many people who twist the truth rather than sticking to it. If you also assume that a little white lie is really not wrong, think again! God expects His children to speak the truth. The Bible calls the Devil the father of lies (see John 8:44) and it is he who incites you to tell lies.

To be able to speak the truth, you need the Spirit of Truth in your life. "When He, the Spirit of truth, comes, He will guide you into all truth," Jesus promises His disciples (John 16:13). Decide now to speak the truth from now on and ask the Lord to help you do so.

Father, please forgive me where there have been times when I too have spoken what is untrue. Make it possible for me to always speak the truth so that I will be a reliable person. Amen.

Hope in the Lord

Yet this I call to mind and therefore I have hope. The LORD is my portion; therefore I will wait for Him (Lamentations 3:21, 24).

Things went so badly for the prophet Jeremiah that he lost all hope. "My splendor is gone and all that I had hoped from the LORD," he confessed in Lamentations 3:18. But then his hope is reignited. The reason for this is that there is no end to the mercies of God; His faithfulness is new every morning; He is good to those who continue to hope in Him.

The reasons Jeremiah had for hoping in spite of his unbearable circumstances is still applicable to you. If you believe in Jesus, you know that your hope will never be put to shame. Because hope is not a feeling, but a Person, "Christ in you, the hope of glory." Paul wrote to the people in Colosse (Col. 1:27).

Thus you can fix your hope on God because Christian hope is the certain knowledge that the promises of God will come true for you in the future; that heavenly glory awaits you. This hope can never be taken away from you because it is fixed in God Himself.

May your hope become ever stronger until the day Jesus returns.

Lord Jesus, thank You that You are my hope for glory. That I can know for certain that You are busy preparing a place for me in heaven where I will one day be with You forever. Amen.

Diligence

Our people must learn to devote themselves to doing what is good, in order that they may provide for daily necessities and not live unproductive lives (Titus 3:14).

Paul writes to the believers in Crete that it is necessary for them to work so that they can help other believers and make sure that they do not lack anything. The emphasis here is not on enjoyable work or important work or well-paying work, but rather on honest work. Diligence is then also the answer for many whose lives are unfruitful, because they cannot provide for their own life necessities.

In many countries there are people who really want to work but who cannot find work; there are others who do indeed have work but are constantly looking for ways to get out of work. It is a privilege and an opportunity to be able to work; never a right or something to try and avoid. If you are fortunate enough to have a job that is at the same time a calling for you, you should thank God for that every day. "I saw that there is nothing better for a man than to enjoy his work, because that is his lot." When God gives any man wealth and possessions, and enables him to enjoy them – "this is a gift from God," says the writer of Ecclesiastes (Eccles. 3:22, 5:19).

Always do your work to the very best of your ability; be thankful that you have a job and reach out to others who are not so fortunate by providing them with the basic necessities of life.

Heavenly Father, thank You so much that I have a job in which I can use my gifts. I pray for all those who cannot find a job. Please show me where I can help them. Amen.

Friendliness

The Lord's servant must not quarrel; instead, he must be kind to everyone, able to teach, not resentful (2 Timothy 2:24).

Mother Teresa is surely one of the people in whom the characteristics of Jesus could be seen clearly. She committed her whole life to helping others and I never saw her in photos or on television without a big smile. "We shall never know all the good that a simple smile can do. We Christians are quick to tell other people that we worship a loving and friendly God. But because they do not see Him they need to see some of His qualities in us. Be a living embodiment of God's love – with compassion in your smile, in your eyes, in your words, in the touch of your hands," she writes.

People ought to be able to see from the friendliness that you radiate that you are a Christian. Some people are by nature friendlier than others, but each one of us can learn to be more friendly; to smile more and to do more for others in an attitude of love and friendliness.

It is not always easy to be friendly; we do not always feel equally friendly. One way of looking at it is to say that a person should put on a smile on the outside and then it will move to the inside.

How friendly are you? A smile is one of the most attractive things that there is. If someone gives one to you, you spontaneously give one back. So make a decision right now that from now on you will deliberately be friendlier to others.

Father, please forgive me for not always being as friendly as I could be. Help me to give a smile to every person I meet. Amen.

Patience

Be completely humble and gentle; be patient, bearing with one another in love (Ephesians 4:2).

God is unbelievably patient with us. When we read the history of the people of God in the Old Testament, we can hardly believe the extent of patience that God reveals. Over and over again He is prepared to forgive His disobedient people. Thankfully God treats us with exactly the same patience – He is always prepared to give us another chance.

Patience is also one of the characteristics of the fruit of the Holy Spirit that Paul writes about in Galatians 5:22-23. It is therefore a quality that God seeks in each one of His children. Paul writes to the Christians in Ephesus that they should always be polite, friendly and patient, and should bear with one another in love. Unfortunately that kind of patience is not often seen among Christians. Christian patience doesn't mean to bear with one another but be bursting with irritation and frustration on the inside. Patience needs to be demonstrated through purposeful, never-ending friendliness.

Are you able to reveal patience through being friendly, even when things turn out differently than you expected them to and you must wait for a long time before your dreams come to pass? If you are by nature an impatient person ask the Lord to grant you more patience.

Heavenly Father, thank You so much for Your great patience with me. I am sorry that I am so impatient with myself and other people. Please make it possible for me to be polite, friendly and patient. Amen.

Dependence

"Blessed are the poor in spirit, for theirs is the kingdom of heaven"
(Matthew 5:3).

In the time in which we live it is not really much of an advantage to be dependent. We would all much rather want to be independent; we want to be able to take care of ourselves without having to rely on someone else.

But in the Sermon on the Mount, Jesus said that it is the person who is aware of his dependence on God who is happy and blessed. He also promises that the kingdom of heaven belongs to these dependent people.

To be honest, it is so important to God that His children should be absolutely and completely dependent on Him, and acknowledge their dependence on Him, that it is the very first sentence of the Sermon on the Mount.

It is usually only when disaster strikes or when you come to the end of your own strength that you are willing to acknowledge your dependence on God. In 2 Corinthians 1:8-10 Paul talks of the problems that they experienced in Asia, and then he testifies, "In our hearts we felt the sentence of death. But this happened that we might not rely on ourselves but on God" (2 Cor. 1:9).

Are you ready to be dependent on God in all things? To give up your independence and your own will so that your life will be lived in dependence on God and in line with His will? Do not put off becoming dependent and acknowledging that you are dependent on the Lord.

Lord, I am still reluctant to be dependent on You. Help me to understand that if I am willing and acknowledge my dependence, I will be part of Your kingdom. Amen.

Holiness

To be made new in the attitude of your minds; and to put on the new self, created to be like God in true righteousness and holiness (Ephesians 4:23-24).

Jesus was a person just like us, with one difference: He was holy and without sin. In fact He came to earth to make it possible for us to also be holy, "Now He has reconciled you by Christ's physical body through death to present you holy in His sight, without blemish and free from accusation," writes Paul to the church in Colosse (Col. 1:22).

God wants each one of His children to be holy just like Jesus was. For this to be possible, we need to undergo a makeover, because each one of us is born in sin. Because God is holy you need to do everything possible to also be holy by getting rid of all the things in your life with which God is not happy. Ask Him to show you what sins are still in your life, confess these sins and let go of them. But be warned, it is not going to be easy.

How to succeed in becoming holy is clearly explained in today's Scripture verse: Your soul and mind must be made new; from now on you should live like a new person who has been created in the image of God.

Your lifestyle must be completely in line with God's will so that you can be holy just as Jesus was.

Heavenly Father, I really want to be holy like You are. Please show me what things in my life I need to get rid of so that I can live and think in a new way and from now on I want to be completely surrendered to You. Amen.

Trustworthiness

Since we have these promises, dear friends, let us purify ourselves from everything that contaminates body and spirit, perfecting holiness out of reverence for God (2 Corinthians 7:1).

God is completely trustworthy. When He promised something to His people He fulfilled those promises to the letter each and every time. They knew that they could trust in these promises. Unfortunately, the same cannot be said of the unfaithful Israelites. They repeatedly promised to be faithful to God and His covenant, and over and over again they broke their promises.

We, like the Israelites, are also unfaithful. When we are in trouble we promise the Lord that we will turn over a new leaf if He will help us, and then we conveniently forget our promise when things go well again. Thankfully, God is still the same as He was in biblical times. Not only does every promise in the Bible apply to you, but God is still as trustworthy as He was then, "Not one of all the LORD's good promises to the house of Israel failed; every one was fulfilled" it says in Joshua 21:45.

You can depend on every promise that has been recorded in the Bible. Don't you want to undertake from now on to be more reliable and to fulfill the promises that You have made to God? If you ask Him to make you more trustworthy, He will gladly do so.

Heavenly Father, please forgive me for having such a history of untrustworthiness. Make it possible for me to be trustworthy from now on and to fulfill all my promises to You to the letter. Amen.

Merciful

"Blessed are the merciful, for they will be shown mercy" (Matthew 5:7).

In the Sermon on the Mount, Jesus promises that the people who are merciful to others will themselves receive mercy. "You're blessed when you care. At the moment of being 'care-full', you will find yourselves cared for," says *The Message*. In Luke's account of the Sermon on the Mount Jesus requests, "Be merciful, just as your Father is merciful" (Luke 6:36).

To be merciful means to have an open heart and open hands to other people. God asks you and me to be merciful just as He is merciful. He asks that we be willing to help other people just as He is always prepared to help us. The compassion of God for the world does not stand apart from the compassionate actions of His children. The love of God is given visible hands when His children live like His children: by protecting orphans; welcoming strangers into their homes; and helping the poor in need.

If you are prepared to pass the compassion that God has shown to you on to other people, there is a beautiful promise that you can take to your account, "If you spend yourselves in behalf of the hungry and satisfy the needs of the oppressed, then your light will rise in the darkness ... The LORD will guide you always; He will satisfy your needs in a sun-scorched land and will strengthen your frame. You will be like a well-watered garden, like a spring whose waters never fail" (Isa. 58:10-11).

Father, I pray that You will give me a heart for those in need and hands that will offer them help so that I will be merciful as You are merciful. Amen.

October 31

Peace

"Peace I leave with you; My peace I give you. I do not give to you as the world gives. Do not let your hearts be troubled and do not be afraid" (John 14:27).

The coming of Jesus into the world brought us peace. He is not the Reconciler and the Prince of Peace for nothing. When He came into the world He came to make peace between God and people and He made it possible for us to live in peace with one another.

When Jesus went away He promised to leave His peace behind for His children. And this peace that Jesus promised to His children differs in every way from worldly peace, which in most cases means nothing more than a truce. The peace of Jesus includes an inner serenity, an absolute trust that wipes fear out of our lives and equips us to be peacemakers and to promote peace in the lives of others.

Without God in your life this kind of peace is impossible. When all is said and done it is only God who can guarantee true peace for you. "Jesus Himself is our peace," writes Paul to the church in Ephesus (Eph. 2:14).

At this moment we are desperately in need of the peace of God in our country and in the world. He is still prepared to give it to us. Pray that the peace of God will come and settle in your heart; that He will make it possible for you to exchange your many fears for His peace; and that nothing will ever be able to take this peace away from you.

Lord Jesus, I pray that You will give me Your peace in my life; that I will experience tranquility, and will be able to shake off my fears and that You will help me to be a peacemaker. Amen.

rayer

Lord Jesus,
I really want to be more like You
by developing in my life the distinguishing features
that You lived out on earth.
Help me to trust You to
satisfy my desires and to care for me.
Help me to believe in You even though Your promises
have not yet come to pass in my life;
to be able to obey You completely and to follow
the guidelines in Your Word.
Make it possible for me to love God with my whole heart,
soul and mind and to love
my neighbor as myself.
I really want to serve You with the gifts that
I have received from You. I pray for Your wisdom in my life
and a thirst for knowledge of You.
I really do want to persevere in spite of my circumstances;
I want to be willing to serve
and be thankful in all things.
I want to worship You and radiate Your glory.
Make me hospitable to all people, humble, honest, courageous
and willing to be of one mind, and dependent on You.
I praise You because You give me courage
when I am feeling discouraged and forgive my sins.
Thank You for Your joy that I can
pass on to others and for the hope of the glory that lives in me.
Make me diligent and patient with others as
You are with me, trustworthy and prepared to live a holy life.
I ask this in Your wonderful name,

Amen.

November

Experiencing the Holy Spirit

Although a lot has been preached and written about the Holy Spirit, most believers do not know how they can experience the Holy Spirit in an intimate and personal way in their own lives. If you are prepared to submit yourself to the control of the Holy Spirit, He will bring about an unbelievable transformation and the fruit of the Spirit will become evident in your life.

According to the Nicene Creed the Holy Spirit is "the Lord and Giver of life who goes out from the Father and the Son, who should be worshiped and glorified together with the Father and the Son and who spoke through the holy prophets."

This month you can learn to know the Holy Spirit better. It is my prayer that you will understand and experience the Holy Spirit more fully; that by the end of the month you will be aware of a positive change and experience a spiritual deepening and that the fruit of the Spirit will show in your life.

God's Gift to You

Peter replied, "Repent and be baptized, every one of you, in the name of Jesus Christ for the forgiveness of your sins. And you will receive the gift of the Holy Spirit" (Acts 2:38).

When you come to repentance and are born again, you receive the Holy Spirit. The Holy Spirit is the gift of God to His children. "God will forgive your sins and you will receive the gift of the Holy Spirit," Peter promised in his sermon on the Day of Pentecost.

Because God has forgiven your sins, the Spirit gives you the power to be His witness. The Spirit is present in the lives of every Christian: He leads and teaches you, He talks to you through the Word of God, He gives you wisdom and He teaches you to pray. It is also the Holy Spirit who grants you specific gifts.

If you have the Holy Spirit in your life, you will never again want to be without God. It is the Holy Spirit who draws you nearer to God. "The Holy Spirit, whom the Father will send in My name, will teach you all things and will remind you of everything I have said to you," Jesus promised His disciples (John 14:26).

But the Holy Spirit never forces Himself on you. You need to freely choose to allow Him into your life, to follow His guidance and to obey His voice. F. B. Meyer rightly states that the ongoing infilling of the Holy Spirit is only possible for those who obey Him in all things.

Spirit of God, I pray that in the month that lies ahead, You would teach me everything about Yourself so that I will daily be able to surrender more of myself to You. And that I will be willing to obey You in all things. Amen.

Created by the Spirit

The Spirit of God has made me; the breath of the Almighty gives me life (Job 33:4).

When someone nearly drowns or loses consciousness, the first-aid rule is to give the person mouth to mouth resuscitation. The Hebrew word for the Holy Spirit, *ruach*, literally means "breath" – and without breath life is impossible.

We read of the Holy Spirit in the very first and the last verses of the Bible. The Holy Spirit was already present before Creation. Genesis 1:2 reads, "The earth was formless and empty, darkness was over the surface of the deep, and the Spirit of God was hovering over the waters." Genesis 2:7 describes how God created people, "The LORD God formed the man from the dust of the ground and breathed into his nostrils the breath of life, and the man became a living being." In Revelation 22 when Jesus talks about His return, He says, "I am the bright Morning Star. The Spirit and the bride say, 'Come!' Whoever is thirsty, let him come" (Rev. 22:16-17).

Job testifies that the Spirit of God made him; that the breath of the Almighty gave him life. The Spirit of God created each person with a specific purpose in mind, He has a plan for the lives of each one of us. He planned your life even before you were born. Just like you cannot live without breathing, you need Him so that you can grow spiritually, for Him to recreate you so that you can become more and more like Jesus.

Holy Spirit, thank You that You are present in my life. Please recreate me so that I can become spiritually stronger and be more like Jesus. Amen.

Inspired by the Spirit

Moses said to the Israelites, "See, the Lord has chosen Bezalel son of Uri, and He has filled him with the Spirit of God, with skill, ability and knowledge in all kinds of crafts – to make artistic designs for work in gold, silver and bronze, to cut and set stones, to work in wood and to engage in all kinds of artistic craftsmanship (Exodus 35:30-33).

When Moses told the people what the Lord wanted the fittings of the Tent of Meeting to look like, he told them that every craftsman needed to help with the task, but that the Lord had specially selected Bezalel for this work and that He would equip him through the Holy Spirit for this. Bezalel was capable of the most wonderful creative work when he was filled with the Holy Spirit.

Every Christian has received a specific gift with which he or she can glorify God and with which we can serve our fellow Christians. The gifts differ from person to person but it is always the Holy Spirit who gives special gifts to us. "There are different kinds of gifts, but the same Spirit," explained Paul to the church in Corinth (1 Cor. 12:4).

All your personal gifts and talents therefore come directly from the Holy Spirit. The inspiration of the Holy Spirit in your life can make an artist out of you. Just as a yacht needs the wind to move forward, you need the "wind" or breath of the Holy Spirit so that you can live life to the utmost, to be able to use your gifts fully, so that you can experience the wonderful power of God in your life.

Holy Spirit, I praise You for the gifts that You have given to me. Give me the necessary skills, insight and understanding like You have given Bezalel so that I can make the best use of my gifts. Amen.

Through the Power of the Spirit

"Not by might nor by power, but by My Spirit," says the LORD
Almighty (Zechariah 4:6).

Zerubbabel was the governor of Judah in the time of the prophet
Zechariah. The prophet told him that he would not be able to succeed
in rebuilding the temple with human "might and power" but that
the power of the Holy Spirit was needed to do that. This did not of
course mean that Zerubbabel could now sit back and do nothing
about the matter. It was still his responsibility to use the strength the
Holy Spirit would give him to work hard and ensure that the temple
was rebuilt.

Human ability and human strength cannot bring about salvation
or revival. It is something that the Lord Himself through the Holy
Spirit will bring about. Perhaps you have discovered for yourself that
when you try to do things in your own strength they always result
in failure. But those times when you depend on the power of the
Holy Spirit and ask Him to help you, you can achieve unbelievable
things far above your own ability.

Be warned, before the Holy Spirit will put His power at your
disposal, you will first need to confess your sins. The power of
the Holy Spirit works most efficiently when you realize your own
lack of strength and trust in God alone. The grace of God is always
sufficient for you, because when you are weak the strength of God
comes to full expression in your life (see 2 Cor. 12:8).

*Holy Spirit, thank You for the promise that Your grace is sufficient
for me and that You will always give me strength when I am weak.
Amen.*

Ask for the Holy Spirit

"If you then, though you are evil, know how to give good gifts to your children, how much more will your Father in heaven give the Holy Spirit to those who ask him!" (Luke 11:13).

When you pray to God He answers your prayers, especially when you ask Him for the Holy Spirit. Because He has forgiven your sins the Spirit gives you the power to witness, Jesus promised in His Sermon on the Mount. "The best thing to do when you realize that you are lacking in spiritual maturity is to ask God for the Holy Spirit. The Holy Spirit is the One who will make real to you everything that Jesus did for you," writes Oswald Chambers.

You already have the Holy Spirit if you are a Christian but that does not mean the Holy Spirit is already playing a leading role in your life. Perhaps you are still doing what you want to do, following your own head rather than obeying God. You are still in control of your life.

If you are willing to leave the control of your life to the Holy Spirit, it might happen that He will lead you to places you do not really want to go; or cause you to do things that you have no desire to do.

It is the Holy Spirit who led Jesus into the wilderness to be tempted by the Devil (see Matt. 4:1). But after the temptation, Jesus was equipped by angels for His work on earth. You too can depend on the Holy Spirit for strength when you go through the wilderness in your own life.

Holy Spirit, please give me the willingness to leave the control of my life to You and please equip me for my calling here on earth. Amen.

The Words of the Spirit

"Whenever you are arrested and brought to trial, do not worry beforehand about what to say. Just say whatever is given you at the time, for it is not you speaking, but the Holy Spirit" (Mark 13:11).

Jesus assured His disciples that when they proclaim the gospel they do not have to worry about what to say. If they are accused the Holy Spirit will give them the words that they need to speak so that the gospel can be spread further.

Many Christians today still have the same problem with this when it comes to witnessing. Just before His ascension Jesus promised His disciples that they would receive power when the Holy Spirit came upon them, so that they could be His witnesses across the world and the gospel would be proclaimed "in Jerusalem, and in all Judea and Samaria, and to the ends of the earth" (see Acts 1:8).

If you really want to carry out the Great Commission which Jesus issued in Matthew 28:19-20 and want to become a disciple-maker, you will need to pray to the Holy Spirit to give you the right words to make the glad tidings of Jesus known to other people.

If you ever become nervous or struggle with this commission, remember the words in Luke 12:12 and make this promise your own, "The Holy Spirit will teach you at that time what you should say" (Luke 12:12).

Holy Spirit, I come and ask You to give me the right words to use to proclaim Your message so that the good tidings of Jesus can be heard all over the earth. Amen.

Know the Truth!

"Then you will know the truth, and the truth will set you free" (John 8:32).

People who believe in Jesus and remain true to His Word are people who know the truth. In John 15:26 Jesus calls the Holy Spirit the "Spirit of truth". It is the true Spirit who also knows the truth well. In John 16:13 Jesus goes even further and says, "But when the Friend comes, the Spirit of the Truth, He will take you by the hand and guide you into all the truth there is" says *The Message*.

It is the Holy Spirit who comes to teach you what the truth of God embraces. He allows you to discover what God sees as sinful and what is important to Him. The more you find out about this, the more you will become like the person God intends you to be: no longer a slave to sin but someone who has been set free by the truth.

The Holy Spirit stands in direct opposition to Satan who is called the Father of Lies (see John 8:44). If you stay close to the Spirit you will find that He will personally point out the wrong things in your life and will also teach you to recognize the truth and to speak it. If you are willing to remain in the truth, you will also be willing to follow the guidance of the Holy Spirit in your life.

Holy Spirit, I praise You because You came to show me what the truth involves. Help me to always speak the truth and to remain in the truth. Amen.

The Outpouring of the Holy Spirit

They saw what seemed to be tongues of fire that separated and came to rest on each of them. All of them were filled with the Holy Spirit and began to speak in other tongues as the Spirit enabled them (Acts 2:3-4).

There were approximately one hundred and twenty believers together in Jerusalem on that first Day of Pentecost after Jesus' ascension. The Day of Pentecost was an important Jewish festival for them. It is always celebrated on the fiftieth day after the first Sunday that directly follows Passover.

On this specific Day of Pentecost the Holy Spirit was poured out on the believers. There was the sound of a storm wind and visible tongues of fire that went through the room where they were gathered. All those who were gathered there were filled with the Holy Spirit, and they began to speak in other languages. Wind and fire are often associated with the appearance of God in the Bible. The wind and fire of that first Day of Pentecost were therefore visible proof that God would be present in His church in a new way. In the past the Holy Spirit had come upon certain prophets and kings but on that Day of Pentecost everything changed. Each person who accepts Jesus as Savior receives the Holy Spirit. We are all temples in which the Spirit lives.

Holy Spirit, thank You so much that I can be Your temple and that I have the assurance that You live in me. Help me to behave like Your child. Amen.

The Spirit Brings Change

All of them were filled with the Holy Spirit and began to speak in other tongues as the Spirit enabled them (Acts 2:4).

The group of believers who were filled with the Holy Spirit were never the same again. We read that their way of life changed radically: They began to speak in other languages, they were full of joy and witnessed with great courage, they praised God and worshiped Him together, they truly cared for one another and experienced miracles (see Acts 2-3).

All these dramatic changes were the work of the Holy Spirit. Peter, who was initially too scared to acknowledge that he was a follower of Jesus, preached with such power on that Day of Pentecost that three thousand people were born again. The Holy Spirit also changed the small group of terrified followers of Jesus into powerful witnesses who spread the gospel over the whole of the then known world.

If you allow the Holy Spirit to control your life you will change. You will live as God wants you to. Your life will also, like the first Christians, be filled with the demonstrations of the powerful presence of the Holy Spirit and your relationships with your fellow Christians and your love for all people will increase and deepen as was the case with them.

If the infilling of the Holy Spirit has not yet brought about a remarkable change in your life, ask the Holy Spirit to change your life for the better so that He can use you optimally in His kingdom.

Spirit of God, I pray that You will change my life for the better so that from now on I can be used optimally in Your kingdom. Amen.

The Holy Spirit and Prayer

Pray in the Spirit on all occasions with all kinds of prayers and requests. With this in mind, be alert and always keep on praying for all the saints. Pray also for me, that whenever I open my mouth, words may be given me so that I will fearlessly make known the mystery of the gospel (Ephesians 6:18-19).

In Ephesians 6 Paul describes the armor of God with which every Christian can defend himself against the attacks of the Devil. However, this armor can only be put on in one way – to pray to God through His Spirit at every opportunity. Paul also asks that believers should be alert and pray regularly for one another; they must also pray for him so that God would give him the right words to be able to proclaim the gospel (see Eph. 6:18-19).

Larry Keefauver says that the key to powerful prayer is not the language you use, your body posture or sounds. Powerful prayer is always prayer through the Spirit.

The Holy Spirit is *the* Person of the Holy Trinity who teaches us to pray. Apart from a life that has been yielded to the Holy Spirit, the secret of a powerful prayer life will continue to evade you. Just as the Holy Spirit gives you the right words to witness, He also gives you the right words to pray. When you do not know what to pray He takes your imperfect prayers to the throne of God's grace.

Does your personal prayer life leave much to be desired? Then ask the Holy Spirit to teach you to pray.

Holy Spirit, thank You very much for the promise that You will teach me the right way and the right words to be able to communicate with God so that my prayers will be in line with His will. Amen.

The Power of the Holy Spirit

The Spirit helps us in our weakness. We do not know what we ought to pray for, but the Spirit Himself intercedes for us with groans that words cannot express. And He who searches our hearts knows the mind of the Spirit, because the Spirit intercedes for the saints in accordance with God's will (Romans 8:26-27).

What a wonderful promise! The Holy Spirit not only teaches you to pray, but also prays for you. And every prayer He prays is completely within the framework of God's will for your life, so that God will understand and answer each one of these prayers.

The Holy Spirit is always finely tuned in to the will of God. And if you are also prepared to tune in to His will and obey it, your life will show the fruit of it. "If we are sensitive to obey the revealed will of God, changes will take place in our thought life because our daily actions will then be controlled by the Holy Spirit. Then the will of God and my own will begin to agree," writes Arnold Mol.

With such an Advocate interceding for you before God, the statement of Paul in Romans 8:28 falls into place: You can live with the assurance that no matter what happens to you, all things will eventually work together for your good.

God's will is always the very best for you, even when it does not seem to agree with your own will.

Spirit of God, I praise You because You not only teach me the right way to pray but You also personally intercede for me according to the will of God so that I can be sure that all things will ultimately work out for my good. Amen.

The Fruit of the Holy Spirit

Now to each one the manifestation of the Spirit is given for the common good (1 Corinthians 12:7).

The Holy Spirit is at work in the lives of the children of God; He transforms us so that we can become more like Jesus so that His characteristics will be revealed more and more in our lives.

In Galatians 5:19-21 Paul describes the practices of the sinful nature with which every person is born and then he tells the church in Corinth how the fruit of the Spirit differs from that, "But the fruit of the Spirit is love, joy, peace, patience, kindness, goodness, faithfulness, gentleness and self-control" (Gal. 5:22-23). The gifts that the Spirit hands out to different Christians differ vastly from one another. Some people receive exceptional gifts while most of us have to be satisfied with ordinary gifts. But the fruit of the Spirit should be visible in the lives of every single Christian.

In the next nine days we are going to look more closely at these characteristics. Through deliberately developing them in your life you can become more like Jesus and play a part in extending His kingdom in the world. When you have a better understanding of the fruit of the Spirit you will be able to practically live out different aspects of the fruit of the Spirit every day.

There is, however, one thing that you need to realize: It is only the Holy Spirit Himself who is able to bring about His fruit in your life – it is impossible to do this in your own strength. Ask the Spirit to do it for you.

Holy Spirit, I really want Your fruit to be evident in my life. Please make this possible for me. Amen.

Love

"A new command I give you: Love one another. As I have loved you, so you must love one another. By this all men will know that you are My disciples, if you love one another" (John 13:34-35).

When Paul described the fruit of the Holy Spirit he put love at the very beginning. The love of which Paul talks in Galatians 5:22 is the unconditional love with which God loves sinful people. This love, which we read about in John 3:16, made Him willing to sacrifice His only Son so that everyone who believes in Him will never perish but will have eternal life. It is also this love that made Jesus willing to leave heaven and come to earth as an ordinary man, to give up His life on the cross so that sinful people could become children of God.

It is humanly impossible to love like Jesus – it is only the Holy Spirit Himself who can bring about this kind of love in your heart, but He is very willing to do so, "God has poured out His love into our hearts by the Holy Spirit, whom He has given us," writes Paul in Romans 5:5.

Ask the Holy Spirit who makes this love of God known to you to also pour it out in your heart so that you can pass it on to other people who come across your path.

Complete: Today I will demonstrate God's love to others by_____
_____
_____

Holy Spirit, I pray that You will pour out the unconditional love of my heavenly Father into my heart. Amen.

Joy

Even though you do not see Him now, you believe in Him and are filled with an inexpressible and glorious joy, for you are receiving the goal of your faith, the salvation of your souls (1 Peter 1:8-9).

Joy as a fruit of the Holy Spirit refers to an inner gladness that no person or circumstance can take away from you, because this joy is based on the knowledge that you have been set free.

You have this joy because you believe in God and because you know that heaven awaits you. Even in difficult times this joy remains the same. "Those who look to Him are radiant; their faces are never covered with shame," announces the psalmist (Ps. 34:5).

Nothing in your life can really go wrong when God is on your side. He is always there to save you and protect you. Even when you lose your life, He guarantees that heaven awaits you. You have perpetual access to this joy if you live in the presence of God. "Surely You have granted him eternal blessings and made him glad with the joy of Your presence," testifies David in Psalm 21:6.

A joy that is connected to your faith is a joy that no one can ever take away from you – it remains forever. From now on you should try to serve the Lord with joy every day of your life.

Complete: Today I am going to demonstrate the inner joy of God in my life by_____
_____

Holy Spirit, I will be glad always, because God is the source of my joy. Help me to cling to Your joy in difficult times. Amen.

Peace

Do not be anxious about anything, but in everything, by prayer and petition, with thanksgiving, present your requests to God. And the peace of God, which transcends all understanding, will guard your hearts and your minds in Christ Jesus (Philippians 4:6-7).

There are few things that can undermine one's joy as much as worry. However, when you get to the point when you know that there is nothing that you actually need to worry about, it is much easier to allow the peace of God to be at home in your heart.

Jesus' coming to the earth brought about reconciliation between you and God and between you and others. He was prepared to give His life so that you could experience the fruit of peace in your life. He is our peace, writes Paul in his letter to Ephesus, "For He Himself is our peace. He came and preached peace to you who were far away and peace to those who were near," (Eph. 2:14, 17).

You can personally take part in this ministry of peace through consciously deciding to be a peacemaker in this world full of unrest and dissatisfaction, so that the kingdom of God can come on earth.

"For the kingdom of God is not a matter of eating and drinking, but of righteousness, peace and joy in the Holy Spirit. Let us therefore make every effort to do what leads to peace and mutual edification" writes Paul in his letter to the Romans (Rom. 14:17, 19).

Complete: Today I am going to make peace with_____

_____

_____

Holy Spirit, please give me Your peace and show me how I can promote mutual peace among Your children. Amen.

Patience

Therefore, as God's chosen people, holy and dearly loved, clothe yourselves with compassion, kindness, humility, gentleness and patience. Bear with each other and forgive whatever grievances you may have against one another. Forgive as the Lord forgave you (Colossians 3:12-13).

Patience as a fruit of the Spirit implies two things: That you will be patient to wait and to persevere. "Being strengthened with all power according to His glorious might so that you may have great endurance and patience," is Paul's wish for the Christians in Colosse (Col. 1:11).

You need to temper your innate impatience by being willing to wait for God. You also need to be patient with other people. The Greek word that is translated as patience literally means to give someone another chance. This is also the drift of *The Message* translation of Colossians 1:13, "Give one another a chance without tearing one another apart with criticism. Also look past one another's faults. After all the Lord overlooked your faults. That is why nothing less is expected of you."

Make up your mind right now not to be impatient with people any longer (especially with your children). Be prepared to give everyone yet another chance and submit your own desires and will to the perfect timing of God.

Also be patient while God uses you in His plan. God does not allow Himself to be hurried or prescribed to – in His right time He will cause all things to work out well for you.

<u>Complete:</u> Today I am going to be patient with_____

_____

Holy Spirit, please make me patient with all people. Amen.

Kindness

We work hard with our own hands. When we are cursed, we bless; when we are persecuted, we endure it; when we are slandered, we answer kindly. Up to this moment we have become the scum of the earth, the refuse of the world (1 Corinthians 4:12-13).

Everyone likes to be around kind and friendly people. Biblical friendliness, which is part of the fruit of the Spirit described as kindness, means somewhat more than just having a friendly smile. It asks you to reach out to other people; to be willing to meet them half way and to make an effort to understand and help them. It is the kind of attitude that was evident in Jesus. He was always concerned for other people and did His best to help them. "A servant of the Lord should always be kind to everyone," writes Paul to Timothy.

But Christian kindness is never limited to a positive attitude towards others; it also requires the ability to remain friendly in spite of the other person's negative actions. It is this kind of kindness that Paul speaks of in 1 Corinthians 4:13, "When we are slandered, we answer kindly."

When you can succeed in bearing injustice and answering with a blessing, to be insulted and remain friendly, other people will not be able to help but be aware that you radiate the kind of friendliness that forms part of the fruit of the Holy Spirit.

<u>Complete</u>: Today I am going to show my kindness by _____

_____

_____

Holy Spirit, please forgive me for often being so grumpy and unfriendly, that I cannot manage to accept injustice against me and still remain friendly. Please give me the kindness that You require. Amen.

Goodness

"Why do you ask Me about what is good?" Jesus replied. "There is only One who is good. If you want to enter life, obey the commandments" (Matthew 19:17).

We are all sinful by nature. When the rich young man went to Jesus and asked Him what good deeds he needed to do so that he could receive eternal life, Jesus said to him that there is only One who is good. If he wanted to inherit eternal life he had to keep the commandments.

When the young man replied that he had done so from a young age, Jesus said, "If you want to be perfect, go, sell your possessions and give to the poor, and you will have treasure in heaven. Then came, follow Me" (Matt. 19:21). The young man was too rich to show his goodness in this way, and went away in despair.

Larry Keefauver says that goodness means to be pure in your motives and actions. The only good that is in us comes from God. As He makes us holy, we are being saturated more and more with the goodness of God.

If you want to understand what goodness really means you can look at the word, good-hearted, and think about its two components: good and heart. This is where the rich young man stumbled: he was more fond of his possessions than of other people.

To be able to be good-hearted, you need to have a good heart, a heart that cares for others as well as being prepared to show your love for them in a practical way. Are you prepared to try?

Complete: Today I am going to be good-hearted by_____

_____

Holy Spirit, please give me a good heart for others; and the willingness to show my love to them in a practical way. Amen.

Faithfulness

You are to hold fast to the L*ORD* *your God, as you have until now (Joshua 23:8).*

Joshua here reminds the people of everything that God did for them in the past, and impresses on their hearts that they should be faithful to God and must love Him.

Faithfulness firstly means to stay faithful to God and not, like His people, follow after idols. Unfortunately, you cannot be absolutely faithful to God in your own strength, but the Holy Spirit can make it possible for you to be faithful. Unlike us, God is absolutely faithful to every promise that is recorded in His Word. And even when we are unfaithful, God can never be unfaithful because He cannot deny Himself (see 2 Tim. 2:13).

Faithfulness also means being reliable in your actions towards people. It is important that you as a child of God are trustworthy in your relationships: that you will be faithful to your marriage partner, "Let love and faithfulness never leave you; bind them around your neck, write them on the tablet of your heart. Then you will win favor and a good name in the sight of God," is the contribution of the writer of the Proverbs (Prov. 3:3-4).

From now on make it your goal to be faithful to God and also faithful to other people; particularly to the person whom you have chosen to spend the rest of your life with.

<u>Complete:</u> Today I am going to demonstrate my faithfulness by_____
_____
_____

Holy Spirit make me faithful to God and to others so that love and faithfulness will distinguish my life. Amen.

Gentleness

Do nothing out of selfish ambition or vain conceit, but in humility consider others better than yourselves. Each of you should look not only to your own interests, but also to the interests of others. Your attitude should be the same as that of Christ Jesus (Philippians 2:3-5).

Gentleness implies humility and meekness. True humility asks of you not to think of yourself and what is to your advantage all the time, but to be prepared to be the least so that others can be the most; to follow the example that Jesus came to set. He was prepared to leave heaven and become an ordinary person so that you could be with God in heaven.

Others first! To regard others more highly than yourself goes against everything in our selfish human nature. After all, we always want what is best for us, unless we allow the Holy Spirit to teach us to be unselfish. My granddaughter (who is just as fond of food as her grandmother!) always used to take the biggest piece of cake for herself until her grandpa explained that children of Jesus always put other people first. Now she often points out to us that she has taken the smallest piece of cake on the plate!

"Everyone who exalts himself will be humbled, and he who humbles himself will be exalted," Jesus said in Luke 14:11. So from now on try to put other people first so that you know that you are acting according to the will of God.

<u>Complete</u>: Today I am going to show gentleness by _____
_____
_____

Holy Spirit, You know that gentleness and humility is the area in which I fail most often. Help me to be as humble as Jesus was so that I will always regard other people as more important. Amen.

November 21

Self-Control

God did not give us a spirit of timidity, but a spirit of power, of love and of self-discipline (2 Timothy 1:7).

Self-control means taking responsibility for your own actions. People who show signs of self-control are people who are in control of their emotions. For some of us this is more difficult than for others. If you lose your temper easily you will find it hard to control your anger when someone opposes you, behaves rudely toward you or is patronizing.

If you think about it you will see that it all has to do with "me and myself." Self-control and gentleness are therefore never separate from one another, because if you really develop an attitude of gentleness, you will not lose your temper if someone offends you. There is only one incident recorded in the Gospels where Jesus lost His temper and that was when the merchants changed the house of His Father into a den of thieves (see John 2:16).

Maybe Spirit-controlled would be a better word than self-control, because it is only when your emotions are completely controlled by the Holy Spirit that you will be completely in control of them. You can readily follow the advice of Paul in Galatians 5:16, "Live by the Spirit, and you will not gratify the desires of the sinful nature."

Complete: Today I am going to practice self-control by_____
_____
_____

Holy Spirit, from now on I want to give You complete control of my life. Please fill me day by day with Your strength, love and self-control. Amen.

Gifts of the Spirit

There are different kinds of gifts, but the same Spirit. There are different kinds of working, but the same God works all of them in all men (1 Corinthians 12:4, 6).

Without the fruit of the Spirit, the gifts that the Holy Spirit has given to you are nothing more than talents that can be used – mostly for your own best interests and advantage. Most people are also not shy to take advantage of other people in this process.

The fruit of the Spirit in your life should control and channel the specific gifts that the Holy Spirit has given to you so that they will always be used for the glory of God and in the service of other people.

Determine what your personal gifts are because every Christian has received some gift from the Holy Spirit – and know that your personal gifts are essential for the kingdom of God.

The Holy Spirit works in a unique way in your life. Therefore guard against being jealous of the gifts of others and if you have received some exceptional gifts, be careful not to be arrogant and think too highly of yourself. Every gift that you have received is precisely that: a gift from God. "What do you have that you did not receive? And if you did receive it, why do you boast as though you did not?" Paul asked the church in Corinth (1 Cor. 4:7).

Always use your gifts of grace for the glory of God and not to your own benefit.

Lord, thank You for the gifts that You, by Your grace, have given me. Help me to identify these gifts and to use them for Your glory. Amen.

Nurture Your Gifts

Do not neglect your gift, which was given you through a prophetic message when the body of elders laid their hands on you. Be diligent in these matters; give yourself wholly to them, so that everyone may see your progress (1 Timothy 4:14-15).

Paul writes to Timothy that he should not neglect the gifts of grace that he received when he was ordained for ministry. He encouraged him to be diligent and use his gifts wisely.

One way of experiencing the Holy Spirit is to yield to the working of His gifts in you, writes Larry Keefauver. If you are an athlete you will know very well that if you do not practice often you cannot expect to win. Something that is never used will deteriorate in due course. If you bury your gifts like the unfaithful slave in the parable of the talents, you will discover after a while that you have lost those gifts.

But if you use and develop the gifts that the Holy Spirit has personally entrusted to you, you will in addition receive even more gifts and God will bless the specific ministry in which you use your gifts.

Always remember that your church and community need your specific gifts. Fulfill the calling of God for your life by applying your gifts in ministry to your fellow Christians and to the glory of God.

Heavenly Father, I am sorry that I am guilty of neglecting my gifts instead of nurturing and developing them. Help me to be enthusiastic about using my gifts so that Your kingdom can be extended through them. Amen.

Keep the Spirit's Fire

Do not put out the Spirit's fire; do not treat prophecies with contempt. Test everything. Hold on to the good. Avoid every kind of evil (1 Thessalonians 5:19-22).

It is possible that the Holy Spirit lives in you, but that you still refuse to surrender your life to Him. Paul says that we must not put out the Holy Spirit's fire, ignore the Spirit or reject the gifts that come from Him.

There are various ways in which you could oppose the Holy Spirit, for example by refusing to confess your sins and continuing in them, by refusing to forgive other people, through your arrogant actions, wrong use of time, selfishness and lack of love for others.

There are three ways in which you can neutralize the work of the Holy Spirit in your life. You can resist the Holy Spirit, grieve Him and even quench Him, the Bible teaches us. More than likely you know the area in which you oppose the Spirit. Make a point of not doing so any longer and make time to listen to the voice of the Holy Spirit with sensitivity.

One of our friends likes to say that the Holy Spirit is a "gentleman". He will never force Himself on you, and surrender to Him is always completely up to you. The more time you set aside for Him, the more clearly you will be aware of His voice in your life and the easier it will be for you to obey Him and surrender control of your whole life to Him.

Holy Spirit, please forgive me for my stubbornness and for continuing to oppose You in so many areas in my life. From now on I want to be sensitive to Your voice, surrender the control of my life to You and obey You. Amen.

The Spirit Makes You Strong

I pray that out of His glorious riches He may strengthen you with power through His Spirit in your inner being (Ephesians 3:16).

In his beautiful prayer for the Ephesians, Paul prays that God, through the Holy Spirit in their lives, will strengthen their inner beings to be able to stand spiritually.

When your life is controlled by the Holy Spirit it will be defined by His power, love and self-control. Other people who look at your actions will clearly see that the strength of God is evident in your life; that His love radiates through you and that at all times you reveal self-control – or rather control through the Holy Spirit. When you live by the Spirit He will determine your behavior (see Gal. 5:22).

This strength that is given by the Holy Spirit is described in Ephesians 1:19-20 as, "That power is like the working of His mighty strength, which He exerted in Christ when He raised Him from the dead and seated Him at His right hand in the heavenly realms." In verse 20 Paul promises that God is able to do far more than you could ever think or imagine through the power that is in Him. And this life-giving power is available to you personally every day if you are prepared to give the reins of your life over to the Holy Spirit.

Do not put off any longer utilizing the power of the Holy Spirit in your life.

Holy Spirit, I pray for Your life-giving power in my life so that I can be strong in my inner being and that from now on You will determine my behavior. Amen.

Set Apart for the Spirit

We ought always to thank God for you, brothers loved by the Lord, because from the beginning God chose you to be saved through the sanctifying work of the Spirit and through belief in the truth. He called you to this through our gospel, that you might share in the glory of our Lord Jesus Christ (2 Thessalonians 2:13-14).

God personally chooses His children to believe in Him. We have in fact been saved because the Holy Spirit has set us apart for Him and because we believe in Jesus. It is also the Holy Spirit who convicts us of sin. "When He comes, He will convict the world of guilt in regard to sin and righteousness and judgment: in regard to sin, because men do not believe in Me," Jesus says to His disciples (John 16:8-9).

To be set apart for the Holy Spirit means to be willing to be put aside for the sole use of God; to belong to God absolutely and completely and to be obedient to Him – so much so that you will disappear and only God will remain, "I no longer live, but Christ lives in me," testifies Paul in Galatians 2:20.

The Holy Spirit really wants to make you new, to set you apart for Himself, renew you and transform you so that you will be pure and holy like Jesus. So that from now on you will think, speak and behave differently. Are you prepared to allow the Holy Spirit to do this?

Holy Spirit, please make me new and set me apart for You so that I will become more and more like Jesus and will be able to partake of Your glory. Amen.

Spirit of Truth

Jesus answered, "I am the way and the truth and the life. No one comes to the Father except through Me" (John 14:6).

In John 15:26 Jesus promised His disciples that when the Mediator came, who He would send from His Father, He would testify about Jesus and would empower the gospel message that He came to deliver to the world.

When that happens the children of God will also receive the power to be His witnesses and to carry the gospel message into the whole world. Here Jesus calls the Holy Spirit the "Spirit of truth" because He will guide His children "into all truth. And He will tell you what is yet to come" (see John 16:13).

The Holy Spirit is still available to lead you in truth, to show you the truth about Jesus and to remind you of the words of Jesus. Because Jesus is the way, the truth and the life, it is impossible to be a child of God if you do not believe in Him. The Holy Spirit also makes it possible for you to witness about your faith and when you are busy with the Word of God He reveals the truth of the Scriptures to you.

Without the Holy Spirit who opens the Word of God for you and who gives you the insight to understand it you will never really comprehend it. You can readily ask the Spirit of truth to make the truth of the Word a reality in your life.

Holy Spirit, I praise You for coming and teaching me what the truth is, that You are indeed the Spirit of truth. Lead me in this truth and remind me of what Jesus has done for me every day. Amen.

The Spirit Works in You

The Spirit of the Sovereign LORD *is on me, because the* LORD *has anointed me to preach good news to the poor. He has sent me to bind up the brokenhearted, to proclaim freedom for the captives ... to proclaim the year of the* LORD's *favor and the day of vengeance of our God, to comfort all who mourn (Isaiah 61:1-2).*

The prophet Isaiah testifies that the Spirit of God came over Him and anointed him to take a positive message to people who were in need, to encourage those who were in despair and to proclaim that God's mercy had arrived for the people of God. When that happened there really would be reason to rejoice: God would punish their enemies, exchange the sorrow of the people for joy and restore the possessions they had lost.

The Holy Spirit is always at work in the hearts of God's children. He marks out a specific field of work for us and He wants that mission field to be the place where you are living at the moment. It is also the terrain where you will be able to use the talents that you have received from Him.

The Spirit wants to have a life-renewing effect on your life so that from now on you, like Isaiah, can be used by Him so that your sorrow can be exchanged for joy and you will be able to encourage those in despair with your words and by delivering the message of God's grace to other people.

From today, obey the call of Galatians 5:25, "We live by the Spirit, let us keep in step with the Spirit."

Holy Spirit, I undertake from today on to live through You so that from now on You will be able to determine my behavior. Please use me to give Your message to others in the place where You have set me. Amen.

The Spirit Remains in You

As for you, the anointing you received from Him remains in you, and you do not need anyone to teach you. But as His anointing teaches you about all things and as that anointing is real, not counterfeit – just as it has taught you, remain in Him (1 John 2:27).

Before Jesus ascended to heaven, He promised His disciples that He would send them Someone who would teach them all things and would remind them of everything that He had said (see John 14:26).

In his epistle John emphasizes the fact that we do not need anyone else to teach us: His Spirit remains in us and He will teach us everything that we need to know. He will also teach us what is right and what is wrong.

Larry Keefauver believes that, it is very easy to ignore the voice of the Holy Spirit when He warns you about the wrong things that you do not really want to let go of. And the Holy Spirit will not play a submissive role in your life. Either He takes the leading role or He absolutely takes no role at all, writes Keefauver.

Every Christian has received the Holy Spirit in His completeness in his or her life. But the Holy Spirit does not always have all there is of us. Perhaps the time has come for you to think carefully about how big a role you are allowing the Holy Spirit to take in your life.

Holy Spirit, thank You for the assurance that You live in me and that You will teach me all things. I really want to obey You – make me willing to follow Your lead. Amen.

A Spring of Living Water

"Whoever believes in Me, as the Scripture has said, streams of living water will flow from within him. By this He meant the Spirit, whom those who believed in Him were later to receive. Up to that time the Spirit had not been given, since Jesus had not yet been glorified" *(John 7:38-39).*

You cannot keep the influence of the Holy Spirit in your life for yourself. His presence flowing in your life is like a spring from which fresh water is continuously bubbling up. Jesus told the Samaritan woman who came to draw water from the well, "If you knew the gift of God and who it is that asks you for a drink, you would have asked Him and He would have given you living water" (John 4:10.) When the woman asked Him more about this water, Jesus said, "Whoever drinks the water I give him will never thirst. Indeed, the water I give him will become in him a spring of water welling up to eternal life" (John 4:14).

When you receive the Holy Spirit in your life you become someone whose innermost being is overflowing with living water. Water that ensures that one day you will live forever. Sin in your life can cause this water to run dry, but if you live close to God and obey Him, this living water of the Spirit will be like a spring in your life that will never run dry but will flow out to others, and will be a blessing to other people.

Holy Spirit, let Your living water flow from within me so that it will be a blessing to other people with whom I come into contact. Amen.

rayer

Holy Spirit,
I praise You as God who lives in me;
the Spirit of truth who comes to make the truth known to me.
Thank You that You are not only
present in my life every day but that You also want
to renew me so that I will be
more and more like Jesus.
Please give me Your miracle-working power in my life
and the right words to be able to proclaim Your message.
Change me so that
I can live as God wants me to.
I come and ask that You will teach me to pray
according to the will of God – that You will intercede for me
and that all the fruit of Your Spirit
will be clearly visible in my life. Make me loving, joyful,
filled with peace, patient, kind, good, faithful,
gentle and self-controlled,
so that people who look at me will see Jesus.
Thank You for the gifts of grace that You have entrusted to me –
help me to discover what they are, to nurture and develop
them and to use them optimally for Your glory.
Protect me from opposing, grieving or quenching Your Spirit.
I now truly want to place my whole life under Your control
so that You will determine my behavior.
Set me apart for You so that I will be able to
partake in the glory of Jesus.
Remain in me and work in me until I become a spring of
living water that will be a great blessing to other people.

Amen.

December

The Coming of Jesus Christ

At Christmas we commemorate the day, more than two thousand years ago, when the Son of God became a person and was born on earth to come and make the good news of God known to people and to bring us peace. Christians still celebrate this birth of Jesus every year with great joy and thankfulness – it is a very special time of the year for us. "Advent is not a time for tense excitement about something spectacular that is going to happen. Just the opposite, Advent is a time of a growing inner peace and deep joy because I realize that He whose coming we are anticipating has already come and has spoken to me in the quietness of my heart" writes Henri Nouwen.

During this Advent season we are going to become quiet together and meditate on the meaning of the coming of Jesus to this world for you and me. We are going to once again make our relationship with God more intimate and prepare ourselves for the day when Jesus will come again.

A Time of Expectation

I wait for the LORD, *my soul waits, and in His word I put my hope. My soul waits for the Lord more than watchmen wait for the morning, more than watchmen wait for the morning (Psalm 130:5-6).*

In the beautiful Psalm 130 David declares that he is willing to wait for the fulfilling of God's Word. The period before Christmas should be a time of anticipation for every Christian.

The time just before Christmas is referred to as "Advent" – and the first four Sundays before Christmas, of which the first usually falls at the end of November – are also referred to as Advent Sundays. The word Advent comes from the Latin word *adventus* (*ad* = after and *venire* = come) and it refers to the approaching arrival of Jesus – His first coming at that first Christmas when He was born as a human baby in a stable in Bethlehem. But it also refers to His Second Coming for which we are still waiting; His coming again to the world when He will fetch His children so that they can be with Him forever.

You can make productive use of the time before Christmas every year by anticipating the coming of Jesus and preparing yourself for it and setting your mind on it. It remains a miracle that Jesus was willing to leave heaven and come to earth, to come and die a cruel death on the cross to make it possible for you to go to heaven. And an even greater miracle is that He has promised to come again to defeat the powers of sin for all time.

Lord Jesus, I praise You for Your first coming to this world that made it possible for me to become the child of God, but also for the promise that You will come again to take me to be with You forever. Amen.

God Loves You!

You will be called Hephzibah, for the Lord *will take delight in you, and your land will be married. I have posted watchmen on your walls, O Jerusalem; they will never be silent day or night. You who call on the* Lord, *give yourselves no rest (Isaiah 62:4, 6).*

In this chapter God once again commits Himself to Jerusalem. The prophet Isaiah delivers the message of God, saying that He still loves Jerusalem and will restore the city to her previous glory. He will care for her and hold her like a crown in His hand, and confirm His love for her and give her a new name: *The One Whom the Lord Loves.*

God also wants to restore His relationship with the disobedient Israel. It was the work of the watchmen on the walls to make sure that the city was not unexpectedly attacked. Isaiah asks the citizens of Jerusalem to be alert and remind God of His promises, and he promised that the segment of the people who had already gone into exile would return to their land.

The coming of Jesus into the world had one message that was crystal clear: God loved the world so much that He sent His Son to a sinful world die on a cross so that it would be possible, because of the work of reconciliation of His Son, for your sins and mine to be forgiven. At this Advent time think about the extent of God's love for you, while you are waiting for His Second Coming, and remind Him of His covenant promises.

Heavenly Father, thank You so much that You saw Your way clear to placing the life of Your Son at stake so that my sins could be forgiven. Every day during this Christmas month I want to meditate on the extent of Your love for me. Amen.

A House for God

"Go and tell My servant David, 'This is what the LORD says: Are you the one to build Me a house to dwell in? I have not dwelt in a house from the day I brought the Israelites up out of Egypt to this day'" (2 Samuel 7:5-6).

It worried King David that he was living in a smart house while the ark of the Lord was still in a tent. But the prophet Nathan got a word that it was not God's will that David should build a house for Him. The Lord had no need of houses made with human hands. "I have not dwelt in a house from the day I brought the Israelites up out of Egypt to this day," He said to Nathan. The Lord let David know that He did not need a house built by human hands but that He would build a house for David, and that his son would be the one who would construct a house for Him (see 2 Sam. 7:12-16).

During the Christmas season we are reminded once again that Jesus came to live among us, "The Word became flesh and made His dwelling among us. We have seen His glory" testifies John (John 1:14).

There is a world of difference between the true house of God and the houses that we construct for Him. Literally what John is saying in John 1:14 is that He came to put up His tent among us. God is now living in people. We are His temples in which His Holy Spirit makes His home. And because He lives in you, you should be a house worthy of Him.

Lord Jesus, thank You that You came into the world to put up Your tent in my life and that I can now be Your temple because the Holy Spirit lives in me. Amen.

Be Compliant

In the sixth month, God sent the angel Gabriel to Nazareth, a town in Galilee, to a virgin pledged to be married to a man named Joseph, a descendant of David. The virgin's name was Mary (Luke 1:26-27).

When the angel brought the message to the young Mary that she would be the mother of the long promised Messiah, he addressed her as "highly favored". Actually, Mary was a surprising choice to be the mother of the Messiah. This young girl whom God chose to favor was not yet married and moreover she was really someone who had no status. But the way in which she received the angel's rather worrisome message is an example for each one of us at Christmastime. After she, half afraid, asked the angel how this could be possible as she was a virgin, the angel told her that the Holy Spirit would come over her and the power of God would create the life in her (see Luke 1:34-35). Mary's answer to this was, "I am the Lord's servant. May it be to me as you have said" (verse 38).

If you have chosen Jesus as your Savior, you are still, like Mary back then, the favored one of God. More than likely you are not as compliant as she was about bringing God's plan to pass in your life. We all have many excuses about why we behave so differently from what the Bible prescribes. As Christmas approaches, let us try to respond as Mary did and to make ourselves available to God.

Heavenly Father, like Mary I truly want to make my life available to You. Use me where and as You will so that Your plan for my life can be carried out. Amen.

God's Intervention

There were shepherds living out in the fields nearby, keeping watch over their flocks at night. Suddenly a great company of the heavenly host appeared with the angel, praising God and saying, "Glory to God in the highest, and on earth peace to men on whom His favor rests" (Luke 2:8, 13-14).

God intervened in the history of Israel after they had lost all hope of the long promised Messiah ever coming. With the announcement of the birth of Jesus, the angel proclaimed a new era of peace. And the first to hear this message of peace was a group of terrified shepherds who were busy looking after their sheep. The prophet Isaiah had already prophesied many years before that the King who was to be born would be a Prince of Peace, a King of peace whose reign would extend and would ensure the peace and prosperity of the children of God for all time (see Isa. 9:5-6).

Jesus can still intervene in our history and change the world in which we live that is so full of turmoil. With the coming of Jesus into the world everything changed for the better. He came to make peace between us and God, as well as among people here. Our world has never had such need of a positive, peaceful transformation as it does right now. People are poorer than ever before, there is more violence, more crime, uncertain political conditions and discord between different races. During this Christmas month ask that God would once again bring His promise of peace to pass for us.

Heavenly Father, we are in need of Your peace more than ever before. I pray that You will give this peace to us in our lives, hearts and world so that Your kingdom of peace will last forever. Amen.

Time for Mercy

The Spirit of the Sovereign LORD is on me, because the LORD has anointed me to preach good news to the poor. To proclaim the year of the LORD's favor and the day of vengeance of our God, to comfort all who mourn (Isaiah 61:1-2).

The prophet Isaiah testified that God had especially anointed him to bring a joyful message to His people in their trouble; to proclaim to them that the time of God's mercy had dawned for them. This is exactly the same message that the angel came to give the small group of shepherds outside Bethlehem many years later, "Do not be afraid. I bring you good news of great joy that will be for all the people. Today in the town of David a Savior has been born to you; He is Christ the Lord" (Luke 2:10-11). Christmas is still the time of God's grace; the time when we are reminded about how God poured out His mercy on the world: He sacrificed His Son to die in our place.

The coming of Jesus into the world was the beginning of a new era – on the cross He achieved a definite victory over the evil powers even though the final defeat will only take place when He comes again. You and I live in a time of grace – it is our responsibility to communicate the grace of God to others. And there is no better time to do so than during the Christmas season. This Christmas, look around you to see where you can help so that other people can experience the grace of God in their lives.

Lord Jesus, at Christmastime make me an instrument of Your grace in the place where I live so that other people can experience Your mercy through my actions. Amen.

December 7

December 7 Read Isaiah 61:8-11

Be Glad in the Lord!

I delight greatly in the LORD; my soul rejoices in my God. For He has clothed me with garments of salvation and arrayed me in a robe of righteousness, as a bridegroom adorns his head like a priest, and as a bride adorns herself with her jewels (Isaiah 61:10).

The Spirit of the Lord, through the mouth of the prophet Isaiah, brings a joyful message to His people who are in despair. When the prophet received this message he praised the Lord in advance for the salvation that He was going to bring about for them. He expressed his joy in two significant images: in his joy he is like a bridegroom who is wearing a priestly crown; he rejoices like a bride who is adorned in her jewels and who is ready for her bridegroom. Just as the earth sprouts forth plants and the plants bear fruit, so too will God give His people the victory and will all the nations hear the song of praise sung to glorify Him.

Advent is a time of joy for the children of God because the coming of Jesus into the world always makes us glad. In fact, it reminds us each year about the unconditional love that God has for us and also of the fact that Jesus, whose birth we are celebrating, brought about our redemption from sin. Therefore you should be glad as Christmas comes nearer. Together with Zechariah, you can testify: "Praise be to the Lord, the God of Israel, because He has come and has redeemed His people. He has raised up a horn of salvation for us in the house of his servant David" (Luke 1:68-69).

Heavenly Father, this Christmastime I want to rejoice because I can partake in the redemption that Jesus brought. Thank You that I can take pleasure in the wonder of Your love for me. Amen.

Let the Christ Child Change You

"A new command I give you: Love one another. As I have loved you, so you must love one another. By this all men will know that you are My disciples, if you love one another" (John 13:34-35).

We rejoice at Christmastime over the birth of the Child in the manger, but this Child as an adult came to show us that the world around us and we ourselves need to change. Jesus brought a new commandment: that people should love one another in exactly the same way in which He loves us. God uses us for this: through our actions other people should be able to see the love of Jesus revealed in our lives; that we, like Him, will help people; that our love for one another should not simply be said, but will be shown through our deeds. It is in fact through our love for others that people will be able to see that we are Christians.

On that first Christmas day, the angels sang of love and peace and the goodwill of God toward people. Unfortunately we do not actually see very much of this in the world we live in today. This year, as Christmas draws nearer, you should do your best to fulfill Jesus' commandment to love; to change the relationships around you for the better. First put your relationship with God right and then your relationships with other people so that the love of the Christ Child will change your whole life for the better.

Lord Jesus, I try so hard to love as You do but I just cannot manage to get it right. This Christmastime please make it possible for me, through the working of Your Spirit in my life, to love other people so that they will all know that I am Your disciple. Amen.

Do Your Part!

Do not forget this one thing, dear friends: With the Lord a day is like a thousand years, and a thousand years are like a day. The Lord is not slow in keeping His promise, as some understand slowness. He is patient with you, not wanting anyone to perish, but everyone to come to repentance (2 Peter 3:8-9).

The Christians in the time in which Peter lived were already impatient for the return of Christ. Just think how much time has passed since then – and we are still waiting for Jesus to come back again to put an end to all our suffering on earth for good.

Perhaps you too have wondered why Jesus is waiting so long to come. But the fact that the Lord has put off the return of Jesus for so long is in fact evidence for us of His never-ending patience with us, reports Peter.

He is not putting off the fulfilling of His promises, but He also does not want one single person to be lost. For this reason He is still giving you another chance to invite Jesus into your life. If you are not yet a Christian do not wait any longer to give your life to God. And if you already belong to God, you should do your part to hasten the return of Jesus by sharing the gospel message; by praying for people who have not yet had the privilege of hearing it and by giving, so that everyone will have a chance to hear this good news and to respond to it.

Lord Jesus, I realize that I do not yet do enough to hasten Your return. Please help me to share Your message with others, to pray and to contribute so that You will come sooner. Amen.

The New Branch

A shoot will come up from the stump of Jesse; from his roots a Branch will bear fruit. The Spirit of the LORD will rest on him – the Spirit of wisdom and of understanding, the Spirit of counsel and of power, the Spirit of knowledge and of the fear of the LORD (Isaiah 11:1-2).

Isaiah prophesied that the judgment of God against Judah and Israel was on its way: they would be destroyed by the Assyrians. But there would also be a remnant of the people of God who would be the inheritors of the new future. God would cause a new branch to begin to grow out of the dead tree stump of Judah; a new branch that would once again bear fruit. God would give new, perfect David to His people, a King on whom the Spirit of God would rest, someone who would have wisdom, insight, governance and strength. A King who would rule in righteousness. This new David would bring a perfect realm of peace into existence. One where leopards would lie down among the deer, and lions would eat grass like the cows do.

With the birth of Jesus this prophecy was partially fulfilled. He came to restore the broken world and to bring the peace of God into the world. One day when He comes back again, this realm of peace will reach its culmination; then the children of God will live in heaven with Him in perfect peace forever.

If we look at the condition of the world at the moment – at the increasing number of natural disasters, global warming, wars, famine and crime, we cannot help but to yearn for God's new world where all these negative things will be something of the past forever.

Lord Jesus, I look forward to Your reign of peace where deer will graze alongside predators and the whole world will be filled with the knowledge of You. Amen.

When Jesus Returns ...

"In those days, 'the sun will be darkened, and the moon will not give its light; the stars will fall from the sky, and the heavenly bodies will be shaken.' At that time men will see the Son of Man coming in clouds with great power and glory" (Mark 13:24-26).

Not many people were aware of the first coming of Jesus and it took place without any pomp and splendor. The King of the world was born in a dirty stable. The Second Coming will be something quite different, though. There has been much deliberation about the date it will take place. From time to time one or other so-called 'prophet' announces that it is going to happen within a week or a month. But this kind of speculation is worthless because no one apart from God knows when Jesus will come again.

The Bible does indeed give us indications of what we can expect with the Second Coming. There will be visible signs in nature and after that Jesus and His angels will appear with great power and majesty in the clouds. One of my husband's former colleagues used to enjoy describing the clouds massed over the Helderberg Mountains in the Western Cape as the "Second Coming Clouds". Each time I look at these clouds I cannot help but wonder exactly how the return of Jesus will happen.

We do not of course know the date or the day when this will happen – not even Jesus knows – but we well know that the Second Coming will be glorious and that we will see Him "coming on the clouds of heaven" (Matt. 26:64). With this coming, Jesus will send out His angels to gather His followers together, writes Luke. Therefore be watchful so that you will be ready when it happens.

Lord Jesus, Your first coming was without any majesty but I know that Your Second Coming will take place in power and majesty. Make me ready for it. Amen.

Be Prepared!

"Be on guard! Be alert! You do not know when that time will come. What I say to you, I say to everyone: 'Watch!'" (Mark 13:33, 37).

Although we do not know when Jesus will come again, His Second Coming is a given. There are some things that will happen before the return: when we see these things happening it is a sign for us that the Second Coming is imminent, Jesus said to His disciples (see Mark 13:29). The disciples of Jesus actually expected the Second Coming to take place within their life times and when this did not happen, many of them were very disappointed. We no longer expect the coming of Jesus to take place tomorrow or the day after but you should never get too comfortable, because the coming of Jesus in your own life is as close as the day on which you will die, and not one of us knows when that will be.

In this Christmas month we celebrate the first coming of Jesus. Perhaps it will be good if at the same time you make sure that His Second Coming will not catch you by surprise. The Bible gives you some basic guidelines: The coming of Jesus is close – live with that in mind, be alert so that you will not be caught sleeping. And while you wait do not do so inactively but make sure that you imitate the behavior of Jesus through being a disciple maker who tells other people about Him.

Lord Jesus, I am sorry that I am so relaxed about Your coming. Make me alert so that I will anticipate that coming, and while I wait I will share Your Good News. Amen.

December 13

Read John 14:16-27

A Time for Gifts

"I will ask the Father, and He will give you another Counselor to be with you forever. Peace I leave with you; My peace I give you. I do not give to you as the world gives. Do not let your hearts be troubled and do not be afraid" (John 14:16, 27).

Christmas is traditionally the time when we give gifts to one another – simply because it is the time when we celebrate God's gift to us – Jesus. We sometimes lose sight of the fact that Jesus, when He returned to His Father, also left two precious gifts for us. In His talk to His disciples just before the crucifixion, He told them about it: He promised that His Father would send them a Mediator, the Holy Spirit, in His place, and straight after this He said that He would leave His peace for them.

The value of these two precious gifts cannot be calculated: With the Holy Spirit with you to teach and guide you, to pray for you and teach you to pray, and to make it possible for you to witness, you will never again be without God. You can now also experience true peace through the working of the Holy Spirit in your life.

Take ownership of these two gifts of Jesus today; give the control of your life to the Holy Spirit and focus on the peace of God that does not depend on your physical circumstances, so that this Christmastime you will be a healthier, happier person.

Lord Jesus, thank You so much for the gift of the Holy Spirit and Your gift of peace that makes it possible for me to live each day with joy, tranquility and peace. Amen.

A Time to Give

"For God so loved the world that He gave His one and only Son, that whoever believes in Him shall not perish but have eternal life" (John 3:16).

One beautiful Cape autumn morning our doorbell rang before eight. As things would happen, my husband – who is usually up and dressed by six o' clock – was sick that morning. I had actually been awake since half past six, but was still enjoying lying in bed and doing my Bible study.

I was thus not all that happy about this early visitor and went downstairs mumbling, wondering who was about to see me with no make-up on. When I opened the front door our gardener was standing there with a beautiful bunch of white and yellow daisies which he put into my arms with a huge smile. "But Joseph, where did you get these beautiful flowers?" I asked in surprise. The smile got even bigger, "In my garden, madam, in my garden. A person after all can't just receive. You've got to give too," said Joseph.

Christmas is by definition the time of giving. Let us make Joseph's thought our own this Christmas and decide not just to be on the receiving end but to give lavishly in the Spirit of Christmas, as God did. Because He was willing to show His love for you by giving His Son so that you can celebrate Christmas as a child of God.

Heavenly Father, I praise You because You were willing to give Your Son so that I can live for ever. Make me willing to give to others out of thankfulness for everything that I receive from You. Amen.

How Do You Respond to Jesus?

After Jesus was born in Bethlehem in Judea, during the time of King Herod, Magi from the east came to Jerusalem and asked, "Where is the one who has been born King of the Jews? We saw His star in the east and have come to worship Him" (Matthew 2:1-2).

We have become so used to the story of the star gazers who came from the east to seek the Baby that had been born, that we tend not to notice the strangeness of this story anymore. The astrologers were heathens who undertook a very long journey to Jerusalem to go and meet the new King of the Jews. They were not even members of the nation of God who had grown up with the promise of a Messiah that was coming to redeem His people. Yet, when they met Jesus they recognized Him immediately even though He more than likely looked nothing like what they had expected.

Instead of an impressive king, they got a newly born baby in a simple manger. These important visitors knelt before Him and gave Him the best that they had: gold, frankincense and myrrh. In contrast with these astrologers, the actual king of Israel wanted to kill Baby Jesus. The scribes were also rather unenthusiastic about Him – even though they knew the prophecies off by heart about where He would be born.

We need to beware that the unbelievers do not go ahead of us in the kingdom of God. This month be especially tuned in to the impact that Jesus came to make. At Christmas kneel once again before Him and offer Him your best and make sure that you never become unenthusiastic about Him.

Lord Jesus, forgive me for sometimes being lukewarm about You. I want to use this Christmastime to kneel before You and offer You my life. Amen.

A Wish for Reconciliation

May God Himself, the God of peace, sanctify you through and through. May your whole spirit, soul and body be kept blameless at the coming of our Lord Jesus Christ (1 Thessalonians 5:23).

In South Africa we celebrate the Day of Reconciliation today. This day used to be called the Day of the Vow. The celebrations of the Day of the Vow stirred up mixed feelings; the largest segment of the population of South Africa was opposed to it and it even led to intense conflict. A small group of people continued to cling to it though, because it represented the intervention of God in history for them.

In 1938 a quarter of a million white South Africans descended on Pretoria when the Voortrekker Monument was unveiled, which was erected in commemoration of the Battle of Blood River when a group of about 470 Boers defeated more than ten thousand Zulus.

It is in fact far better that on this historic day we are reconciled with God and our neighbor. It is also only God who can bring about reconciliation in our land. You need to trust Him for that but also play your part so that it can come to pass. It is my wish for the Day of Reconciliation that not only every South African, but everyone who is reading this, will keep the good from the past and will live so committed to God that we will truly experience His peace and His reconciliation in our hearts so that it can also be reflected in the history of our land. "The one who calls you is faithful and He will do it" writes Paul (1 Thess. 5:24).

Heavenly Father, I pray that You will make true reconciliation possible among all groups in the world and that this reconciliation will endure so that Your lasting peace will once again rule in our hearts. Amen.

A Life of Love and Light

Live a life of love, just as Christ loved us and gave Himself up for us as a fragrant offering and sacrifice to God (Ephesians 5:2).

The Christmas story of the redeeming love of God that appeared to all people should elicit a response from us – it appeals to us at this Christmastime to do the same – to, like Jesus, live a life of unconditional love here on earth. If you see your way clear to doing so, it will require that you treat all other people with the same love and mercy that Jesus shows to you. Make a decision right now to do your best to live like Jesus for the rest of the month and for the rest of your life; to care as He does and to love as He does.

With the first Christmas the light of God shone brightly over the fields of Bethlehem when the choir of angels sang of the love and peace of God. From then on the light would always be stronger than the darkness. In Ephesians 5:8 Paul encourages the Ephesians to be people of the light. This meant that they needed to obey the will of God and share His message of light with others. In the Sermon on the Mount, Jesus said that we are the light of the world. Let that light shine this year at Christmas in such a way that other people will see the good things that you do and will honor God for them.

Lord Jesus, please would You make it possible for me to be a person of the light who will live in love and will follow in Your footsteps for the rest of my life. Amen.

The Christmas Gospel

The kindness and love of God our Savior appeared (Titus 3:4).

With the birth of Jesus on that very first Christmas, the love of God was made visible to us and we discovered precisely what that love included. People could now see it with their own eyes and tell others about it. We no longer need to doubt God's purpose for us. Even though we deserve the love of God even less than Adam and Eve, even though we still commit sin every day, God does not withdraw Himself from us and He is no longer the unreachable God. Through the birth of His Son He made it possible for us to reach Him – He became our Father God; and we can now be His children.

In Jesus, God Himself became a person for us. With the coming of Jesus, a new dimension of the covenant was unveiled, wrote Henri Nouwen, "In Jesus, God was born, God grew to adulthood, lived, suffered and died like us and amongst us. God is God with us." Because Jesus came, you and I now always have God with us and we are assured of His presence. And because God forsook Jesus on the cross we need never again fear that we will need to get by without God. Through His Holy Spirit He still lives in us – He is closer to us than ever before. God wants to breathe in us so that everything that we say, think and do will be absolutely and completely inspired by God, writes Nouwen.

It is my prayer that you will experience the presence of God more clearly this Christmastime than ever before.

Lord God, I praise You for the Christmas message that You are always with me; that I will never again have to get by without You. Amen.

A King for Israel

Every warrior's boot used in battle and every garment rolled in blood will be destined for burning, will be fuel for the fire. For to us a child is born, to us a son is given, and the government will be on His shoulders. And He will be called Wonderful Counselor, Mighty God, Everlasting Father, Prince of Peace (Isaiah 9:5-6).

The prophet Isaiah prophesied that the Messiah, whom the people of God had been looking forward to for so many years, already would be a king over Israel who would rule with wisdom. He would be clothed with power and eternal glory. He would be responsible for the peace and prosperity of the people and, furthermore, He would ensure right and justice. He would sit on the throne of David forever and rule His kingdom with justice and righteousness.

If someone were to read this prophetic utterance very carefully it could seem like a rather selfish expectation, but the hope of people has much to do with one's own desires and needs. For the Jews, the most important task of the Messiah was to bring about their liberation from the might of the Romans. It was their dream that He would establish their own little kingdom where they would, as of old, live under a righteous Jewish king.

Our own dreams for the future are also very often selfish. We hope and long for those things that are important to us and which we need. This selfish hope is however not what God requires. This Christmas fix your hope in God and not in your own desires. People who hope in God are never disappointed.

Lord Jesus, I praise You as the King of my life. I now want to fix my hope in You and stop serving You in a selfish way. Amen.

A Christmas Wish for You

We had hoped that He was the one who was going to redeem Israel. And what is more, it is the third day since all this took place (Luke 24:21).

The men on the road to Emmaus were shattered by the crucifixion of Jesus. They had so hoped that He was the one who would set Israel free. The word *hope* plays a very prominent role at Christmastime. It is after all about the hope that had lived in the hearts of Israel that the Messiah would come and bring them a new era of hope and peace. They fiercely hoped that there would now eventually be an end to the Roman oppression.

Hope is always good. People who have no hope have pretty much given up living, and yet you need to tread lightly with regard to wishful thinking at Christmas. If you only hope for the things that will be an advantage to you, then you are a poor person. Christmas is the time when you should be reaching out to other people and hoping for good things for them. At Christmas you get the chance to once again channel your hope in the right direction. I want to offer Romans 15:13 as a Christmas wish for you this year: "May the God of hope fill you with all joy and peace as you trust in Him, so that you may overflow with hope by the power of the Holy Spirit!"

It is only God who can put true hope in your heart. Through the working of the Holy Spirit in your life this hope becomes even stronger and your peace and joy even richer and more intense. May this be true for you this year!

Lord Jesus, thank You so much that You came to teach me to hope – that You are the Source of my hope. Because I believe in You I know for sure that heaven awaits me. Amen.

The Time That God has Appointed

When the time had fully come, God sent His Son, born of a woman, born under law, to redeem those under law, that we might receive the full rights of sons (Galatians 4:4-5).

God Himself determined the time when Jesus would be born. He sent His Son, who had no sin, into the sinful world to make it possible for sinners to be His children. Before this it was impossible to obey the law of God. Because Jesus was without sin He, through His death on the cross, paid the ransom for our debt of sin so that there would no longer be a deep gully between sinful people and a holy God. By bearing the punishment for our sins, He made it possible for God to forgive our sins.

Thus the birth of Jesus means that you are set free from your sins. He redeemed you when His blood flowed on the cross just as slaves were set free in the old days through having a freedom price paid for them, so that you can now be the child of God. God also appointed the time when you would accept Jesus as your Savior. If you already belong to God, you are already experiencing that freedom in your own life and you are no longer a slave to sin. If not, do not wait any longer to respond to God's time – Jesus came so that you could be free. Therefore, make that freedom your own through acknowledging Him as your Redeemer!

Heavenly Father, it is wonderful that You appointed a specific time to send Your Son into the world and that You also appointed the time when I could acknowledge Him as my Savior. I do not want to wait any longer to accept Your invitation. Amen.

Portrait of God

No one has ever seen God, but God the One and Only, who is at the Father's side, has made Him known (John 1:18).

In the month of December we are focusing on the birth of Jesus. Through the centuries His birth has been synonymous with the things that He brought to this world – peace, joy, mercy and truth. We must also never lose sight of the fact that it was Jesus who came to show us what God looks like. "Anyone who has seen Me has seen the Father," Jesus Himself said to Philip when he asked to see the Father.

Through His words, life and actions Jesus came to show us exactly what God looks like and how much God loves us. "The Son is the radiance of God's glory and the exact representation of His being," declares the writer to the Hebrews (see Heb. 1:3). This love portrait of God is seen most clearly when we remember that the Son of God died on the cross so that our sins could be forgiven. If you ever doubt the love God has for you, you simply have to look at the crucified Jesus.

If you want to know what God looks like, look at Jesus. Try your best to live and act this Christmastime in such a way that people who look at you will not only be aware of Jesus, but that the love of God will also be clear to them through your actions. Through the things that you say and do may they have a new experience of the love of God and His mercy to all people, and may they experience His closeness through your example.

Lord Jesus, I praise You that through Your coming You came to show me what God looks like by acting like Him. Please help me to be able to demonstrate the love of God to others through my life. Amen.

Christmas All Year Round!

"The virgin will be with child and will give birth to a son, and they will call Him Immanuel" – which means, "God with us" (Matthew 1:23).

In 1981 we visited the German Medieval town of Rothenburg with our three little ones. It was a wonderful experience for them – especially the little Christmas shops that sold the prettiest Christmas decorations – in June! While the children were excitedly admiring the delicate wood figurines, I was thinking that the shop owners in Rothenburg actually had a point. It should be Christmas all year round for the children of God. We do not have to only celebrate the coming of Jesus to the world in the month of December or on Christmas Day. We should be celebrating it every day.

You too can meditate every day on the miracle of the Son of God who became a person for you, who came to the world as an ordinary baby to die here on a cross so that you could be the child of God.

Quite a few years later when we were visiting our children overseas in Washington we discovered a charming shop with all kinds of trinkets. Here I bought the most charming little wooden angels as gifts for my friends. I did not have the heart to give all the little angels away, however, so I kept three that now hang on my wall lamps all year round – to remind me that I ought to celebrate Christmas all year through. When I look at the little angels I remember that Jesus was born for me and came to die for me and then I thank God.

Lord Jesus, make it Christmas all year in my heart so that I will think every day about the miracle of the Son of God who became a person – for me! Amen.

A Surprising Secret

Now to Him who is able to establish you by my gospel and the proclamation of Jesus Christ, according to the revelation of the mystery hidden for long ages past, but now revealed and made known through the prophetic writings by the command of the eternal God, so that all nations might believe and obey Him (Romans 16:25-26).

It is easy to become sentimental about Christmas. And that is moreover a trap into which we often fall when we look at the Christmas decorations in the shops and listen to Christmas music; we run ourselves ragged buying presents and wrapping them and getting the Christmas dinner on the table.

The final words of Paul in his letter to the Romans lead us away from sentimentality and point us in the direction of how we should really understand the Christmas message: It includes a surprising secret for every believer. A secret that needs to be uncovered. A secret that should make hearts glad and strengthen them for the road. A secret that needs to be proclaimed in the church and in the world. This secret that once lay in a manger as a little Child, now lies in the hearts and mouths of believers. Every ear must hear of Him, every eye must see Him, including the eyes and ears of little children. If this does not happen, the mystery of Christmas will remain a secret; and we will still be caught up in the wrapping paper, the artificial nativity scenes and the tinsel and cards and festivities of Christmas.

Make sure that this year your family will embody this secret, so that you can exchange the sweet sentimentality into which Christmas can so easily fall for a renewal of your relationship with the Christmas Child.

Lord Jesus, thank You that You came to earth so that I can believe in You and learn first hand of the love of God for me. Amen.

Birth of a King

"You will be with child and give birth to a son, and you are to give Him the name Jesus. He will be great and will be called the Son of the Most High. The Lord God will give Him the throne of His father David, and He will reign over the house of Jacob forever; His kingdom will never end" (Luke 1:31-33).

The angel told Mary that her Baby would rule as King over the descendants of Jacob and that there would be no end to His kingship. Jesus, the greatest of all kings, voluntarily laid aside His kingship in heaven to come to earth as a human baby. A newborn baby is probably the most helpless creature there is – he can do nothing for himself and is absolutely and completely dependent on his mother.

Jesus was completely human, but we must also never lose sight of the fact that He was still King. This is what the star and the choir of angels and the light of God that flooded the fields outside Bethlehem bore testimony to. The Jews really wanted Him to be king but allowed Him to be crucified when He did not meet up to their expectations of a king. It is ironic that Pilate hung a board above the cross of Jesus on which "the King of the Jews" was written. Have you yet acknowledged the kingship of Jesus over your life? Are you willing to obey Him in all things? This Christmas Day you should not only celebrate the Baby in a manger but also the birth of the King.

Lord Jesus, on Christmas Day I honor You as the greatest of all Kings, One who was willing to set aside Your kingship for me. Thank You for being the King of my life. Amen.

The Day of Goodwill

If you spend yourselves in behalf of the hungry and satisfy the needs of the oppressed, then your light will rise in the darkness, and your night will become like the noonday (Isaiah 58:10).

The day after Christmas is known as the Day of Goodwill in South Africa. In the month that has past we have rejoiced over the birth of Jesus and told one another exactly what that means for us. We have shown our goodwill towards our family and friends by giving them gifts and visiting together around well-laden Christmas tables.

On the Day of Goodwill we need to reach out beyond those to the people whom we do not know so that they will be able to see that our faith in Jesus and our relationship with Him has changed our lives. God is almighty but in the world in which we live He can do nothing without us. God reaches out to the poor by using our money; He gives food to those who are hungry when we work in soup kitchens; He prevents people from getting cold when He gets us to hand out warm clothes and blankets.

Today God wants you to be the one to spread His goodwill where you live. He wants you to be aware of the needs of the people around you and to do something about it. Do not wait any longer to show your goodwill to others. If you are willing to do this, God will lead you and make sure that all your needs are met. You will be like a well-watered garden, like a spring where the water will never run dry (Isa. 58:6).

Lord Jesus, I praise You for Your goodwill towards me that led You to leave heaven so that I could become a child of God. I now also want to testify of Your goodwill to others through providing for their needs. Amen.

December 27

Read Exodus 33:7-16

The Goodness of God

The LORD replied, "My Presence will go with you, and I will give you rest" (Exodus 33:14).

The day before yesterday was Christmas – the day on which we celebrate the birth of Jesus – God who became a person for us.

A very long time before this birth Moses requested God to go with the people of Israel on their journey through the wilderness. God was willing to do so and told Moses that he was His friend, that he carried the favor of God. Moses then asked that God would allow him to see His glory. Again God agreed. He did not give Moses a breathtaking display of His might and majesty but instead summed up His glory in one little word, "You have found favor with Me." The glory of God is revealed in His goodness and love that He shows towards people.

It was only many years later when God sent His Son into the world as a very ordinary person that we really grasped how immeasurably great this goodness is that He wants to make known to us. God is great and glorious and He reveals His glory to you through letting you see Jesus. God became human for you – so that you can experience His goodness first hand and can realize how wonderful it is to be able to be His child. And that is exactly what Jesus' coming into this world was able to do for you: it allows you to be aware of the goodness of God in your own life.

Lord Jesus, I praise You because You came into the world so that I could see something of the Father's goodness towards me, and understand it. Thank You that I can take that goodness for myself every day and can share it with all the people with whom I come into contact. Amen.

The Things for Which You Hope

We want each of you to show this same diligence to the very end, in order to make your hope sure. We do not want you to become lazy, but to imitate those who through faith and patience inherit what has been promised (Hebrews 6:11-12).

We all know the well-known myth of Pandora who received a box that she was forbidden to open. She could not curb her curiosity and when she did actually open the box all kinds of catastrophic things such as sickness, old age, crime, hardships and disasters were released into the world. Luckily there was also one good thing in Pandora's box, that is hope. It is only hope that makes it possible for us to be able to handle the disastrous contents of the box that was let loose in the world.

The writer to the Hebrews encourages the readers of his letter to hold fast to the things in which they hope until that hope is fulfilled. And people who believe in God can always be hopeful. After all, they know that heaven is already a reality for them. Therefore, you should hold fast to the "hope of glory" about which Paul talks in his letter to the Christians in Colosse. Take a look at the content of that hope, "To them God has chosen to make known among the Gentiles the glorious riches of this mystery, which is Christ in you, the hope of glory," writes Paul (Col. 1:27). Because your hope is actually a person, no one can take it away from you. Make a point in this month of the birth of Jesus to keep your hope in Him shining brightly.

Lord Jesus, I praise You as my hope in glory. Thank You that You have made heaven possible for me because You were willing to come to earth. Amen.

God As Our Only Hope

Save me from all my transgressions; do not make me the scorn of fools
(Psalm 39:8).

The psalmist here found himself in a troubled physical position. He comes to the conclusion that he does not have much time left on earth. He also has little hope and as a person he is deeply conscious of his mortality. "My hope is in You," he confesses to God (verse 7).

In the light of your own human mortality and fragility, if you are sick or if your life is threatened, there is nothing more you can do than to acknowledge God as your only hope. In 2 Corinthians 4:16 Paul writes, "Though outwardly we are wasting away, yet inwardly we are being renewed day by day." In contrast with the visible indications of the mortality that each one of us can feel in our bodies when we get sick or as we grow older, there is the promise of eternal life in God. And we can hold fast to this hope because God always fulfills each one of His promises to the letter.

The secret of how you can continue to hope in spite of your negative circumstances is to know Christ. If He lives in you then you have a hope in glory. Then you know for sure that your earthly hardships are negligible and moreover will only last for a short while, but they will result in an "eternal glory that far outweighs them all ... for what is unseen is eternal." (see 2 Cor. 4:16, 18). You can therefore readily fix your hope in God when nothing else remains for you.

Heavenly Father, I worship You as my only hope who will ultimately cause all things to work out for the best. Because I know that my hardships on earth will one day lead to Your heavenly glory. Amen.

Joy of Life

So I commend the enjoyment of life, because nothing is better for a man under the sun than to eat and drink and be glad. Then joy will accompany him in his work all the days of the life God has given him under the sun (Ecclesiastes 8:15).

The writer of the book of Ecclesiastes was searching for the meaning of life. He saw that it sometimes wicked people get away with things while good people suffer. And yet he comes to the conclusion that every person who has found joy in life is a happy person; that such a person can succeed in giving meaning to his own life as well as to others.

The time between Christmas and New Year is traditionally a time when most people take a holiday. Holidays are times when families come together, when we take a break from work and we enjoy the company of our families and friends. Make the most of your holidays this year. Enjoy the time to rest with the people whom you love; eat, drink and be merry so that you can be fully rested for all the work that will lie ahead for you next year. Try to live each day with joy so that you will also be able to generate joy for others – there are few things that are as contagious as a smile and a positive attitude. Make sure that God is always an integral part of your life, because without Him you will never know the real meaning of joy.

Lord, thank You so much for the joy of holidays, for relaxing together with loved ones and friends and for the joy that this being together brings me. Help me to be joyful and give me that inner joy that distinguishes Your children every day. Amen.

God's Inexpressibly Great Love

Because of His great love for us, God, who is rich in mercy, made us alive with Christ even when we were dead in transgressions – it is by grace you have been saved (Ephesians 2:4-5).

For Christmas 2006 my husband gave me a copy of John Ortberg's book *Love Without Reason* as a gift. In the front of the book he wrote, "May the inexpressibly great love of God be a new experience for you this Christmas." Christmas had already passed when I began to read the book, but the contents and the dedication of this exceptional book did in fact ensure that in the year that lay ahead I gained a new glimpse into and a new experience of the love of God.

When you are focused on something, you see it all around you. During my personal Bible studies, in the spiritual books that I read, in my conversations with other Christians, in the things that happened to me, in the beauty of the world around me I could see God's love for me more clearly than ever before.

The very best way to let the light of God shine in the world is by focusing on His love for you and passing it on to all the other people who will cross your path in the year that lies ahead. May you, too, in the year ahead experience the inexpressible love of God for you in a new way and may He enfold you in that love every day of the year that lies before you.

Father, I pray that in every day of the year ahead You will make me aware of Your inexpressibly great love for me, and that You will help me to pass this love on to other people. Amen.

Prayer

Lord Jesus,
I praise You for the privilege of being able
to experience Advent:
a time in which I could become quietly joyful because
You were born as a human baby.
And because You died on a cross so that I can live forever.
A time during which I could once again work on my relationship
with You and could look forward to Your Second Coming.
This Christmas I could particularly focus on
Your immeasurable love for me.
I now want to make my whole life available to You so that Your
master plan for my life can be carried out.
Thank You for the gifts that You have given me:
Your peace that passes all my understanding, and Your Spirit
that lives in me so that I need never again be without God.
Change me, Lord, so that I will love
all other people the way You love me,
that I will do my part to spread Your Good News
around the world and that every day I can look forward
to Your return, and will be ready for it.
Make me willing to notice the needs of others
and to help them because of my gratitude for You.
Please let there once again be true reconciliation
among the people in our country.
I praise You as the King of my life –
I want to fix my hope for today and for the future in You.
Thank You that You are the source of my hope.
Make it Christmas all year for me so that I will be reminded each day
about the miracle of God who became man
and help me to celebrate Your goodness every day.

Amen.

Scripture Verse Index

Proverbs

Galatians

Ephesians

Philippians

Bibliography

Magazines:
Discipleship Journal, No. 132, Dec/Jan 2002.

Books:
Brazelton, Katie. 2005. *Pathway to Purpose*. Grand Rapids, Michigan: Zondervan, 2005.

Cowman, L. B. *Streams in the Desert* (Updated edition). Grand Rapids, Michigan: Zondervan, 1997.

Farrel, Pam. *Woman of Influence*. Madison: Intervarsity Press, 2006.

Hughes, Selwyn. *Every Day with Jesus*. Surrey: Waverley Abbey House, 1981.

Keefauver, Larry. *Experiencing the Holy Spirit*. Nashville, TN: Thomas Nelson, 2000

L'Engle, Madeleine. *Walking on Water*. New York: North Point Press, 1980.

Lewis, C. S. *Miracles*. New York: MacMillan, 1947.

Lucado, Max. *The Great House of God*. Nashville, TN: Thomas Nelson, 2001.

Mandela, Nelson R. *A Long Walk to Freedom*. Great Britain: Little, Brown and Company, 1994.

Niven, David. *The 100 Simple Secrets of Happy People*. Francisco: Harper San, 2000.

Ortberg, John. *If You Want to Walk on Water You've Got to Get Out of the Boat*. Grand Rapids, Michigan: Zondervan, 2007.

Ortberg, John. *Love Beyond Reason*. Grand Rapids, Michigan: Zondervan, 1998.

Peck, Scott M. *The Road Less Travelled*. Great Britain: Hutchinson & Co., 1983.

Peterson, Eugene H. *Eat This Book*. Grand Rapids, Michigan: Zondervan, 2007.

Rinker, Rosalind. *Communicating Love through Prayer*. Grand Rapids, Michigan, 1966.

Smith, Hannah W. *Safe within Your Love*. Ada, MI: Bethany House

Publishers, 1992.

Weaver, Joanna. *Having a Mary Heart in a Martha World.* Colorado Springs: Waterbrook Press, 2006.

Yancey, Philip. *Prayer.* Grand Rapids, Michigan: Zondervan, 2006.

Yancey, Philip. *Reaching for the Invisible God.* Grand Rapids, Michigan: Zondervan, 2000.